END
OF AN EXILE

ISRAEL, THE JEWS AND THE GENTILE WORLD

James Parkes

micah publications

End of An Exile, by James Parkes: New Edition
Copyright © 1982 by Micah Publications, 255 Humphrey St.,
Marblehead, Massachusetts 01945, U.S.A.

Library of Congress Cataloging in Publication Data
Parkes, James William, 1896-1981
End of an exile
Includes index
1. Israel. 2. Zionism. 3. Israel and the Diaspora. 4. Judaism-
Relations-Christianity. 5. Christianity and other religions-
Judaism. I. Title
DS126.5.P29 1982   956.94'001   82-60880
ISBN: 0-916288-12-9

Printed by McNaughton & Gunn, Ann Arbor, Michigan

Acknowledgements:
Robert A Everett, "A Christian Apology for Israel," Christian-
Jewish Relations, Sept., 1980; reprinted with permission of
author.
Carl Hermann Voss, "The American Christian Palestine Committee,"
The Herzl Year Book, Vol. 8, Essays in American Zionism,
1917-1948 (Herzl Press, New York, 1978); reprinted with per-
mission of author and publisher.
Reinhold Niebuhr, "Jews After The War," The Nation, Feb. 21
and Feb. 28, 1942.
Rose G. Lewis, "James Parkes: Christianity without Anti-
Semitism," Midstream, Jan., 1982;Reprinted with permission
of author and publisher.
James Parkes,'The Parkes Library," Studies in Bibliography
and Booklore (Library of Hebrew Union College--Jewish Institute
of Religion), Vol. iv, June, 1960. Reprinted with permission of
publisher.
A. Roy Eckardt, "In Memoriam James Parkes: 1896-1981,"
Journal of Ecumenical Studies, 19:1, Winter, 1982. Reprinted
with permission of publisher and author.
Every effort has been made to locate copyright owners of other
material quoted in this book. Any omissions will be corrected in
subsequent editions, if brought to the attention of the publishers.

To Jewish friends
in many lands and of many different opinions
encountered during twenty-five years of wandering and study
this interpretation of their history is offered in gratitude
by the Author

CONTENTS

Page

PART FOUR

E PLURIBUS UNUM

INTRODUCTION

The purpose in republishing this book, first published in 1954, is not only to repeat the arguments on behalf of the return of the Jewish people to Zion; but to make known its author, Dr. James Parkes, who is unknown to all but a circle of scholars though he was a major influence in current Christian theology and in contemporary Christian Zionism. He is unknown to most Jews and Christians alike, yet he devoted his life to explaining the Jewish people to the Christian world; he became the second Gentile to hold the position of president of the Jewish Historical Society in London (1949-1951); spent his life in the effort to understand and to elucidate the roots of antisemitism; espoused Zionism; established a private library in his home in Barley, England with books of Jewish history and on Gentile-Jewish relations, now housed at Southampton University; irreversibly changed Christian understanding of its Jewish past; taught the Christian world its contribution towards shaping antisemitism, first as Church policy grounded in what he felt was a fundamental error, then as a means of political and social control; helped rewrite the Medieval record of Jewish life; and finally, as a result of his studies as an historian and a theologian, became an influential Christian Zionist.

Robert A. Everett commented on the prestigious pedigree of intellect behind this movement--"Scratch an American Christian Zionist and you'll find James Parkes or Reinhold Niebuhr beneath."

This movement, begun in the nineteenth century, predates Parkes' work, but was given a theological basis through him, in addition to the humanistic and moral bases which early motivated it. Parkes was supported in his advocacy of Christian Zionism by other outstanding theologians, scholars and clergymen in the twentieth century: Niebuhr, Albright, Lowdermilk and Mumford, to name a few. The history of this movement in the United States

is ably written by Reverend Carl Hermann Voss in his article in
the appendix of this edition. His knowledge of American Christian Zionism and of the contribution to it of such men as Parkes
and Niebuhr added considerably to my knowledge and decision
to include the articles by Niebuhr, first published in The Nation
in 1942, as well as Dr. Voss' article on the American Christian
Palestine Committee, all of which I must thank him for. These
articles not only reflect a history of thought and effort embedded
in a period, but the stature of the men who engaged in the struggle
for Zionism.

A third reason for republishing this book is its usefulness as
a gauge of history. Journalism creates an illusion of "breathless
pace" to events, and addicts us to this pace. Yet anyone who
reads End of An Exile will be startled to discover how little has
changed in the problems of the Middle East; which must lead us
to observe that "understanding" is not the same thing as "information"; and that to be "informed" is not the same thing as to "understand." We read our daily newspapers as we read a daily thermo-
meter; that is, we take a "reading" of events, but this is not the
same thing as understanding what is meant by "weather" or
"climate."

To those lacking information, Parkes' books on the Middle
East, End of An Exile, Whose Land, and A History of the Palestine Peoples, has much to contribute for sheer facticity on such
subjects as demography, history, the ethnic composition of the
people, soil erosion and peasant technology, for as a social
historian he left no aspect of the life of this area out of his ac-
counting in his search for justice in the Middle East. Nor was
anyone more aware than he that ignorance was Israel's worst
enemy, whether that ignorance suggested itself in statements that
this disputed territory was the "birthplace of the three monotheistic faiths," or that "Jerusalem was equally holy to Judaism,
Christianity, and Islam," or that "the Arabs" had lived in this
territory as long as had the Jews.

Nor is it his advocacy of Zionism which alone claims our attention with respect to this issue, but his definition of the movement as organically related to the history and religion of the
Jews, and which has had a value and spiritual orientation for
them which has shaped the conduct of post-Biblical Jewry.

Edmund Wilson once said that "After the fall of Jerusalem,
there is no Jewish history, only a series of sad anecdotes."

ii

After James Parkes, as well as the work of other post-Biblical
historians such as Salo Baron, Moore and Herford, Jewish
history after the fall of Jerusalem has come of age. The record
of the Medieval Jew takes its place alongside that of the Biblical
Jew. We can now trace the political and social institutions of
Medieval Jewry, its everyday life and working habits, its intellectual and scholarly communities, its public life in both Gentile
and Jewish worlds, the special "treaties" which existed between
them, the abrogation of those treaties which led to the expulsions;
--and, most significantly, the writings of Jewish philosophers,
poets and rabbis, particularly that immense and remarkable
record of Jewish thought known as the Responsa, residing today
in 1500 volumes.

It was the discovery of this record and what it suggested of
religious vitality, which led Parkes to a major theological re-
vision, as he wrote in Whose Land: ". . . it is only politically
that the defeat by Rome, and the scattering of the Jewish population made a decisive change in the history of the Land. That
which had been created by more than a thousand years of Jewish
history remained." (p. 31). This shift in perspective cannot be
overemphasized for its theological implications for Christianity.
The Jewish Scriptures is shared, and disputed, by Jews and
Christians; but Rabbinic literature is not. While it sometimes
influenced Christian thought in the Middle Ages, as indeed Christian thought and practice sometimes influenced Jewish tradition,
the world of the Talmud and the Responsa is not "shared ground."
There is no disputed theological territory here. It lies outside
the directions of Christianity and assures the independent nature
of its religion which Judaism always claimed for itself, but which
Christianity was led to deny on behalf of its own theological claims.

Perhaps the insight seems commonplace to some now. That
is only the mark of its extraordinary veracity and of how well
James Parkes did his work. In his autobiography, Voyage of
Discoveries he comments that in 1928, at a conference between
nationalist and Jewish student organizations they "had combed
Europe unsuccessfully for a Christian scholar who could talk
objectively either about Jewish history or about the contemporary
Jewish situation." (p. 114). His work in the International Student
Service on the continent during the 1920s was decisive for his
career, for it was through this work and involvement with student
organizations that he became aware of the diabolism of Europe.

iii

His autobiography is important for its picture of student life and organizations during these years. Troubled by the marked nature of antisemitism on the continent, a problem he had not encountered in Guernsey where he was born and raised, he wished to know something of its origins but, he complains, that in 1929 neither could he find "a competent short study of antisemitism in English."

That problem might have discouraged others, but it aroused in Parkes the insatiable curiosity of the scholar and the writer who came to view the problem as, he quixotically describes it, "a theological whodunit." Confronting the problem with something of a tabula rasa, he immediately sensed the irrational in it. The occasion was an international Christian student conference in Switzerland in 1925 which he chaired on the discussion of "the Jewish question." One lone Rumanian Jewish student had been invited to state the case for the Jewish people. In Voyage of Discoveries, Parkes describes the opening Christian's position:

> The Christian's speech was so venemous, contained
> so many accusations and innuendoes that I was sure
> were false that I took the unusual step of saying from
> the Chair that I could not accept the speech as the
> introduction to a discussion among Christians of the
> problem. I would invite no one else to speak until
> the speech was withdrawn. I then sat down, and a
> deathly silence ensued.

A model, surely, for U.N. members!

The experience led him to formulate a simple question: "Were the Jewish people eccentric, or were they a normal people with an eccentric history?" He writes in Prelude to Dialogue that he "had reached the conviction that the right answer to this question was more important than any sociological or political studies." (p. 192). Concluding that their history was eccentric, he began a lifelong investigation into what had caused the eccentric history. "My subject was an enquiry into the origins of antisemitism. I could not more closely define it, as I was in considerable doubt as to what I should find." (Voyage of Discoveries, p. 120). The result of this "enquiry" was that august monument to scholarship, The Conflict Between Church and Synagogue, written as a thesis for his Ph.D. degree in philosophy from Oxford in 1930. The consequences of this thesis reverberated in him for the rest of his life as well as for this century of Christians:

iv

. . .I was completely unprepared for the discovery that
it was the Christian Church, and the Christian Church
alone, which turned a normal xenophobia and normal
good and bad communal relations between two human
societies into the unique evil of antisemitism, the most
evil, and, as I gradually came to realise, the most crip-
pling sin of historic Christianity. It was not any particular contemporary fact on either side which led to this
tragic result, nor was it any deduction by the Christians
of any one period from the behaviour of their Jewish
contemporaries.

Antisemitism arises from the picture of the Jews which
Christian theologians extracted from their reading of the
Old Testament, a work for whose every word they claimed
divine authority. The Old Testament is very frank about
Jewish sins and very definite in its certainty that they
earned divine punishment. But it also dwelt on the love
between God and Israel, and the promises of the Messianic
Age. So long as both elements in the story are accepted
as being about a single people, a lofty balance is retained.
But Christian theologians divided it into the story of two
peoples--the virtuous Hebrews, who were pre-incarnation
Christians, had all the praise and the promise; and the
wicked Jews had all the crimes and denunciations. This
was the interpretation repeated over and over again, in
every possible variation, and in every century from the
third onwards. In the leading Church historian of the
fourth century, Eusebius of Caesarea, Jews and Hebrews
are biologically two distinct races. . . .I carried my
study right down to the end of the Roman influence on the
first barbarian societies, Visigoths, Vandals and the rest,
and ended in the Dark Ages. It was longer than was
necessary for a doctorate, but it completed a period,
and left the Middle Ages for subsequent study.
                    Voyage of Discoveries (p. 123).
Indeed it did! The consequence of this was Parkes' study,
The Jew in The Medieval Community.

It is more or less ironic that a good deal of the recovery of
Jewish history since the fall of Jerusalem has been in the hands
of Christian philosophers and historians. The turn of the tide
came in the sixteenth century when the relationship between

V

political philosophy and Christian theology was being reassessed. "Harmonious social relations," Reinhold Niebuhr has written in Moral Man and Immoral Society, "depend upon the sense of justice as much as, or even more than, upon the sentiment of benevolence." The pursuit of justice, as both Parkes and Niebuhr were concerned to observe, lies outside the Christian theology of salvation. As concern with communal man rather than with individual man engrossed early thinkers such as Jean Bodin, John Selden and Willian Surenhuysen, Jewry was reconsidered as an exemplar of "natural law" and "natural religion." The first a French political philosopher and free-thinking Catholic, the second a lawyer, Orientalist, and Anglican, and the third a Calvinist and a professor of Hebrew at the Academy of Amsterdam, all three, as Parkes comments in Voyage of Discoveries, accepted the Old Testament as a revelation of natural law and natural religion in "concrete form" given to the Jews, "rightly continued and interpreted by them in their rabbinical academies and writings"; and, most influential for Parkes, "that Judaism was consequently still a living religion. . . ." (p.48). It is difficult to say how much of his theology he owes to these sixteenth and seventeenth century thinkers, but his interpretation of the Trinity as a "creative tension" between social man, individual man and man as thinker, or as between the pursuits of justice, love and knowledge, and his interpretation of the covenant at Sinai as between God and His people in their life as a nation (i.e. kingdom of priests,holy nation) finds accord with these early views. Given the history of deliberate and coercive misinterpretation of Jewish concepts, it is a matter of applause that such words as Pharisee, Torah, and Chosen People are restored to their original meanings. If Parkes had done nothing more than edit a Dictionary of Right Terms it would have been enough.

He believed that the flow of these early ideas had been interrupted for lack of an "adequate post-biblical Jewish history," the kind of historical accountability which could lend credence to ideas, philosophy and theology. It was his lifelong quarrel (among others) that "no good theology can arise from bad history," and he believed that much of Christian theology concerning the Jews was based on bad--or indeed no--history. In this respect the first post-Biblical history was written at the beginning of the eighteenth century by Jacques Basnages, a Huguenot, who was also the first to point out "the appalling responsibility of the

Christian Church for the persecution of the Jews "; and it was
not until the nineteenth century that two more post-Biblical
histories of the Jewish people were written, both also by Christians: Dean Milman and E.A. Abbott. (The neglect of a Jewish
historian of this history is a matter of present inquiry among
Jewish scholars.)

The history of Christian thought on the subject of the Jews,
from the time of Jerome who assiduously studied Hebrew and
"read the works of the Jews" so that he "could quote them against
the Jews," through the Christian Hebraists of the sixteenth century who studied the Talmud for secret admissions that Jesus
was the Messiah and for buried confessions in the Trinity, for,
as Parkes aptly describes such scholars in Prelude to Dialogue,
"the game of discovering Christian beliefs in rabbinic writings,"
is not in the main morally edifying; and when we reflect that
Parkes is only the fourth historian to follow in the footsteps of
Basnages, we appreciate his description of himself as a "pioneer."

The discipline of history shaped his theology and his conviction
that there was no scriptural or historical proof that Christianity
had superceded Judaism, and his belief that Judaism and Christianity are distinct and co-equal religions.

But apart from theological departures, as a scholar Parkes
was even more rare. He was able to take the esoteric, the
emotionally-laden, the superstitiously-saturated matter of
Christian-Jewish relationship, the accumulation of centuries of
obscure laws, Medieval logic and legal terminology, forgotten
definitions and suppressed social nuances, and subject a mass of
details to lines of discourse. He was rare in the ability to bring
together scholarship and readability without sacrificing either. The
matter at hand might be a seventh century Roman law on property,
requiring a page of footnotes--the subject might be tedious, elusive,
obscure--the writing never was. He never cultivated sententious-
ness or ambiguity. He required few rhetorical devices. He knew
that the subject itself, the origins of antisemitism, needed only
excellent scholarship, clear thinking, unflagging scrutiny of
material, a sense of reasonableness and proportion among the
myriad details and implications; and with it all, plain speaking.
He brought to scholarship the qualities of character evident in his
response as chairman of the International Christian Students
Conference: rectitude, common sense, and tenacious honesty.
He was the best of scholars: the scholar with a cause, the

vii

embattled scholar, the passionate scholar; and his was the optimism
of a great scholar with faith in the scholarly process. Surely he was
one to whom Isaiah would have said, with confidence in the man he
was addressing, "Come, let us reason together."

We wish to understand a great man. We hunt his personality
for qualities which will explain him. For without understanding
we cannot hope to imitate, only to admire. But we know from
biographies of other great people that biography will not yield
the secret, however much we compile a collectible of traits. We
note in Parkes a boyhood belief in ghosts--apparently what was
due a Guernsey citizen--balanced with a strong sense of the
practical, an English "facing up to facts" attitude. At the same
time he confesses to irritability and a quick temper, particularly
with the unceasing round of committee work--the occupational
hazard of clerics and activists. He noticed that women who knit
through the interminable stretch of meetings kept their tempers
sweet. In pursuit of equanimity, he took up tapestry work, but
that his nerves were at times stretched too far is evidenced by
the fact that he collapsed from strain on several occasions.
Immersed in Jewish history and the practical problems of both
Jewish and Christian organizational work, he still remained an
Anglican clergyman concerned for the daily lives of his fellow
Christians. He wrote a series of popular books on Christianity
and God under the pseudynom of John Hadham, and during the
war did a series of religious broadcasts in England. If he had
many gifts he also had many loyalties, not least among these to
ordinary people and in the Middle East they counted primarily in
his calculations for peace. Nor was his piety ever embarrassed
by problems of practical politics.

The question arises whether his character was formed in the
religious habits of his family. His ancestors had been Unitarians.
The family were divided in their religious habits. His father was
an agnostic, his mother religious. But she died while he was
still young, after a long illness which left the family impoverished.
He and his sister and brother were left free to choose their own
church practice. Parkes opted for attendance at the country
parishes. No uniformity of thought, no family tradition of
religious practice.

There were many illnesses suffered throughout his life, begin -
ning in early boyhood with severe headaches which sometimes
caused him blindness, a nervous collapse while studying for the
Open scholarship for Oxford, "Dupuytren's contraction of the
planta fascia of one foot, which they decided to fillet," an operation
which caused "clinical death"; a bout of influenza which led to
delirium, several later cases of cardiac arrest, and again physical
and nervous collapse during a lecture tour in the United States.

He reports fatalities and losses in his autobiography in dry,
factual fashion. His brother was killed during the first world war,
his sister lost at sea when the S. S. Leinster was torpedoed in the
Irish Sea; himself so severely gassed during the war his doctors
did not expect him to reach the age of thirty. He was almost
eighty-five when he died. The emotional vibrations are reserved
for his descriptions of nature. He knew, and was proud of knowing,
every stone, bird and flower on the island of Guernsey. Conval-
escence of spirit takes place when the resources of nature are
available to him. He deplored "scriptural infallibility," but believed in the doctrine of Atonement, in the Incarnation and the
Trinity, and in an afterworld, which he regarded as the only
possible victory over evil. To this he added a Jewish perception
of God, expressed at the end of his life, in Voyage of Discoveries:
". . . it is my deepening understanding of the traditional attitudes
of Judaism that has come most to my assistance. It is God the
Creator, not God 'the wholly other,' whose reality overwhelms
me with happiness and expectation." (p. 249).

A career begun unexpectedly at a student conference in the
mid 1920s brought him into confrontation with the whole of Jewish
history and, in the consequences of this century, with the Nazis
as his struggle against antisemitism, his support for the Jews,
and his rescue of refugees, came to their attention. Inevitably,
they attempted to assassinate him, and seriously wounded his
servant in his place. Gilbert Murray, the great Classical scholar,
commented to him of this event: "I hope you are not upset. This
is probably the greatest honour you will ever be paid." But many
of his benevolent friends came to regard him as "dotty" in his
role of Gentile watcher of Jewish affairs. In the end, his career
transcended the estimates of the malignant and the benevolent.
He became for this fated century of Christians and Jews: historian,
theologian, true iconoclast, righteous Gentile. Insight after
insight unfolded in him, his reward and ours:

I had come to reject the whole of the traditional view
of Judaism, as expressed by the universal opinion of
Christian theologians of the eastern and western churches,
of the fundamentalist or liberal, alike. To them, Judaism was the now dead predecessor of Christianity,
but to me it was now a living and contemporary religion.

The title of this book, End of An Exile, is not precisely suitable, as Parkes himself knew. The word "exile" for Jews does
not suggest entirely what it does for Christians. While it borrows
meaning from the circumstances of political exile, it conveys the
religious meaning of "exile from God," a condition which can occur
in several ways, one of which being the loss of Zion as the center
of Jewish life, another being subjection to "the yoke of foreign
nations," an evil of such paramount importance it is referred to
several times in the Talmud. The full evil of "exile" is conveyed
in the Hebrew word, "galut," which Yitzhak Baer, defines:
> The word "Galut" embraces a whole world of facts and
> ideas that have appeared with varying strength and
> clarity in every age of Jewish history. Political serv-
> itude and dispersions, the longing for liberation and
> reunion, sin and repentance and atonement: these are
> the larger elements that must go to make up the concept
> of Galut if the word is to retain any real meaning.
To the extent that Israel "bears the yoke of foreign nations,"
and its political life is contingent, it cannot be said that the exile
has come to an end, but the process has begun.

The word, as Parkes intended it, relates to his interpretation
of Jewish history as a recurrent pattern of Exile and Return, as
seen in the histories of the Exodus, the Babylonian Exile, and the
Diaspora. The earliest of these, the Exodus, bears a title which
has led to a misjudgment of the event. The word "exodus" is a
misdirection--it is not a matter of "going out" but a matter of
"going back in."

There is now archeological evidence to support this view that
the Hebrews' return to Canaan is not the invasion of wandering
tribes, but of a people whose religious identity had been molded
in that land and who return to rejoin an ancestral community.
When Moses experienced God in Horeb, before the Burning Bush,
God identifies Himself as "the God of thy fathers." God

does not identify Himself as a new god, but as the immemorial
God whose presence had been known in Canaan and had been
testified to by Abraham, Isaac and Jacob. Buber raises the
matter in his book, Moses:

> Nowadays. . .there is a widely held view that no twelve
> tribes of Israel were ever in Egypt, that those who were
> in the country were 'the tribes of Joseph' and their
> followers; and that in Canaan these united for the first
> time into a complete twelve-tribe association with
> the tribes that had remained there and which had
> previously constituted a 'six-tribe amphictyony.'

Yehekial Kaufman, in The Religion of Israel, describes the
political process in more detail:

> . . .the consciousness of unity that the Israelite tribes
> display throughout their history cannot be explained
> as a late development. For the isolation and separate
> destinies of the Israelite tribes once settled in Canaan
> and Transjordan would have been sufficient under nor-
> mal circumstances to dissolve even a united people. . . .
> Inexplicable on the basis of later history this sense
> of unity must have had its roots in the period before
> the entry in Canaan. The tribal confederation is
> therefore primary.

Kathleen Kenyon in Archeology in The Holy Land corroborates
this view:

> A theory that has gained acceptance from a number of
> scholars is that there is evidence in the biblical account
> that not all the tribes which made up the subsequent
> Israelite nation took part in the Exodus. This school
> of thought holds that the religious significance of the
> Exodus was such that in the course of time all the
> tribes came to believe that their ancestors took part
> in it. Such a theory has many attractions, particularly
> since it goes far to reconciling biblical account with
> other historical records and with the archeological
> evidence.

It is often assumed that monotheism evolved out of polytheism--
and so it does for the Greeks and for others. But in Canaan, the
Bible suggests that monotheism always existed, at least in Canaan,
alongside other religious structures. When Abraham arrives in
Jerusalem, the knowledge and worship of "the Most High" is

already present, as expressed by Melchizedek. The Bible does
not know of a time when this God does not exist; it does not know
of a theory of deistic evolution. It knows of other gods as it knows
of other people and their histories. But of the historical substance
of the Hebrews themselves, as God's answer to Moses suggests,
it knows only one God. Through this God, the relationship between
Canaan and Egypt remains bridged. Religiously, the people who
had left Canaan--though they were gone four centuries--were the
same people who returned to "the God of their fathers." It is often
said that in Judaism, God is a God who enters history. It is
through the return of the Hebrews to Canaan that God the creator
of the world is conjoined with God the maker of nations.

For reasons that are not clear, but suggest an historical mystique,
it is the exilic experience which usurps attention from the people
who remain in the land. Parkes quarreled with the Zionist organizations for not emphasizing the continuity of Jewish settlement
in Palestine, a continuity which present archeological evidence
now suggests predates the Exodus by several centuries. But it
is the exilic events which impress themselves upon Jewish consciousness. In the Exodus, the returning tribes are molded into
nationhood. They are given a code of law, they are given a
covenant and a moral destiny. They return to the land with riches
of mind and soul. The history of the land begins again with the
drama of their return.

Aside from the fact that contemporary views of the Exodus
suggest that the tribes who remained in Canaan were indigenous,
or at least as old as any other people mentioned in the Bible
(Kathleen Kenyon writes: "Therefore at the period at which the
Hyksos appear in Palestine and Egypt, we have on the move
groups of Hurrians and Habirus. . . ."), it limns the basic
historical Jewish pattern vis a vis Canaan-Palestine-Israel,
expressed more relevantly in the Jewish concept of "Return,"
with its religious implications of "returning" to God--such a
fundamental Jewish thought.

For Parkes, the exilic emphases falsify the history of Zionism
which, he argued persuasively and justifiably, belongs as much
to the continual presence of Jewry in Canaan-Palestine-Israel,
as it does to the scattered communities: "For the fact is that the
majority of the Jewish inhabitants of Israel have never, in the
more than three thousand years of their recorded history, lived
in any other continent or among any other nations." (Prelude to

xii

Dialogue, pp. 132-124). In our day modern political Zionism has usurped attention from this older history of Zionism, as Herzl acknowledged in Der Judenstaat:

The idea which I have developed in this pamphlet is an ancient one. It is the restoration of the Jewish state. . . . I have discovered neither the Jewish situation as it has crystallized in history, nor the means to remedy it.

That history or aspects of a history are often forgotten is not startling news, and a good deal of Parkes' work was a matter of bringing to the surface again such forgotten histories as the Jewishness of Jesus, the continuity of Zionism, ". . .the recurrent emergence of the Holy Land into the very centre of Jewish life " (Prelude to Dialogue, p. 120), and the independent nationhood of the Jews in European history, throughout, from Roman times. Recognition of the Jews as a separate nation was implicit in Roman laws respecting the Jews, and their relationship to Jerusalem was upheld, even after Roman legions drove them from the city. In the fifth century, the Empress Eudocia, widow of Theodosuis ll, secured permission for them to return to Jerusalem. Yitzhak Baer, in Galut, notes that until the seventh century of the common era, Jews still fought for possession of Palestine. There were rabbinical schools and priestly families in the Galilee; in Usha, near Haifa; in Sepphoris and in Tiberias. In Whose Land, Parkes notes that Peki-in "claims a continuous Jewish settlement from Biblical to modern times," and the Middle Ages are marked with the periodic establishment and destruction of Jewish communities in Palestine. Individuals as famous as Maimonides and Judah ha-Levy went to Palestine to live, and groups as cohesive as that of the three hundred rabbis in the thirteenth century left Europe and went to Palestine. Communities were constantly established--and overrun by Persians, Muslims and Crusaders-- but always re-established again. As Parkes notes, the succinct difference in attitude towards this land between Christian and Jew is that for the Christian the Holy Land is a traditional place of pilgrimage--for the Jew a place of settlement. (Prelude to Dialgoue, p. 120).

Throughout the Middle Ages, the concept of Zion was central in the Jewish religion, often interpenetrated with the concept of the Messiah. In Whose Land, Parkes points out that St. Jerome reported that at the time he lived in Bethlehem, "there were few

Christians and that most of the people in the country were Jews."
(p. 47). Indeed, with respect to the claim that the "Holy Land" is
"equally" holy to the three monotheistic faiths, Parkes points out
that only a number of holy sites, built over original Jewish holy
places, are holy in Islam; and that Jerusalem, as a holy city, is
only the third holiest city. As for the sacral nature of the "Holy
Land" in the development of Christianity, he says:

> For Christianity the organizational break was complete.
> In all its subsequent history it never again regarded the
> Holy Land as either its intellectual or geographical centre.
> No bishop of Jerusalem ever contested the primacy of the
> Pope of Rome or the Patriarch of Constantinople; no special
> authority ever attached to the opinions of the scholars
> of the Holy Land; and no permanent centres of learning
> came into existence in the country. (Whose Land , p. 32.)

The magnetic pull of Zion on Jewry throughout the centuries
of dispersion shaped their political conduct in their other lands.
The absence of effort at rebellions, revolutions and coup d'etats
or effort at territorial acquisitions elsewhere was not due to
lack of opportunity (in Portugal in the fourteenth century the pre-
ponderance of armaments manufactury was in the hands of Jews--
it surely would not have been difficult for them to arm themselves for an uprising) or cowardice, but to lack of motivation:
the Jewish people never identified their national aspirations with
any other territory. It is this identification which contstrained
their behavior and which explains why, of the three monotheistic
religions, they have never produced a world conqueror or an
empire. They have never produced an Alexander, a Julius Caesar,
a Napoleon (nor a Hitler, needless to say), nor movements comparable to the armies which followed Mahomet, Ghengis Khan, or
Richard the Lionhearted ; nor have they ever acquired overseas
colonies, possessions, or territories, nor made claims of such
in the name of a Jewish esprit. It is not only antisemitism which
has made their history eccentric.

> For the religion which was developing into a universal-
> istic ethical monotheism never lost its roots in The
> Land: and the people, increasingly dispersed, con-
> sidered residence in any other part of the globe,
> however prosperous it might be, to be 'an exile,'
> or at least 'a dispersion.'
> (Whose Land , p. 26)

xiv

Parkes fought adamantly for this view of Zionism against competing versions, which linked the origins of Zionism to modern forms of nationalism; and he based his theology of the Jewish people as being both particularistic and universalistic on the history and continuity of the Jews in Canaan-Palestine-Israel on the one hand; and on the other hand on the diaspora experiences, as two basic "roots" of Judaism.

Shrewdly, Parkes realized that the modern Zionist political argument was an expression of its secular and adversary position to Orthodoxy, as both groups wrestled for mastery of Jewish history:

> Up to the present the whole tradition of Jewish historiography has been to present the Jew of Europe, and later of America, as the heir to an earlier Jew of the Middle East. He has indeed provided the central figure of Jewish history since about the thirteenth century. At that time Puritan reactionaries destroyed in Fatimid Egypt and the Western Caliphate the happy symbiosis of Jews and Chrisians with their Moslem rulers and their Moslem neighbours. Because of the long stagnation of the area, the Jewish historian tended to forget that substantial Jewish communities went on living there except when there was a European Jewish iruption such as populated sixteenth-century Safed. European Jewish history was more exciting in its continuous incidents, whether tragic or inspiring.
>
> (Prelude to Dialogue, p. 125)

If world history written by Europeans, until recently, was western oriented, so was Zionism written by western Jews, both suffering in focus as a consequence. The correction of this led Parkes to the conclusion that ". . . if more than half the Jews in Israel were in their family background and tradition even more deeply rooted in the countries of the Middle East and North Africa than the Arabs themselves--who only erupted from the peninsula in the seventh Christian century--it was increasingly absurd to maintain that Israel was a totally inacceptable foreign intrusion." (Voyage of Discoveries, p. 236).

Though Parkes greatly respected the Rabbinic traditon as it had developed from the time of Ezra through the Middle Ages, theological and moral problems led him to oppose Orthodoxy and Fundamentalism in both Judaism and Christianity. A

Fundamentalist acceptance of the Bible as "the word of God"
led one into the moral cul de sac of claiming Biblical authority
for slavery, polygamy and the burning of witches; it presented
Christians with the dilemma of a Jesus as messiah and son of
God who damned whole cities and classes of people "without
regard to any distinction between the innocent and the guilty";
of commitment to a belief in hell, "because the parables of the
Gospels constantly terminate with a division of men into sheep
and goats"; and to accept a Jesus who "behaves in a way which,
to contemporary moral standards, not merely denies that he is
God incarnate but makes him a figure unworthy of our admiration."
(Prelude to Dialogue, p. 203.) Finally, it commits the Christian
to antisemitism. Parkes believed that the only way for the churches
to free themselves of this was to throw off the shackles of Biblical
infallibility. The problems in doing this were profound, but he
believed that the evil of not doing this was worse. The views of
the Pharisees and of the Jews as set forth in the New Testament
being not only unfair, but factually untrue, as he argues in
Prelude to Dialogue, the antisemitism it encouraged led the Christian to a false posture.

As an historian Parkes knew that all interpretation was condi-
tional. ". . .the Bible describes the activity of God, as interpreted by men who with their whole heart believed in Him. But
the men who wrote it were men of widely different understanding,
and of widely different time and environment. The literature they
composed covers more than a thousand years of history."
(Prelude to Dialogue, p. 202).

The New Testament is not only the record of the love of a prophet for his people and the courage of his martyrdom, it is also
the record of the disputatiousness of human beings, of argument,
resentment and vindictiveness. It is the record of the range of
human reaction of a people caught in the crisis of change, feeling
the weight and the desperation of responsibility for each decision.
But the crisis is past, and it is time to ask whether we cannot have
the wheat without the chaff? Parkes would have agreed with
Frederick Grant's appraisal in his Foreword to Judaism and The
Christian Predicament:

> Someday the Bible will be loosed from its chains and
> will be understood in a natural and intelligent way.
> Then its real treasure, hitherto in 'earthen vessels,'
> will begin to be apparent--as the poet Coleridge said

long ago. That treasure is its purely religious
teachings. These must be separated from human
prejudices and antagonisms and bigotries. Combined with these religious treasures are the moral
teachings that underlie its whole structure, in both
the Jewish and the Christian scriptures.

What allows Parkes to accept the whole of the Biblical scriptures is his view that underlying them "is the common conviction
of its writers that material power and intellectual activity are
not the central dynamic of history, but that the real dynamic is
the activity of God in His creation." (Prelude to Dialogue, p. 203)

Parkes believed that the relationship between Christianity and
Judaism did not have parallels between Christianity and other non-
Christian religions. Judaism was not another non-Christian religion vis a vis Christianity, but had a unique relationship to it,
which he hoped to expound in a "theology of the Jewish-Christian
Relationship," and he believed that his interpretation of the
Trinity as a manifestation of man as social being, as individual,
and as seeker of knowledge, not only spoke to this theology, but
was "anthropologically" correct. Though he recognized that
theology was alien to the Jewish spirit (and was critical of this,
erroneously, I think), and though his interpretation of the Trinity
is too abstract to solace ordinary Christians (committing the
same error which much theology does), he believed there could
be no future fruitful relationship between Judaism and Christianity
unless the balance was restored, and unless the "work" of Judaism
was allowed to continue to reflect the "work of Divine Action."
To this end, the missionary attitude was a negation of the meaning
of Judaism, of its "mission in the world as a covenanted community,"
in search for laws which governed and led to social harmony or,
as the Bible exhorted: "Justice, justice thou shalt seek." Unfortunately, as Parkes knew, a good deal of the work of interfaith
dialogue is still undertaken in the spirit of missionary work, and
wherever this is so it damages the endeavor.

Parkes was at times too schematic and wrote too decisively
about the differences between Christians and Jews (for we all
need justice, social harmony, love and mercy, and intersect
historically as individuals, as families and as communities).
Obligations and perceptions are often forced on one by time and
place and circumstance. Then, too, to distinguish between
Christians and Jews on the basis of developments in the Bible(s)

xvii

leads one to overlook other developments and attitudes as, for example, towards sex, virginity, monasticism, congregationalism or its absence. The presence of hagiographical literature in Christianity, and its virtual absence in Judaism, suggests and makes for as much difference between the two religions as the differences in their hierarchical structures. In the long run, every difference is a difference, and over two thousand years differences become compounded. Yet, one can say this and not gainsay at the same time the central, overlapping, ever magnetizing centrality of interests stemming from the Bible which may hold them in deadly and dear combat forever.

Parkes' perception of the role of the Jewish people was possibly heightened by his concern with the failure of Christianity to solve political problems--a concern which arose, as with so many others, in the aftermath of the first world war. In Prelude to Dialogue, he writes that he had come to realize "that there was nothing central in the Christian tradition which could be called a doctrine of the natural community. . .but that there was a strong and uninhibited Christian tradition which denied the relevance of the Christian insight to the political field. . . ." (p.193), whereas Judaism "met the reality of the human situation at a different point"; it spoke to "the Divine Action in politics and international relations."

He quarreled with Church teaching "that Christ is the solution to every problem," (Prelude to Dialogue, p.209), a view, he wrote, which reflected the optimism of first century Christianity, but which nineteen hundred years of history should have taught better. The doctrine of "salvation in Christ has led to excommunication of Christians by other Christians and to the total negligence of the 'universal responsibility of a Creator,' and denial of the existence of holiness within other religions." (ibid.) The "Christocentric" nature of Christianity had led to such absurdities as the thirty-nine articles which states "that God considers it to be sinful if any man perform a good work save through faith in Jesus Christ." (Prelude, p. 210).

As a pastor and as an historian, Parkes believed in the principle of human responsibility, with divine intervention and he criticized Christianity for its failure to create "a theology of politics": "The influence of the Church in the transformation of society has been negligible. In the field of law. . .it had been disastrous." (Prelude, pp. 206-207). Its ethic of brotherly love, as Niebuhr

had pointed out in Moral Man and Immoral Society, suitable in
individual relationships, was irrelevant to nations and had contributed to confusion in modern political thinking by obliterating
the distinction between different levels of moral action; while
the shock of political confrontation has assailed Israel in debate
about the use of political power--"a subject into which the Jewish
world has now been plunged in an extreme form with the creation
of the state of Israel in defiance of the united hostility of the Arab
world." (Prelude, p. 184).

His Zionism grounded in theology as well as history, he believed missionary work among the Jews a frustration of this "Divine Action,"
and that ignorance of Jews and Judaism often went hand in hand
with a pro-missionary posture and an anti-Zionist position. Parkes
recognized the connection between subliminal missionary hopes on
the part of all the Christian groups and their posture in the Middle
East, and he was outspoken in his vehemence towards this. Of
one of his trips to the Middle East, he wrote in Voyage of Discoveries:

> I went with personal introductions to all the Christian
> agencies, academic like the Near East Foundation, or
> religious, whether Catholic, Protestant or Quaker. The
> experience was horrfying. The ignorance of Israel was
> as complete as identification with the refugees. A Quaker
> lady, whose views would have pleased Goebbels, explained
> to me that, if they did not identify their opinions com-
> pletely with those of the refugees, they would not be al-
> lowed to work in the camps. This hideous and destruc-
> tive moral cowardice was common to Catholics, Protes-
> tants and Quakers. It is a curious fact that I have never
> met a pro-Israel Christian with whom one could not dis-
> cuss in a rational and friendly way any question concern-
> ing the Arab world. Every Christian I have met who is
> "pro-Arab" is not merely anti-Israel but both ignorant
> and mildly or virulently antisemitic. It is a most
> tragic problem, and does immense harm to the un-
> fortunate Palestinian Arabs whom it encourages to
> live in a world of fantasy, where none of the limitations
> which apply to the rest of humanity apply to them, and
> where they have no responsibility for any sins they
> have committed.
>
> (p. 219).

Never have so many who were badly informed or not informed
at all, or morally inadequate been called to an historical challenge:
to render justice in the Middle East--for the fellahin, for the Jew,
for the Kurd and for the Christian. Among Parkes' greatest
gifts, as Roy Eckardt points out in his eulogy, "greatest of all
was his empathy," for beyond all historical and political arguments his concern was with the ordinary Christian, Jew or Muslim
who would continue to live here after the armies and the diplomats
went home.

After thirty years, End of An Exile holds up exceptionally well.
For anyone who wishes to begin to "know" rather than to be merely
informed, the book is a good beginning. Ideally, it should be only
a beginning, and serve to introduce the reader to Parkes' other
work on antisemitism, on Jewish history, and on the Middle East.
His later books on this last subject, Whose Land and A History
of The Palestine Peoples amplifies many details, extends some
arguments and, of course, updates his position on Jerusalem,
which in End of An Exile is necessarily out-of-date. Parkes was
too ill to revise it at the time of this republication and requested
that it stay in the book as it is. Written in 1954, it offers no
solution, but it offers insight. Later, in Whose Land he wrote
of Jerusalem, that of the three monotheistic religions:
>Each is there by its own right, but each is not there
>because Jerusalem is the heart and nerve centre of
>its world-wide community. That applies only to
>Jewry and Judaism.
>
>That Jerusalem should remain united and within
>the political sovereignty of Israel is right and
>proper; for, though both Christendom and Islam
>venerate it as a holy city, neither religion could
>claim that it has ever had the place in their
>thought that it has had for nearly three millennia of
>Jewry.
>
>   (p. 321).
Parkes' subsequent writing on the subject of Jews and
Arabs reveals some peripheral changes, but no substantive
change. Since there is so much misinformation on the subject,
it is important here to quote him on the demographic aspect of
the problem:

It is false to oppose to this Jewish position either
the idea that it automatically overrides the rights
of the Arabs, or, on the other hand, a conception
of an Arab Palestine, fully populated by the ancestors of the present Arab population for a period of
centuries and millennia. The frontiers created in
1919 are quite new and artificial frontiers; they do
not correspond to any historic Turkish or Arab
divisions. They were created to divide the British
and French Mandates, roughly along the line of the
Biblical frontier of the Holy Land. Historically
Palestine is part of "Syria," and the Arabs of Palestine are Syrians. Considerably more than half of
those living at present in Palestine originally lived,
or are descended from Arabs who lived, in the
northern part of Syria or in other Arab countries,
until the prosperity consequent on Zionist colonisation gradually drew them by the prospect of work
and high wages. Very many Arabs have actually
entered the country since 1920.

(An Enemy of The People: Antisemitism, p. 134)

Of those "Arabs," roughly the peasant conservative population
who trace their origins back for millennia and are pre-Islamic,
they are originally of Christian, pagan, or Jewish origin:

Palestine did not become a Moslem land through the
entry of new inhabitants professing Islam, for the
Arab conquest involved practically no change in the
population. Insofar as the peasantry are concerned,
the Moslems of today are in large measure descendants of the Jews, Christians and pagans of earlier
centuries. As in most countries, it is the urban
population and the landowners who represent more
recent immigrations. Among the latter in particular are some ancient Arab families, but in general
the word Arab, before its modern nationalist use
came into fashion, applied only to the Beduin, and
it would have been no compliment to a fellah to call
him an "Arab."

(Prelude to Dialogue, p. 115).

Paradoxically--perhaps--it was this aspect of the fellahin background, rooted in the ancient peasantry of the land, which gave

xxi

Parkes reason for hope in the sociological elements, if not in the political ones. As for the latter, he was opposed to binationalism on the grounds that if it is just to create two separate states, it would not be just to create them in such a way that one or the other or neither would be viable. States that are not viable, or chained together in a disastrous fashion, are not better than no state. ". . . all the evidence is that it would not work. It is. . . yoking together two horses, one of which cannot stop and the other of which does not wish to start." (An Enemy of the People, p. 136.)

In End of An Exile, he regarded the espousal of the cause of the Palestinian Arabs by the other Arab nations as altruistic. By 1969, when he published his various lectures in Prelude to Dialogue, he appraised the relationship of the Arab states to the Arabs living in Israel differently:

> They are an embarrassed minority, because as long as
> Israel is surrounded by hostile Arab states, so long do
> her Arab citizens know that a peculiarly beastly fate
> would await them were there a sudden attack on Israel,
> and did they fall prisoners to their brother Arabs. Many
> dare not show excessive Israeli patriotism, and the
> Israelies are realists enough not to expect them to.
> Much of the propaganda alleging that they are treated
> as second-class citizens ignores these obvious facts.
> It is part of the paradox of Israel that only the sur-
> rounding Arab states can make the Arabs of Israel
> into first-class Israeli citizens. But within Israel,
> their difficult and isolated situation is well understood
> but little talked of.

> (p. 133).

To render justice in the Middle East it is not sufficient to have the attention of the media, to have a microphone, a format, a briefcase and a diplomat's license plate. It is not even sufficient to lend the weight of institutional, papal or state or parliamentary authority declaiming "the legitimate rights of the Palestinian Arabs." To approach the problem, one must be James Parkes.

I wish to express my thanks to Donald Altschiller of the American Jewish Historical Society, who kept me alert and sent me the necessary articles he thought I should read, to Dr. Carl

Voss again, and to those journals and institutions and people who have generously allowed me to republish their articles in the appendix. The article on The Parkes Library was written by James Parkes himself and will give the reader an idea of the style of the man as a scholar and a writer. Robert A. Everett's article and Rose G. Lewis' article each develops an aspect of Parkes' thought in his contribution to the study of Jewish history, and Jewish-Christian relations. Carl Hermann Voss' article is invaluable for its background and history of the American Christian Palestine Committee. I thought it fitting to conclude the articles in the appendix with A. Roy Eckardt's eulogy and summation: "A great man has left us."

The assessment of James Parkes' work is beginning. He knew better than anyone how long it would take. Once when he described his work to a friend as "pioneering to reverse a verdict with nearly two thousand years behind it," he was asked how long he thought it would take. "Three hundred years," he said. To which we must respond, "The work is long and the Master is impatient."

Roberta Kalechofsky
September, 1982

Acknowledgments

When an historian ' sticks to his last,' and confines his attention to the record of men's past activities, his acknowledgments should be to the sources which he has consulted, and the authorities of whom he has made use. But when the same historian seeks to interpret contemporary events in the light of his understanding of history, then, if he is wise, he will consult with living contemporaries of as many outlooks and as diverse experience as he can collect.

The chapters of this book were originally composed at various times, some in their present form, some first in more tentative expositions. While the opinions ultimately expressed are inevitably and properly my own, I should be lacking in courtesy if I did not thank the Jewish Historical Society of England for the opportunity to deliver before them chapters ten and thirteen in the form of the Presidential lectures for 1950 and 1949 ; and if likewise I did not thank for their comments on the manuscript or on the subjects which it treats, Professor Horace M. Kallen and Rabbi Dr. Maurice N. Eisendrath in New York ; Professors Norman Bentwich and L. A. Mayer, Dr. Leo Kohn, Rabbi Jacob Herzog, and Dr. Chaim Wardi in Jerusalem ; and Rabbi Dr. Altmann, the Very Rev. C. Witton Davies, and Dr. Walter Zander in England. There are others whom I should have mentioned by name, and I beg them to forgive me for having omitted them. For in truth, as my dedication should make clear, my gratitude goes to an innumerable company with whom I have discussed things Jewish over twenty-five years and three continents.

James Parkes

Foreword

THE story of the Jews embodies the longest period of continuous *creativity* to be found in the annals of any nation. Other peoples may claim a longer *existence,* others may have reached a high level of culture earlier, and have maintained it undisturbed until the modern world irrupted into its life. But for more than three thousand years the Jews have known no conditions which would allow them either to sit back in tranquillity, satisfied with their past achievements, or to watch with incurious eyes an indifferent world passing their doors and not seeking to enter. Somewhere within the Jewish people there was always curiosity about the world outside ; and the cultures and religions of the world were always pressing in on them, whether with the seductive allurements of a less puritanical existence, or through the harsh demands of missionary zeal. Even the strange life of the Eastern European ghettoes, where they wove and re-wove in ever more intimate detail patterns of life venerated and defined by centuries of tradition, was lived against a background of constant wariness, of persecution, and sometimes of flight and emigration to totally different environments. The youngest state in the world embodies the oldest memories. And those memories have yet another claim to our attention.

The place of any people in the gallery of the nations rests on three factors : what it expresses through its own genius, what it has drawn into its life from its contacts with others, and what it has passed out into the common pool of the world's heritage to mould the life of others. All these factors have been experienced in special measure by this people. No other people can show the maintenance and development of its national genius under such exceptional and unpropitious circumstances. No other people has lived in such intimate contact with so many cultures, or watched so many nations rise and fall with which it had such entangling links. And a nation whose religion is the parent of the two other monotheisms of the world could rest its claim to an exceptional place in the world's gallery of nations on that alone, even if its influences had not—

as they have—also expressed themselves in a dozen other fruitful forms.

Today the Jews are passing through a period of dynamic and even chaotic change, following on a tragedy which still sears their memories and strengthens their determination. The infant state of Israel is grasping in its inexperienced hands threads which bind it to the destinies of almost every other people in the world by the treble plait of its own dispersed brethren, its geographical position at the heart of one of the world's storm centres, and its own population which is neither eastern nor western but both, which is neither socialist nor capitalist but both.

The title chosen for the book, *End of an Exile,* however, refers to far more than just the establishment of a Jewish state in the land of Israel, epoch-making though that event is. Denial of a place among the free peoples of the world was but one of the exiles imposed on Jewry for nearly two thousand years. For a longer period than that their dispersion has been a fundamental part of the Jewish story, and the long struggles for emancipation likewise mark the end of an exile, partial or total, from the life and thought of non-Jewish civilisations. Nor is that all: modern scholarship is just beginning to challenge the exile of the post-biblical contribution of Judaism from the religious story of mankind, and to realise that Judaism did not cease to grow with the coming of Christianity.

The purpose of these essays is to survey some of the factors in this complex situation, both as they affect the destiny of the Jews, and as they touch us who are not Jews and whose religion is not Judaism, but who cannot be indifferent or unaffected by what future the Jewish people mould for themselves out of factors of such fascinating complexity. It would be kind if history would stand still, and allow them to tackle their immense problems one by one. But their whole past has risen up—not *against* but *with* them— at a moment when there are no stable values anywhere in the world, and when every people, albeit with less poignancy, is passing through some aspect of the same confusion which marks the passing of an epoch in the world's history.

James Parkes

PART ONE

The Roots of Israel

In other volumes I have recounted the story of the Balfour Declaration and the history of the Mandate. They will be found in particular in The Emergence of the Jewish Problem, 1878-1939, *and in* A History of Palestine from A.D. 135 to 1948. *No one can pretend that the story is simple, or that it is easy to move objectively through the maze of promises made by the British during the first world war, or assess fairly the relative rights of Jews and Arabs on which those promises rested.*

But whereas the Arab case is a normal one, and easy to understand, for it rests on the normal association of a people with the land in which it has lived for centuries, the Jewish case is not so easy to appreciate. For it rests not on the immediate political situation in which the promises were given, but on a long history, little known even to many Jews, and not easy to assess in terms of a political decision. But without some knowledge of that past association no fair judgment can be made ; and, however dimly appreciated, it was acceptance of that past connection which moved many Englishmen, Lord Balfour among them, to take a unique decision.

The tree of Israel springs from five roots deeply embedded in the experience of the Jewish people. The first and deepest is Judaism, as the religion of a community. The second is the Messianic hope, intimately connected ever since the destruction of the Jewish state with the expectation of a return to the Promised Land. The third is Jewish history, and the long experience of dispersion and insecurity. The fourth is the continuity of Jewish life in Palestine. The fifth is the unique relationship between the Jewry of Palestine and the whole Jewish people. The word ' Palestine ' is used in this section, as it is the name which covered all the population of the country from the time of Hadrian to that of the establishment of Israel (A.D. 135-1948).

3

CHAPTER I

The First Root : Judaism

THE Jewish world to-day is as much under the influence of secularism as any part of its Christian environment, and Zionism has in very large measure expressed itself in the normal terms of political nationalism. A certain group of religious Jews makes a sharp distinction between the political activities of Zionism, which they condemn, and the true character of Jewry, which they claim to be a religious fellowship ; and they find ample justification for their attitude in the secularist philosophy of Zionism, and the secularist, and even at times chauvinist, tone of Zionist claims.

Nevertheless, just as contemporary secularism cannot undo the influence of Christendom in the formation of European civilisation over the past millennium, so secularist Zionism cannot alter the fact that the deepest root from which the state of Israel has sprung is the Jewish religion. And by this is meant not merely the obvious historical fact that it was the peculiar form and intensity which monotheism took among the Jewish people which alone assured their survival. It is more than that. The nature of Judaism is such that, in all his wanderings, each individual Jew was conscious that he was a member of a single people—he would not have understood had he been asked whether that people constituted a religious or a national community—and that the fulfilment of his own destiny was inextricably bound up with the safety and restoration of his people.

Judaism presents the paradox to an outsider of claiming to be a universal religion while at the same time it is bound up with the Jewish nation. If we think of its content primarily as the mono-theistic and ethical beliefs of individuals, then the claim that only by entrance into the Jewish nation is it possible to hold these beliefs is obviously absurd. The same beliefs are shared by Unitarians, and many elements in them are common to both the Jewish and Christian faiths. If we look at Judaism from the opposite point of

5

view as being a national religion, in which Jews claim to enjoy a special protection and privilege by the mere fact of physical birth, then those who are not Jews are entitled to reject its pretensions as inconsistent with any belief in the common fatherhood of God, and to refuse to give any sanctity to political claims which Jews may base on a literal interpretation of their own scriptures.

But, in fact, to bring Judaism into either of these categories is to miss its essential characteristic. Judaism is the religion of a community, because essential concerns of the religion itself are communal. It emphasises as much as any Protestant Church the ultimate responsibility of each individual for his destiny before God, but yet it is not a religion basically concerned with individual salvation. It believes in the divine society as much as any Christian of the Catholic tradition ; but it regards this divine society not primarily as a body of believers separate from the larger ethnic or national community in which they live, but as the national unit itself, in all its political, social, commercial, educational, and other responsibilities and relationships. The place which the Church occupies in Christian thought is occupied in Judaism by the whole people, good, bad and indifferent, faithful and unfaithful. Christian thought, even before St. Augustine, thought in terms of two cities, the City of God, and a city of this world, whose ruler was not God. Judaism knows no such dualism, and to speak of a ' Jewish Church ' is a complete misnomer, if by the phrase is meant a community composed exclusively of members drawn together by a common belief (even if some hold it lightly) contrasted with a world outside of those who do not belong to it, even though they belong to the same people or nation. The vast body of rabbinic writings is little concerned with what Christians would recognise as theological or religious topics ; but it is intimately concerned with aspects of common life over which the Churches have only slowly come to claim any authority. The belief of the individual Jew in the maintenance of his people is, therefore, basically religious not political, because it rests on the belief of the ancient Israelite and the medieval rabbi alike that a national society was essential to the maintenance of the Jewish religion : through the life of a nation the revealed will of God was done.

While the issue is not in reality whether Jews are right or wrong in their beliefs, but only what in fact their beliefs imply, yet, since the endorsement of the Balfour Declaration involved the world as

6

a whole, it should be added that this belief in themselves as a chosen people is not, as sometimes said, a Jewish version of the Nazi belief in themselves as a *Herrenvolk*. Of course, there have been in every generation Jews who have interpreted this faith in terms of contempt and hostility for the non-Jewish world. In times of misery and persecution such Jews were usually numerous. But this cannot be made a reproach against the religion itself ; for prophets and rabbis alike regarded the choice as a responsibility and not a privilege, and reinforced their teaching with illustration, legend, and folk-lore. It was said that the Law had been given in all the languages of the world, so that all might consider whether to accept it, and that Israel alone was willing to bear its yoke. It was pointed out that the Law was given in the desert at Sinai, outside Israel's frontiers, and this was used to remind Jews that they could never consider it their exclusive possession.

Jews, then, believed that at Sinai Israel was called to a particular vocation *as a people* ; and the religion which developed from Sinai, alike in the message of the prophets, in the books of the Law, and in the codes of the rabbis, presupposes a responsibility before God of and for the whole people. That is why rabbinic legislation covered every aspect of social and communal life, and dealt with a man's business relations as much as with his personal religion. That also is why a Jew could not live a full religious life in isolation ; for that he needed to be a member of a synagogue. In all of Judaism there is this pervading sense of a whole community, in all its affairs devoted to the fulfilment of a divine purpose ; and it is therefore natural that the restoration of the people as a whole should always have survived in the belief of the individual Jew.

This survival is all the more remarkable in that during almost the whole period in which rabbinic Judaism was being formulated, Jews were not independent, and that in all the formulations of rabbinic practice reference had to be made to the validity of the laws of the people among whom they lived. But centuries of this tradition only accentuated the belief that one day these non-Jewish laws would have no more validity over Jewish lives ; and the 'times of the exile' were always contrasted, as a temporary phenomenon, with the times of fulfilment when Israel, sovereign in its own home, would be able to devote itself entirely to obedience to the divine law of Sinai.

Even though many of those who created the modern Zionist

7

movement were in reaction against the orthodoxy of their day, they inherited to the full this deep feeling for the whole people which orthodoxy had implanted in them. They might speak of Jewish culture instead of Jewish religion ; in modern jargon they may speak of ' folk-ways,' but the essential idea remains unchanged.

At no time was this restoration of the community thought of as taking place in another world. Even those who looked to its coming through a miracle, envisaged the miracle as occurring within the space and time of our present history. However distressed Jewish life might be, however restricted the opportunities allowed them by Christian or Muslim law, it was in this world that they expected the restoration to take place ; and that it *would* take place they had no doubt.

The long centuries of the dispersion had largely stripped the belief of any precise political tinge ; it did not turn Jews into revolutionary or subversive elements within the states wherein they dwelt. Within the broad framework of nineteenth-century liberal democracy the Jewish ethic was so perfectly compatible with citizenship that many Jews accepted assimilation within the society of which they were citizens as an ideal compatible with their religious loyalty. For them the restoration of a Jewish people was indeed relegated to a remote future ; but it must always be remembered that those who found this assimilation possible were never more than a small minority during a brief period of history. And even with these assimilated Jews the conception of a single Jewish community remained alive in one field, and that field was the one in which it was relevant in practice. Prosperous Jews of nineteenth or twentieth-century London, Paris or New York might be ready to ignore a religious unity with the poor Jews of Warsaw, Baghdad or Tunis ; they did not think in terms of a common privilege, divinely given, which they should share with them. Many had ceased to believe in their religion. But they did not forget that they and the Jews of Warsaw, Baghdad, and Tunis were all alike ' Jews ' when the latter were persecuted or in distress. Modern history is full of the organisations established by Jews in Western Europe and America to fight for political rights and social progress for Jews in Eastern Europe, in Asia, and in Africa ; their philanthropy knew no bounds ; and there is probably no voluntary organisation anywhere with such a record of solidarity with the unpopular distressed as the American Joint Distribution Committee to which American Jewry has contributed annually since the first world war millions and tens of millions of dollars.

This, then, is the first, as it is also the deepest, root of Israel—that the whole Jewish religious tradition has impressed on every successive generation of Jews, as a fundamental consequence of the first divine call at Sinai, that *as a people* they are called to fulfil a divine purpose which can only be fully expressed through the life of an independent society.

CHAPTER II

The Second Root : The Messianic Hope

ONCE we appreciate the extent to which the idea of a whole community devoted to the fulfilment of a divine order in society permeates the structure of historic Judaism, it is easy to understand the different development which the Messianic idea underwent in the Synagogue and the Church. Almost within the lifetime of the apostles Christian thought, as the Book of Revelation shows us, had turned away from interest in the actual city of Jerusalem and the land of Palestine to a heavenly Jerusalem associated with the second coming of the Messiah and with the vision of eternal life. But with the Jewish people the enforced dispersion which followed the two unsuccessful rebellions against Rome only intensified their love of the actual soil and stones of their holy land and city ; and the Messianic hope was linked ever more intimately with the restoration to the one and the rebuilding in freedom of the other. Both developments were natural ; for Christians were building a universal community out of personal surrenders in which national traditions played no part ; whereas the Jewish concern was inevitably linked to the space and time of history within which alone a community can be a reality.

In centuries when the verbal infallibility of the Bible was the common belief of Jews and Christians alike, it is natural that the many promises of restoration which are to be found in the prophets should have played an important part in sustaining the courage and giving certainty to the hope of Jewry amid the sorrows of exile and the miseries of persecution ; and these prophecies of restoration become ever more intimately identified with the expectation of the coming of the Messiah. In the first century many different ideas as to his nature and function competed for recognition, and there were sections of Jewry who were little interested in the idea at all, relegating it to a distant future. As the sorrows of exile came to affect almost the whole people—for only a small minority inhabited the Holy Land after the second war

10

with Rome—so the concept of the person and the function of the Messiah became clearer ; a single picture came to be more generally accepted ; and the question of his coming came to be of common interest. In Jewish thought the Messiah, though divinely called and divinely inspired, had little in common with the Divine Person whom the Christians saw in Jesus Christ. Whatever thought of universal judgment and redemption from the burden of sin and evil Jews might associate with his coming, they did not think of him himself as ' redeemer ' ; and although hopes of universal peace and brother-hood were indissolubly linked with the concept of the Messianic Age, the realisation of these hopes was not the main function which the Messiah himself was expected to fulfil. His prime function was the gathering in of the dispersion, and the restoration of the Jewish people to the land of their fathers, the land they believed to be theirs by divine promise. There he would rule as the righteous king ; all nations would come to accept him—whether voluntarily or by conquest ; and after a period of rule he would deliver up his kingdom to God.

Again and again in their history rumour spread through the Jewish world that somewhere the Messiah had appeared, and the consequences were always the same. Jews began to sell their homes, dispose of their goods, and gather themselves to await the summons of the Holy Land. Some in their excitement expected the sea to open before them ; others sought ships to transport them ; but that the Messiah summoned them *home* none doubted. On many occasions men arose believing that they were themselves the promised Messiah ; and if some were charlatans, some were mistaken enthusiasts. One summoned Christendom to fight with them against the Turks ; one demanded of the Vatican the release of all Jews within Christendom ; one hoped for this same release from the sultan in Constantinople. Messianic rumour and the Messianic hope took many forms ; but the return to Palestine was central in all. There could be no redemption which was not redemption from foreign rule.

Even when no Messianic rumour was in the air, the hope of return found expression every year in the Passover service celebrated in every Jewish home. There in the commemoration of the deliverance from Egypt each generation associated itself with those who had eaten the bitter bread of exile in the land of the Pharaohs ; and each generation felt that it participated in the great journey to the promised land as the last words of the festival service echoed in the hearts of each family: Next year in Jerusalem.

Although ancient pamphleteers and modern antisemites have at times pretended alarm that Jews were coming to assume that one of the lands of the dispersion was to be their promised land, and would be acquired by their gold, or conquered for them by supernatural power, such an idea never occurs in Jewish history. However numerous a Jewish community, however prosperous, it had no thought but that in due course it would abandon its temporary abode for the one promised land. Of course, ‘ordinary’ Jews thought of it as a belief which would not affect themselves, in exactly the same way as ‘ordinary’ Christians relegated the End of the World to a period after they themselves had safely died in the full possession of their property—*après moi le deluge* is an attitude common to all. But this does not affect the reality or the universality of the belief, even if, when things were going well, its edges became blurred and its political implications were lost in a vision of a remote future.

Although the Messianic belief continued to develop in exile and at a distance from the land involved, Jews were at no period ignorant of what was happening in the Holy Land itself. Travellers visited it constantly ; and emissaries from the communities of the Land visited the synagogues of the dispersion. And all that both had to tell fitted into the picture which the Jews drew from the Bible itself. They knew that since their departure no new kingdom had arisen within its borders, and that it was never, under all its successive rulers (except the Latin kings of Jerusalem), more than a province, usually a neglected one, of an empire whose centre was elsewhere. They knew of its increasing desolation after the Arab conquest. For the Arabs had conquered the three richest areas of the ancient world, the valleys of the Nile and the Euphrates and the province of Syria, and their own failures, aided by the invasions of Mongols, Tartars, Mamluks, and Turks, had turned them all into as near a desert as the bounty of nature made possible.

Century by century travellers told them how literally the words of their ancient prophets were being fulfilled. God had said that their cities should be desolate and without inhabitant ; and they learned that it was so, and that the land was covered with ruins. The owl and the jackal dwelt in their ancient palaces and holy places, and Jerusalem itself had to bemoan the poverty and oppression under which its inhabitants laboured. Throughout the land the goats of the peasant pastured where rich communities had grown their wine and their corn and their olives. The wells were filled up ; the boundaries were broken down. In the constant feuds between Arab villages, and in the constant exposure of all to the raiding, murder, and looting of the bedouin, it was no exaggeration to speak of a land where every man's hand was against his neighbour and where oppression and unrighteousness flourished. The picture was not inaccurate ; it is amply confirmed by Christian travellers right down to the middle of the nineteenth century ; and if descriptions are thought unreliable or subjective it is amply borne out by archæology ; it is visible in the ruins which are the most prominent feature of most photographs of the country taken before 1914 ; and it is finally confirmed by the statistics which show that at the beginning of the nineteenth century, when the population of most countries was still expanding, that of Palestine had sunk to little more than half a million and was still diminishing.

The slogan of Israel Zangwill : ' the land without a people for the people without a land ' was exaggerated, but it had quite enough truth in it to veil the difficulties which would inevitably arise out of a return based on a political decision, and realised in terms of day-to-day practical possibilities.

CHAPTER III

The Third Root : Jewish History

FOR more than a millennium almost the whole Jewish people was divided up into innumerable separate communities which lived as local minorities somewhere within the territories of either Christendom or Islam. And neither religion could grant them equality. The Christian Church within a hundred years of its peace with the Roman Empire early in the fourth century had begun to deprive Jews of their civic and political rights ; and the final status which was allotted to the Jewish communities of Christendom, that of witnesses to the crime of deicide by the misery and humiliation of their existence, precluded any idea of regarding them as equals. It was from other than Christian sources that the movement for emancipation sprang at the time of the French revolution. Likewise, Islam, by the authority of Muhammad himself, could not grant equality to those who were not Muslims ; and though some groups were more privileged than others, the assumption of equality with a true believer, even in dress and deportment, was always an act punishable by law. In such conditions it might be argued that Jews should have migrated elsewhere. But, in actual fact, there was no alternative but to live within the domain of one religion or the other. Between them they covered the whole viable territory of the then known world. Even if some alternative territory had existed, the conditions of the time would have made a mass migration of men, women, children, and movable property impossible. Jews had no army ; in many countries they had no training in the use of arms and were forbidden to bear them. In any case Christian and Muslim rulers, who drew considerable profit from their presence, would have prevented their departure by force.

Both religions granted them that measure of autonomy which just made their communal life possible, and just permitted, in however restricted a measure, the preservation of the essential quality of Judaism. But the restriction was always there ; and therefore, even when conditions were temporarily tolerable or even favourable, Jewish life always looked beyond the present to some future development which the present could not realise. Only for a small minority of Jews, and for a brief period, has there been an exception to this statement. In the western world in the nineteenth and twentieth centuries it was possible for some Jews to accept an assimilation so complete that they lost entirely the basic qualities of the Jewish tradition, and saw in their Jewishness nothing more than a personal religious choice, or the memory of a vanished past.

This picture of the compulsive influence of desire to fulfil a religious destiny may appear to some remote from the motives which move ordinary men. Human nature is astonishingly adaptable. It has a way of finding satisfaction for its ideals in the achievement of what is possible. It may then well seem too idealistic to argue that the inability of Jews under alien rule to practise in full their religion could, of itself, have kept alive a Messianic hope. If all that were at stake were the hopes of idealists for perfection, then, it might be said, it was for Judaism to make an adjustment with reality, and not for Jews to follow a chimæra.

But it was not all. The deficiencies in their conditions made themselves felt, not only to religious idealists, but to ordinary Jewish men, women, and children. The autonomy which both religions granted, and the basic toleration on which it rested, were both strictly limited. Christendom tolerated the Jews because it was held, on the evidence of St. Paul's epistle to the Romans, that their conversion would prelude the second coming of the Messiah. With literal minds, Christians believed that if no Jews survived to fulfil this expectation, then no second coming could take place. But Christendom likewise ordained precisely the status of inferiority which Jews must observe as a deicide people. The badge, the ghetto, the censorship of books, the limitation of travel, of rights of justice, and many other details, certified their peculiar position ; and some of these conditions survived into the twentieth century, for instance, for the large section of the Jewish world which lived in Tsarist Russia.

In the same way Muslims tolerated the Jews, because Muhammad had laid down that the ' peoples of the Book,' that is, the Jews and Christians, were to be protected and allowed to live anywhere under Muslim rule save in the Arabian peninsula itself. But it was equally laid down that no non-Muslim was in any way to pretend equality with a Muslim. This in itself was serious ; but what was of universal significance to Jewries in Muslim lands was that no non-Muslim had any right to protect himself against attack

15

by a Muslim. He might not lift his hand against a Muslim even in self-defence. In Muslim law it was laid down that if the government failed to protect a Jew against such attack, it was bound to return to him the special tax which he had paid for such protection. Here indeed is evidence of the noble intentions of Muslim law-makers—but how often in fact was even this cold comfort available to the victim ?

Popes and imams, princes and amirs, were usually ready to guarantee their Jewish communities the rights the law allowed them ; and the more noble among them would even do it without thought of reward and without the stimulation of a bribe, though it has to be admitted that such nobility was rare. All alike would deplore and condemn popular violence. But leaders of both religions equally insisted on the status of inferiority which the laws demanded ; and it is a universally valid psychological fact that you cannot permanently maintain a carefully graded superiority and inferiority between two groups of people living together. One of two things must happen. The inferior group will gather power and climb to equality, or the superior group, especially among its less educated members, will accept the official inferiority as an excuse for the physical oppression more agreeable to its temperament, and will indulge in violence. And the net results will always be the same: a deterioration of character on both sides.

It is often said that Jews must have given some excuse for the hardships from which they suffered ; and, of course, Jews are no more perfect than any other human group. But basically it was their status, and not either their religion or their ethnic characteristics, which was at the bottom of their tragedy. No group could maintain undimmed through a millennuim those qualities which are characteristic of a free people, and which men easily notice and admire, when they have to live in the positions of inferiority and often daily humiliation which both the dominant religions imposed on them. They were cringing ? They were clannish and secretive ? They kept two standards, one for dealing with their own people, one for outsiders ? They secretly despised their masters and would plot against them when they could ? They were untruthful, ungenerous, unreliable, unclean ? So it has always been with groups submitted to such treatment ; and the answer is always that which Abbé Gregoire flung at his opponents in the French Revolutionary Assembly which first granted Jews emancipation: ' if you must

16

once again rake up the misbehaviour of Jews in the past, and their rottenness in the present, then do it only in order to repent of your own handiwork.' Of course, not all Jews suffered this deterioration ; but where it was true, it was no more true of them than of others who have endured similar misfortunes.

A second consequence of their dependence was that Jewish life was always insecure. Everywhere the most everyday necessities depended on the good will of others. It is difficult for the contemporary non-Jew to realise how widespread this condition was, how long it lasted, and how small a page in the long story is occupied by conditions such as we Christians believe Jews to enjoy today in England or the United States, where, we are convinced, Jews have nothing to fear from the society around them and will be judged, as are their neighbours, for their own qualities, good or bad. So felt the Jews and Christians of Germany in 1932 ; and the rumblings of fascism and antisemitism which may sound trivial to our ears must, to Jewish ears, carry an evil undercurrent of remembrance.

In this disillusioned world after the second world war it is perhaps easier for us than for our parents forty years ago to enter into an understanding of the tragedy of the last hundred years of Jewish history. Emancipation in the increasingly democratic countries of Western Europe and the United States seemed to the Jews of a hundred years ago to have closed for ever the long epoch of misery, frustration, and restriction. With what a passion Jews embraced the culture, the philosophy, the music of nineteenth-century Germany! With what affection they regarded France, who had first freed them from their medieval shackles! Even to the Russia of the Tsars liberalism seemed destined inevitably to spread. Between 1879 and 1900 the dream was shattered. In Russia, Germany, Austria, and Hungary political antisemitism spread like a forest fire through the powerful parties of reactionary nationalism ; in all these countries and all through the Balkans the medieval and half-forgotten accusation of ritual murder was heard again. In France the streets of Paris echoed to the cry of *à bas les Juifs* during the *affaire Dreyfus*. In Russia pogroms such as they had not known for centuries, backed by the blind hostility of an all-powerful bureaucracy, sent two million fugitives to pour through the industrial cities of the west and the United States.

Nor must the Jews of Asia and Africa be forgotten in this

17

general picture. In the heyday of nineteenth-century European optimism it seemed possible to the members of the Alliance Israélite Universelle and the Anglo-Jewish Association that it was but a matter of time before the ancient and miserably depressed Jewries of the East would benefit from the general rise in the standard of living and education. In the French possessions of Africa Jews were beginning to taste the joys and responsibilities of citizenship. In Egypt Jews benefited from the security of a British administration. Elsewhere schools were springing up ; constitutions were guaranteeing equality ; progress and prosperity seemed but just round the corner. But even before 1914 the rising nationalism of the eastern peoples revealed how unsubstantial some of these dreams were likely to prove, and greater knowledge showed how little basic change was taking place within the miserable quarters in which most Jews lived under the stagnation of Muslim rule.

The situation which confronted Jewish leaders before and during the first world war gave everywhere reasons for anxiety and alarm. The Russian bureaucracy gave little sign that it had any intention of making a radical change in its anti-Jewish policy ; but it was evident that the period of free immigration into the western world was coming to an end. Neither Britain nor the countries of Western Europe were likely to be able or willing to absorb more immigrants ; and in the United States there were signs that the door was closing. Rumania was as hostile as she ever had been, and an increase in her territory was likely to bring more Jews under her corrupt and nationalistic bureaucracy. A new Poland was an enigma, but again there was an evil record in the past, and the new government and people would be overwhelmed by problems of Polish revival, and little likely to be able to give time or sympathy to their three million Jewish subjects. True, there were dreams of a better world ; there were projects for the protection of minorities ; but many Jewish leaders were inevitably and, as the future showed, rightly, sceptical that any reshuffle of the old ingredients could remove the inferiority and insecurity which had become the normal lot of the immense majority of European and Asiatic Jewry.

Here, then, in Jewish history is the third root of Israel, based on long experience of inequality and insecurity under the rule of both Christendom and Islam, and on the shattering disillusion which followed the high hopes of complete emancipation in the liberal democracies of nineteenth-century Europe.

CHAPTER IV

The Fourth Root: The Continuity of Jewish Life in Israel

THE fourth root is the actual continuity of Jewish life in Palestine from Roman up to modern times. If the number of Jewish inhabitants has constantly varied, it has been because of circumstances outside Jewish control, and not because Jews had themselves lost interest in living in their ' promised land.' On the whole it may be said that it was always as large as was possible in view of conditions existing at any one time.

After the defeat of Bar Cochba in A.D. 135 much of Judaea was left a desert, and some towns of Galilee were also ravaged. But in the remoter corners of the south, and in the north, a substantial Jewish community survived ; and by the end of the second century it was enjoying a relatively great measure of autonomy under a patriarch whose seat was at Tiberias, and who had both religious and secular jurisdiction over the Jews of the country, as well as a certain status over all Jews within the Roman empire. The Jewish population consisted basically of landowners, artisans, and peasants ; much of the urban population was Greek or foreign ; that of the coast was, as always, mixed. Many of the merchants were Syrians ; but in the south and north the bulk of the land was cultivated by Jews. This was the formative period of rabbinic Judaism, and it was at Tiberias that the Mishna was composed at the beginning of the second century.

This situation changed for the worse in the time of the Christian Emperor Theodosius II (408-450). He deprived the patriarch of his authority, and a good deal of Jewish autonomy was lost with it. Moreover, the country had become a Christian shrine, and Jews had to suffer a good deal from the fanaticism of eastern monks. When in the sixth century Justinian withdrew citizenship from all who were not members of the ' orthodox ' Church, Jewish numbers probably declined, partly by emigration to the kindlier atmosphere of Babylon (Mesopotamia), partly by conversion to the dominant religion. Together with the formal loss of citizenship, Jews had, ever since the fourth century, been losing their civic equality with their neighbours ; and it is not surprising if, when the Persians invaded the country at the beginning of the seventh century, Jews sided with the invaders. They paid heavily when the Emperor Heraclius reconquered the country ; so that again they looked with pleasure on the invasion of the Muslims, though there is no record of their giving them active help.

During the early period of Arab rule they prospered. The conquest had at first made little difference in the distribution of the population ; military posts were established at Lydda and Tiberias, and Arab landowners replaced wealthy Christians who had fled. But the Arabs despised agriculture, and their great trade routes did not pass through Jewish sections of the country. The Jewish towns and villages remained Jewish, paying taxes to Muslim, instead of Christian, rulers, but otherwise continuing their normal life. At the end of the seventh and at the beginning of the eighth century the situation began to change for the worse, and the long decline set in which was to last almost as long as Muslim rule.

Under the first rulers so few Arabs had the necessary qualifications for administration that the local system and its officials were left untouched. Jews and Christians were freely employed, and even the records were kept in Syriac or Greek. At the turn of the century it became possible to demand Arabic of an official, and only in exceptional cases was one who was not a Muslim accepted. This led to conversions among the wealthier section of both Jews and Christians.

The other change which began to show itself at this time was much more serious. It was a permanent weakness of the Arabs and their Muslim successors that they never developed a capacity for establishing and maintaining honest and efficient local government. Many caliphs were men of noble character who erected public buildings, endowed charities, and fostered agriculture. But there was no continuity. Good administrators saw their work swept away by bad successors, and the rulers were indifferent. By the middle of the ninth century the rot had extended to the centre itself. The caliphs were no more than ecclesiastical prisoners of their Turkish mercenaries, and, for the hundred years which preceded the establishment of the Fatimids at the end of the tenth century, Palestine

20

suffered from a succession of rapacious and indifferent administrations, sometimes from Baghdad, but more often from Egypt, which effectively destroyed the relics of the rich culture and efficient government which the Romans had bequeathed to their conquerors. All the population suffered ; but the minorities had to bear the additional burden of the unchecked violence and arrogance of the Muslims. Even the establishment of Fatimid rule made no substantial change. For if some of the new rulers were wise and tolerant, there was still not that continuity which could secure a real restoration of prosperity.

During all this period Jewish strength lay in Galilee, not in the south. Jerusalem was empty of Jews from the second century to the fifth, when a new community was allowed to settle. Under the sway of the early Muslims it increased considerably. But it was wiped out by the Crusaders when they captured the city in 1099. For the next century such evidence as we have shows a continuing decline in numbers. Other city Jewries were massacred when the cities were captured by assault. Elsewhere Jews fled before the Christian invaders, taking refuge in Muslim lands. Yet some Jewish villages remained intact, and they survived because the Crusaders needed the food which they produced.

With the passing of the Latins and the coming of the Ayyubids and Mamluks, the situation gravely deteriorated. The coastal towns were deliberately destroyed, to give no foothold to an invader. The rich coastal plain became a malarial swamp pastured only by the flocks of the bedouin. Constant struggles between rival governors, the constant rapacity of all alike, weighed heavily upon the inhabitants. That the Jewish community did not die out was henceforth largely due to immigration. Muslim rulers, whatever their intolerance or incapacity, never prevented Jews from settling in the country before the days of Abdul Hamid at the end of the nineteenth century ; and immigrants came singly or in little groups from all parts of the Jewish world. Immediately after the Muslim conquest large numbers had come from Arabia itself. As the conquest spread they came from all parts of the Muslim world, from North Africa, from Cairo, and from Baghdad. But they were also permitted to come from Christian countries, although Christians themselves were admitted only for temporary visits of pilgrimage. During the Middle Ages Jews came from England and France, from Spain and Italy, from Germany and Poland, sometimes alone, sometimes in groups.

21

Distinguished rabbis were among them, like the two hundred who settled in Acre at the beginning of the thirteenth century, or Nachmanides after his defeat of his Christian antagonist in a disputation at Barcelona. A new community was re-established in Jerusalem, which survived in the southern quarters of the old city until 1948: but the strength of the Jewish population was still in the villages and little towns of the north. The most important Jewish city was Safed.

In the sixteenth century a remarkable event took place. Don Joseph Nasi, favourite of the sultan and made by him Duke of Naxos, was given a tract of land with the city of Tiberias, in which to establish a Jewish community with considerable powers of self-government. It was the period after the expulsion from Spain and Portugal, when the counter-reformation was increasing intolerance also in Italy, and the new commercial centres of North-Western Europe were not yet ready to extend toleration to Jewish citizens. Thousands, great and small, had taken refuge in some part of the Turkish dominions. Now there seemed an opportunity for something more substantial. Some hundreds succeeded in reaching Tiberias or Safed. But the settlement failed, for various reasons. Don Joseph could not leave the court in order to supervise his project, lest rivals should procure his fall from favour. Immigrants could not reach the land by sea, because the degenerate descendants of the Knights Hospitallers, from their strongholds in Rhodes, had taken to piracy and had made the seas impassible for Jewish refugees. And in Galilee itself there was no local government interested in protecting the new settlers from the jealousy of Muslim villagers or the raids of the bedouin. Nevertheless, sixteenth-century Palestine witnessed a Jewish life which was intensely vigorous, in comparison with the long decline which had preceded it.

Though the communities of Don Joseph fell into rapid decline, immigrants continued to come from various directions, making the few thousand Jews of the country into a unique microcosm of the whole Jewish people ; and this variety emphasised the affection and respect which this Jewish community enjoyed all through the Jewish world. They were regarded as in some sense ambassadors for the whole people in the land of their ancestors, and their presence was a token of the return which was to take place in the future. They were preparing for the coming of the Messiah. This affectionate respect had an increasingly practical side. The disorder and decay into which the land had fallen by the seventeenth century was such that it was no longer possible for the few thousand Jews who were scattered in its towns and villages to earn even the miserable livelihood of their non-Jewish neighbours, such was the extra burden of oppression and insecurity under which they lay. But rather than see the ancient association perish, Jewish communities all over the world raised annually considerable sums to support them. In the nineteenth century these annual contributions amounted to nearly £60,000. In return the Palestinian community was supposed to spend its life in prayer and study, and most indeed did so. But they suffered morally from their destitution and dependence, and the struggle to rediscover for them a basis on which they could support themselves became a problem whose solution paved the way for early Zionist settlement.

In the nineteenth century a new type of immigrant began to come, young Jews who were determined to wrest somehow a living from the land of their fathers. They began to come long before there was an organised Zionist movement, long before the Balfour Declaration gave international sanction to their return. To settle on the land was still almost impossible. If they escaped dying of malaria, they saw their fields deliberately laid waste and their fruit trees torn up by bedouins or neighbouring fellaheen. Only in the neighbourhood of the towns was anything possible, and near Jaffa in 1875 the Alliance Israélite Universelle gave the Jews of Palestine their first institute for teaching agricultural production. Native Jews of Jerusalem in the same year made their first attempt at an agricultural settlement. Then in the 1880s came the first fugitives from persecution in Russia and Rumania, and agricultural settlement began in earnest. With the vicissitudes and struggles of these early Zionists it is scarcely necessary to deal. Their story is well known. What is important for our present purpose is that they were successors and reinforcements to a Jewish community which through all vicissitudes had remained in the land of Israel, and of immigrants from all parts of the Jewish world who, in every century, had braved its dangers and accepted its hardships in order to live and die upon its holy soil.

CHAPTER V

The Fifth Root : The Relation of Palestine Jewry to the Jewish World

THE previous section has indicated the continuous, if sometimes tenuous, thread which bound all Jews geographically to their ancient homeland through the permanent settlement of some Jews in its towns and villages. Of even greater significance is the extraordinary part which that small community played at four critical moments in Jewish history. From that standpoint the Palestine community is unique. No other Jewry in the world, however great its numbers, its power, or its intellectual eminence, can claim to show anything parallel.

Jewish life in its troubled passage through the last two thousand years has on four occasions found itself with but the narrowest margin separating it from final destruction.

The first occasion was after the disastrous wars with Rome, when the Temple, which was the centre of its national life. was destroyed ; when its political institutions were abolished ; when its religious practices were proscribed ; and when it was challenged from within by the increasing power and intransigence of emerging Christianity.

The second occasion was when Turkish invasions destroyed the prosperity and stability of the Baghdad caliphate, at a time when Babylonian Jewry was the centre of the Jewish world, and had no visible successors, either elsewhere in Muslim lands or in Europe.

The third occasion was after the torch had been, for centuries, transferred to Europe, and when two centuries of persecution, expulsion, and the destruction of their centres of learning, culminated in the tragedies of the double expulsion from the Iberian peninsula in 1492 and 1496. Again, there were no visible successors. Jewish life in Muslim countries was at a low ebb ; in Eastern Europe it was still building ; the new Jewries of the Protestant countries, Holland and England, were but tiny seedlings. For a generation the centre of the Jewish world was Safed, in the mountains of Galilee.

24

Finally, when Tsarist persecution changed the whole face of Jewry, and the train of modern antisemitism was laid which was to lead to the death camps and D.P.s of Hitler's Europe, came modern Zionism, a movement whose importance we cannot overestimate in Jewish history, but whose significance is still inevitably a contemporary controversy. What, however, is now incontestable, is the part which Zionism played psychologically during fifty troubled years of world Jewry, and the part which it played physically in giving a home to the survivors of Hitlerism when the doors of the rest of the world were closed.

When Jerusalem was captured, and its Temple destroyed by Titus in A.D. 70, the richest and intellectually the most eminent Jewish community in the world was in Alexandria ; and it might well have appeared to be the successor to Jerusalem as the centre of Jewry. In opposition to the political fanaticism and religious narrowness of the latter city, the Jews of Alexandria were tolerant and progressive. They were loyal to their tradition, but ready to reinterpret it in terms of the Hellenistic civilisation around them. The Scriptures had been translated into Greek, and Philo and Josephus willingly explained to the Græco-Roman world the treasures of Judaism with such modifications, allegorisations, and ' modernisations ' as would make them acceptable to a cultured and philosophically minded pagan. Had Alexandria occupied the centre of the picture, Judaism, refined and emasculated, would have titillated the jaded palate of the classical world for a century or two, and then disappeared with all the other oriental religions which competed for the interest of the dominant society before the advance of Christianity.

That Judaism survived with its traditions unbroken it owed to a small group of scholars who withdrew from the siege of Jerusalem, and, after various migrations, settled in Galilee. In the days when they had their own country, Jewry had all the varieties of belief natural to a free people. Zealots, quietists, orthodox, indifferent, modernists, and reactionaries, were all alike members of the nation. This group of scholars recognised that with the loss of political autonomy religious unity was the sole possible basis of survival ; and with infinite skill and patience steered the fragile bark of a defeated and dispirited people between the Scylla of a theological uniformity which would have turned the people into a religious sect, and the Charybdis of a narrow particularism which would have meant but the survival of a mummy. The miracle which they achieved was to turn a political nation into a national community, composed of autonomous local communities, each of which could adapt itself to the very varied life which Jews lived in Europe, Asia, and Africa, and at the same time exhibit, wherever they might be, the same identifiable pattern of life. This pattern had to be not static but dynamic, not dependent on any central authority but capable of adaptation and development anywhere in the Jewish world, under conditions which the scholars of Galilee could not possibly foresee.

The essential institutions of the synagogue and the school they had inherited from their predecessors, working both in Babylon and Palestine. Their task was to give full meaning to Judaism as the religion of Torah. It is unfortunate that this word is usually translated ' law ' ; for it is one of those central words which contain within themselves a wide variety of meanings. Just as the word ' civilisation ' covers political and social forms as well as cultural and artistic traditions, so Torah embraces not merely the actual laws of Judaism, laws of the Pentateuch, and laws of the rabbis, but the whole conception of a revealed order of goodness and morality, and the whole conception of a way of life mediated through the instruction of successive generations.

Their task was to develop and teach the nature of Torah, so that it could become the ultimate authority in Jewish life, replacing king or temple, and yet be something not static, but living and growing so that it was sufficiently flexible to meet the changing conditions of Jewish life. It had both to strengthen the executive powers of the isolated and autonomous communities of which the Jewish world was made up, and be so closely interwoven into the life of the individual Jew that it retained his loyalty and inspired his devotion. The result was the Mishna, and the principle of continual interpretation of Torah, not by single authoritative priests, or a hereditary class of rulers, but by all who were skilled in its understanding. The synagogue became the centre of the community, and continual discussion and elucidation part of its regular life. All matters came to it, covering the whole pattern of daily living, religious, professional, social, and domestic. It may be the elaboration was sometimes carried too far. But this cannot impair the essential grandeur of their achievement. For out of the defeat of their nationalism, and the destruction of their political autonomy, the rabbis of Galilee did, in fact, lay the foundation which allowed the Jewish people not only to survive, but to retain their creative power.

Their task achieved, the community in the Holy Land passed into obscurity for some five hundred years. Then the end of the glory of the Abbasid caliphate in Baghdad marked also the end of the glory of the Jewish academies of Babylon which had taken the torch from the rabbis of Galilee. They in their turn had completed their work. The Talmud stood beside the Mishna ; individual ' responsa ' from learned rabbis could take the place of the discussions in the academies. With a final flicker in two brilliant scholars, Hai Gaon and Saadia Gaon (an Egyptian Jew by birth), the intellectual eminence of Babylon disappears completely from Jewish history. No other Jewish centre was yet ready to receive the torch, but there were urgent tasks to be done. It was to the now tiny, and deeply impoverished community of Galilee that again the succession came.

The interests of Babylonian Jewry had been concentrated largely on the text of the Mishna around which their voluminous commentaries had been built. But the Mishna itself rested ultimately on the Pentateuch and the rest of the Old Testament ; and the text of the Bible needed both clarification and control. Already, while the Talmudic work of the Tiberias academy had appeared of only secondary importance compared with that of the great eastern community, Palestinian scholars had been concerned with the rules of copying and correcting the Biblical text itself, which they called *Masorah*, literally ' the tradition,' then the traditionally transmitted text. In the ninth century the work of the Tiberias Masoretes became of capital importance, and their work was done so thoroughly that it has sufficed up to modern times, though they could scarcely have realised that they were laying the foundation on which Jewish scholars like Rashi and his successors, in the then barbarous regions of Northern France, were going to build medieval Jewish life in Europe. How well they worked in preparing their Masoretic texts has been proved by their identity with the Hebrew scrolls, written nearly a thousand years earlier, and discovered in these last years. Had the work been delayed any longer, we might well claim that it could never have been satisfactorily done ; and we should be confronted today with a diversity of texts and traditions in which it would have been impossible to obtain either certainty or clarity.

During the same period, the same small Jewry, often financially dependent on the richer but less cultured community of Egypt, received the last remnants of Babylonian scholarship; and a shadowy Academy of Gaon-Jacob is to be found, first in Jerusalem, then in other cities of the country, until it disappears in Damascus at the time of the crusades. For the most obscure century of Jewish history it occupies the centre of the picture, waiting to transfer the torch from Babylon to Egypt and to Spain. Their dual task accomplished, the Jewry of the Holy Land lapsed again into obscurity.

The dynamic power within European Christendom which led through the great revival of the twelfth and thirteenth centuries to the new civilisation of the Renaissance and the Reformation, and so to the new world of seventeenth-century science and scholarship, had no parallel in the story of medieval European Jewry. The reverse is true ; the tale is one of increasing gloom, and of a decay not only of security and prosperity, but of scholarship and communal life. The physical disorders which began with the crusaders of 1096 were repeated with enhanced effect in the social and religious fanaticism which at one time or another decimated the communities of England, France, Germany, and Spain in pillage and massacre. The hostility of the Church, which compelled the Jewish badge in the Council of the Lateran in 1215, spawned also the evil charges of ritual murder, of the profanation of the host, of the poisoning of wells and spreading plague, of alliance with the Islamic enemies of Christendom, until no community could know security or rest assured under the protection of the secular princes. Nor could *their* friendship be relied on, did churchmen need conciliation, or did other interests look with jealousy at Jewish privileges. In England the decree of expulsion fell in 1290. In France, after a see-saw of flight and recovery, the final edict was issued a century later. The lack of central authority in Germany made prosperity and desolation an alternating patchwork in its imperial and episcopal cities, its merchant towns and baronies ; but though diversity might often offer a near-by town to which to flee, it could offer no basic guarantee against the necessity of flight.

Finally, in Spain in 1492, after a century of martyrdom, of persecution and of pressure to accept the safety of the baptismal font, the richest and most numerous of all the Jewries of Europe was offered the alternative of conversion or emigration ; and in 1496 the same position prevailed in Portugal.

But the community of Palestine was already arising from the misery and decline of the two centuries of Egyptian Mamluk rule which had followed the expulsion of the crusaders. Small groups of refugees were reaching the country from the south. But the real change was yet to come. It is difficult to realise today that in the fifteenth century the Ottoman empire presented the spectacle of the most powerful, the most tolerant, and the best administered state in the world. But such was the case ; and while the military strength of the janissaries spread terror through the eastern territories of Christendom, the toleration of the sultans invited Jews fleeing from Christian Europe to take shelter within their dominions. This did not at first mean access to the Holy Land itself ; but Spanish and other Jews could take refuge and rebuild their lives in Adrianople, in Salonica, in Constantinople, and on the Asiatic side in Brusa and Smyrna, until in 1517, in a campaign which contained only two battles, Selim I added to his dominions Syria, Egypt, and Arabia. Then indeed the doors of Palestine were opened, even if entry was still limited by the dangers and difficulties of the route.

Nevertheless, as the sixteenth century advanced, the Jewish population of Palestine grew steadily both in numbers and prosperity. Just as its first essential work had been carried on from a city thus far pagan, the Herodian pleasure city of Tiberias, so the new capital of Jewry was a town unknown to Biblical scholars— and indeed we still do not know whether it existed in Biblical or Roman days. In the mountains of Galilee, on a rocky promontory surrounded by deep gorges to east and west and south, and with a vast vista before it of the lake of Tiberias nearly four thousand feet below, stands Safed. West of it rises the still higher mass of Jebel Jarmak, to whose slopes clings the village of Meron, where are the tombs of Hillel and his disciples and of Simeon bar Yochai, the reputed founder of Jewish mysticism. This corner of Galilee had, in consequence, always had an attraction for Jewish students of mysticism ; but it was not until the sixteenth century that the city became the centre not only of Palestinian Jewry, but of the Jewish world. This was made possible not only by its saints and mystics, but by its geographical situation. Secure amid its mountains, it was yet only a few miles from the caravan road from Acre and

Haifa to Damascus ; and Safed developed a prosperous manufacture of woollen goods which it could trade in the markets of Damascus.

The destruction of the great Jewry of Spain was not the only event which stirred the imagination of the Jews of Safed. Christendom itself appeared in dissolution. The movement for reform had broken its theological unity, while the Turk was engaged in an apparently invincible attack upon its territories from south and east. At such a time thoughts of the coming of the Messiah filled Jewish minds ; and Safed presented an extraordinary spectacle of almost continuous religious excitement.

But the Jewry of Palestine, on the occasions when it has been called from its obscurity by the disasters of diaspora life, has never been only a refuge. It has always succeeded in offering a new dynamic for the future ; and among the many scholars who thronged Safed in the sixteenth century two admirably filled that rôle. Joseph Caro was born in Spain a year or two before the expulsion and was taken by his parents to Adrianople. In 1536 he came to Safed, and there in 1555 he completed the Shulchan Aruch, which was to be the text-book of Jewish orthodoxy for centuries to come. Two years before his arrival in Safed there was born in Jerusalem, of Ashkenazi parents, Isaac Luria ; and some time after the middle of the century he also was drawn there, where he quickly became the leader of those Jews who were inclined to mysticism. A new mystical doctrine arose which broke with the older Cabbalism, in that it was not an esoteric doctrine for the few, but a popular movement which inspired the many. It was a movement which was not without its dangers ; and in the following century it provided many followers for the false Messiah, Shabbetai Zvi, and so brought about a grave crisis within Jewry. But it arose again, purged of many of its messianic details, as Polish Chassidism, where it brought life and gaiety to the melancholy and restricted life of the Polish ghettoes. Safed was to be a place of pilgrimage and attempted settlement for Polish Chassidim through the eighteenth and nineteenth centuries.

To the sixteenth-century Jew in the Holy Land the work of Caro and of Luria might have seemed unimportant beside the splendid projects of Don Joseph Nasi. But the political settlement in Tiberias failed, and their work survived. Their task had been accomplished. Richer and more secure Jewries could carry forward the life of the Jewish people ; and the Jewry of Palestine, harried by the bedouin and the peasants, oppressed by the tax-collector and the official, sank still deeper into penury and obscurity, until the beginning of the Zionist movement.

Zionism has a long history, going back well before the foundation by Herzl of the World Zionist Organisation at the end of the nineteenth century. It is a story in which the longings of Jews of Eastern Europe is mingled with the idealism of a few Western Jews, and of some Christians, including notable Englishmen. It runs parallel to the history of emancipation, though at first with no notion of providing a counterblast to the tendencies of assimilation which were tempting the small and seemingly secure Jewries of the U.S.A., Great Britain, and Western European countries. It attracted the idealist, but also the political thinker, non-Jewish as well as Jewish, who was aware of the fragile basis of assimilation, and watched with anxiety the growth after the year of unsuccessful revolutions, 1848, of a nationalist exclusivism which boded ill for minorities such as the Jews. Even before Russian persecution opened the flood gates to the West in 1881, plans were being made for Jews to resettle in the Holy Land ; and hopes were expressed that it might be possible for them to buy some secure autonomy from Turkey, or even be granted it by European powers. As early as the suppression of the ambitions of Mehmet Ali in Syria by the British fleet in 1839, the thought was expressed that Southern Syria, i.e., the Biblical Holy Land, might be restored somehow to the Jews. It was too early for any such ambitious scheme. But the idea had been planted in men's minds. After 1881, though only a tiny trickle accepted the hardships of an agricultural life in a land riddled with malaria and the prey to constant disorder, the psychological influence of the Zionist idea played a part, out of all proportion to the numbers involved, in restoring Jewish self-respect from the shock of renewed persecution and antisemitism.

Resettlement proved a slow and costly business ; not merely the life but the climate was new to Jews from Russia, Poland, or other northern countries. The price paid in lives was heavy, and the adventure was costly in money also. But when Jews approached the British and other governments during the first world war they knew that they could speak of a successful experiment ; they had proved that they could cultivate the soil ; they knew that they could restore fertility to many waste places in the land. During the first ten years of the British administration advance was slow ;

but the National Home was there, capable of great expansion, when the blast of depression reduced hundreds of thousands of Polish Jews to destitution, and when the Nazi régime in Germany sent its hundreds of thousands into exile. And when the relics of European Jewry were gathered together after the second world war only wishful thinking can persuade men that it was propaganda and not a genuine longing which turned the minds of so many of the D.P.s to the possibility of a life where they would not be dependent on Gentile good will. The gates of most of the world were almost completely closed. The gates of Israel, though at infinite cost to the Jews already living there, were open.

PART TWO

Israel and the Nations

There is no doubt that he who would speak of the position of Israel in the world must know that it is impossible to keep religion and politics apart. There are those, neither Jews nor Israelis who loudly protest that they are not antisemitic, but who view the establishment of a State of Israel as a political monstrosity meriting the most whole-hearted condemnation. And there are Jews, some religious and some materialistic, who see in the establishment of a Jewish state the entry of Jewry into the ' normal' and ' ordinary' life of nations. Both groups have grossly deceived themselves. There is little in Israel's relations with the world which could be called normal ; and there is still less which can be understood if religion is kept severely out of the picture.

It is not fair to the Arabs to ask them to accept Israel save on grounds in which contemporary real-politik is inextricably inter-woven with millennial religious claims, whether they accept the latter or not. And it is folly to think that the future of Jerusalem can be settled by ecclesiastical intrigues behind closed doors, or that it will become a City of Peace through the bickerings of the Eastern and Western Churches, or the violence of orthodox Judaism.

I make no apology for introducing God into the argument, for I find no explanation of Israel or of Jerusalem apart from Him. Perhaps in the long run the deepest lesson which Israel may have to learn—and to teach—is just that. Our secular world makes as little sense by itself as does a religious world concerned only with ecclesiastical issues. That which challenges us in Israel, and in Jerusalem, is the meaning of ordinary life, but at its deepest level. That is still true whether at that deepest level we find God—or silence.

35

CHAPTER VI

The National Home and the Arabs

THE essay on *The Roots of Israel* considered the Jewish reasons why the whole development which led to the establishment of a state of Israel must be seen as a natural growth out of the history and religion of the Jews. It took no account of the effects on others of this Jewish situation. But no nation is permitted by the very nature of the world to live entirely to itself ; and certainly this could never be the destiny of a people established in one of the nerve centres of mankind, one of the storm centres of the world's political struggles. All the time such a nation is influencing its neighbours, and being influenced by them. And this is equally true when there are no open relations between them. For the breach of relationship which such a situation implies is pregnant with psychological effects on both sides ; and it can safely be said that these effects will be, for both sides, evil and deleterious.

There is an ' Arab point of view ' which one day Israel will accept. Towards it she will mould what is relevant in her policies ; and out of it she will gather a strength and dignity which will likewise mould the face which she turns towards the outside world beyond the Arab horizon.

There was a time when psychologically as well as factually one could have spoken of the old slogan of ' a land without a people for the people without a land ' as being decisive in the surrender of the Biblical area of Palestine into the hands of the Jewish people. But psychologically that moment was already passing when Zionist colonisation began. For the winds of nationalism blowing through Europe, which had moulded ancient Jewish longings and inherent Jewish needs into the political programme of Zionism, were already being faintly felt by the British in Egypt and the Turks in Syria, Lebanon, and elsewhere. It could already be predicted that an Arab nationalism would revive, even if slowly, from the long stagnation which had followed, and even preceded, the Turkish conquest four hundred years earlier.

The country which became British Mandated Palestine, and

36

to which some tens of thousands of new Jewish immigrants had already come during the preceding thirty years, had for centuries had no separate political identity, and for two thousand years it had been subject to a succession of foreign rulers, few of whom had any interest in the welfare of its inhabitants. The rulers had, for the most part, not sought to colonise, but many factors had led to a continual, if gradual, change in the character of the population. The early Arab rulers had introduced some Arab tribes from the Arabian peninsula, but the main cause of change was not political. Palestine was always part of a larger unit within which movement was natural, and it formed a bridge between Asia and Africa. It was therefore subject to the natural laws of such a situation, and there was a coming and going of the most varied elements, urban and rural, which was neither checked nor noticed by the political authorities.

At the end of the nineteenth century only a few individuals from the ruling families had become attracted by the new movement of Arab nationalism, and their loyalty was not to any unit called ' Palestine ' but either to the Arab people as a whole, rather vaguely conceived, or else to Syria, of which province they felt themselves to be a part. The greater part of the population found their allegiance in the villages or clans to which they belonged, or accepted the ancient, but factually meaningless, division into ' Qais ' and ' Yemen '—' northern ' and ' southern '—as the basis of friendship or hostility with their neighbours.

While, as in most countries, the population of the towns was cosmopolitan and heterogeneous, and reflected the normal movements of an urban class, at least some of the villages could have traced their descent back to Canaanite or even neolithic ancestors. This was shown again and again during the survey of Palestine made in the nineteenth century, when ancient Biblical names, completely forgotten in all written sources, were recovered from the villagers. Most of those who could have shown so long a residence in a single area must at one time have been Jews by religion—for at least during the Maccabean period there was a general policy of religious uniformity—and later Christians, for the same was true at least from the time of Justinian to the Arab conquest. But such memories had perished, and most of them were, and had for centuries been, Muslims with no memory of any other past.

There were, however, important exceptions. There were villages which had, from some period before the Arab conquest, been

Christian and which retained their Christianity against all difficulties and hardships throughout the centuries. Some of these villages were almost completely isolated, but most were in the neighbourhood of the great Christian centres of Jerusalem, Bethlehem, and Nazareth. There were also a few villages which had retained the memory of having been Jewish by religion, though by the time of the Mandate only part of one, Pekiin or al Bukaia, survived in an obscure corner of Galilee.

What was true of the villagers was true also of some of the bedouin tribes whose seasonal movements through the same areas had continued uninterrupted for centuries, possibly even for millennia.

Not all the population, however, has anything like such an ancient tradition of residence. A few of the great families, and some of the urban population, entered the country at or shortly after the Arab conquest, though that conquest affected the countryside but little, for the Arabs took slowly to agriculture. Some were deposits of the crusading period. Still more came during the Mamluk and Turkish epochs—Druse villages in the north, Egyptian in the south, and in quite recent times Bosnian Muslims, Circassians, North Africans, and others. The common feature of these movements was that they were internal to the Turkish empire ; and they were paralleled during the nineteenth century by a similar immigration of Jews from various parts of North Africa and the Middle East. Movements from outside the empire were much fewer. Some Christians, mostly members of Christian religious orders, and small groups of Jewish immigrants, young and old, came from various parts of Europe, but not in sufficient numbers to affect the general balance of the population. The one thing that distinguished these latter groups was that they were not Arabic speaking. For all the rest, indigenous or immigrant, Muslim, Christian, or Jew, one common factor was the Arabic language ; and it was through their common language that the two former came in the present century to feel the beginnings of a common loyalty, and to share a common nationalist aspiration. A large proportion of the pioneers of Arab nationalism in Syria came from the Christian minority, and a few, especially in Egypt, were Jews.

The nationalism which was thus being born in the period before the first world war had, unhappily, but shallow roots either in an economic advance, or in a spreading of education, two fields in which European nationalism had found firm roots. The period of Arab glory to which it looked back had come to an end a thousand years earlier, and had been succeeded by a calamitous and continual decline, a decline which had immensely reduced the population as its means of subsistence had disappeared by soil erosion, by the destruction of forests, and by the passage of fertile plains and valleys into malarial swamps.

It was a nationalism also which rested on no adequate middle class with the political, commercial, professional, and administrative experience which creates and is created by such a class. A few Arab notables participated in the Turkish administration, and even sat in the Turkish Parliament, but the knowledge thus gained was exiguous and not without corrupting elements. Apart from the urban and rural schools established by the Christian missionaries and religious orders in the nineteenth century, there were few opportunities for education, even in the towns ; and in the villages, where the bulk of the inhabitants dwelt, there were none.

These disabilities which accompanied the gradual emergence of Arab nationalism were, in the circumstances, inevitable. No radical improvement could have taken place under Turkish rule ; and the abysmal poverty of the population, together with the lack of any clear picture of the nature of a modern state in the minds of those who were coming to think of themselves as a single ' Arab ' people, made concrete planning extremely difficult. This background affected both the giving of promises during the first world war and the understanding of the promises by those who received them. All that is clear is that, on both sides, the key-note was ' liberation ' and that the general expectation was of progress towards the normal independent twentieth-century state. That this progress would be accompanied by many qualifications of various kinds may have been in the minds of those who made the promises ; but those who received them had neither the experience which would have enabled them to form a sober judgment of the justice or reasonableness of any qualifications involved, nor the temper to admit that such might be necessary.

Inevitably the main responsibility for action lay with the British, who held all political power in their own hands. But at this early stage of the situation the Jewish leaders took the right course in seeking direct agreement with the accepted leader of the Arab people, the Amir Faysal. The Weizmann-Faysal Agreement of

January, 1919, speaks of 'Palestine' and 'the Arab State' as though Palestine were a Jewish 'state' in friendly and co-operative relations with an Arab state covering the whole area inhabited by the Arab people. That friendly relations could be extremely beneficial to the Arab people, only slowly emerging from the stagnation of centuries and extremely suspicious of western imperialism, was obvious to both Faysal and his father, Husayn, Sherif of Mecca. But Faysal inevitably made it clear, in a note appended to his signature, that his agreement depended for its validity on the future of the Arabs being some form of united political society. When Britain and France divided up the Arab world into mandatory areas the agreement lapsed, and the Jewish immigrants into Palestine found themselves confronted with a new political entity, the Palestine Arabs, or rather the Arabs of Western Palestine, for those across the Jordan were formed into yet another new political unit.

The Arab point of view which the Jews will ultimately recognise is the point of view of this particular section of the Arab people, now largely refugee. For at no stage in the negotiations which led to the Balfour Declaration and the Mandate were they consulted. The obvious reason for such an unfortunate omission is that during this early period they had no form of 'national' organisation which could officially collect and express their views, or negotiate and discuss with the British or the Jews. Actually expressions of Palestinian opinion were collected by both Syrian organisations and by the King Crane Commission, and they were unfavourable to Zionism ; but though they were undoubtedly sincere, they were of little use since they were not the product of informed discussion of the actual issues involved. They recorded only the immediate reaction of almost chance Arab groups to any suggestion of infringement of their nationalist ambitions. Later both the British Mandatory and the Jewish Agency worked hard to bring into being a Palestinian Arab body of opinion with which it would be possible to negotiate. But both groups insisted on the negotiations being conducted on the basis of acceptance of the Mandate which embodied the Balfour Declaration, and this was precisely what the Arabs wished to throw back into the melting-pot to re-emerge on a 'democratic' platter.

It can appear doubly academic to raise this issue now. For not only has it already been admitted that the Arabs of Palestine had no national organisation which could have been consulted, but it has also to be admitted that, if they had possessed one, it is extremely unlikely that it would ever have agreed to conditions being established in the country by which they were to share their own political development with, and make its speed dependent on, immigrants whose needs and numbers were still unknown. Modern nationalism, especially among undeveloped peoples, has neither the wisdom nor the knowledge to examine such a proposition impartially. Why then is it raised ? The answer lies not merely in the subsequent story of the Mandate and the final war of liberation, but in the experiences of the British at the moment of writing, in Persia, Africa, and Egypt. An English detective story writer is fond of quoting an ' old Spanish proverb ': Take what you like, says God—and pay for it. The British are learning to-day how much has to be paid for, and that the idealists of yesterday who told them so were not such unrealistic political judges as they then appeared. I remember in my first curacy, twenty-five years ago, saying some such thing about the British Empire. My vicar was furious, and in closing the meeting entirely dissociated himself from my views, saying that it was the British task to preach Christianity to other nations, so that they should forgive us without demanding restitution! Those were his actual words, and they were warmly applauded by the audience. To-day we are learning that there is no such easy blotting out of the past.

The present generation in Israel know that they paid for every dunam of land which they owned, that much of it they brought into cultivation from barren sand or hill side, or malarial swamp, that they claimed nothing that was not legally promised them under the Balfour Declaration and the Mandate, and that they came to the country with no ill-will towards its population. But at some time it will be realised in Israel that the material advantages which they brought (which were substantial) and the goodwill which they offered (which was genuine) still fell short of what the Arab population regarded as the minimum to which they were entitled. For to the Arab majority they did not touch the fundamental issue, that ' their ' country was to be theirs no longer. At best they were to have ' equal rights ' in it ; in all probability they were to become a minority, both in power and numbers.

In all material respects what the British promised, and what the Jews were ready to give, was more than the mass of the population in any Arab country have gained under independence. Likewise, in

41

material respects, what the politically conscious minority had in mind when they clamoured for independence would have brought little relief to the masses they would have ruled. For they dreamed of the financial benefits of power, and of the opportunity to exploit for their own advantage whatever could be exploited. Nevertheless, in the current conception of international relations, these are not matters which one power, however wise and benevolent, can regulate for another. And in the conditions then reigning in Palestine, there is little doubt but that the fellaheen and the townsmen would have supported their landlords and the ruling families in demanding rights which would but have increased their own burdens, and in rejecting a tutelage from outside which would have eased them.

It is not such material calculations that would have appeared in speech and propaganda, but the heady appeal to freedom. And it will be realised that in any other situation this Arab appeal would have been justified, and would have had the sympathetic agreement of the Jewish people the world over. For Jewish rights in Israel, founded on unique historical circumstances, were allowed by the Balfour Declaration and the Mandate to override the normal rights of the Arab population.

There is no reason to ask Israel to reject this situation. But one day she will recognise that it is wrong to evolve far-fetched arguments to deny any Arab rights in the land they had inhabited so long, or to rest her case on the legality of the Balfour Declaration. She was allowed to override normal rights because she had unique claims. But the permission involved a deep debt of honour to those who lost by her gain ; and even those who hold, as I do, that it was right that she should receive this permission, and who recognise— as I do—that she tried hard to cushion the blow to the Arabs, make a grave mistake if they seek to support their attitude by refusing to recognise that all the normal rights were on the Arab side, and that the Arabs were inevitably conscious of this, and bitter at the world's refusal to acknowledge it. Jews as well as Arabs must share responsibility for the bitterness with which the two sides—and their supporters—were divided.

To the Arabs and to their supporters it appears self-evident that the Balfour Declaration and the Jewish National Home are morally indefensible, simply because natural rights were with the Arabs. But factually this is not necessarily so. The Jews may be unique in many ways, but those who supported the Declaration and the terms of the Mandate were not making a unique exception to established custom in their action. It is true—and it is right—that natural rights usually govern political decisions ; but it has long been recognised that there can legitimately be exceptions to this usual rule. Most of them have occurred within the limits of a single nation, but some have involved two or more nations. They are recognised as exceptional ; and each case in which it is suggested that natural rights should be overridden needs to be separately established on its own merits. But if a special case *is* established, it has not been considered either illegal or immoral to set natural rights aside.

Within a nation a typical case would be that in which an expanding city sought to turn a fertile and cultivated valley into a reservoir to increase its water supply. That the farmers had a ' natural right ' to their farms nobody would deny. But the issue would not be left to them, and the government which possessed ultimate authority over both city and farmers would decide irrespective of whether they objected. In a world which is never static every government must possess powers which can override natural rights. In a world as complex and interdependent as ours the exercise of some of these powers is going on continuously and provokes little comment and less refusal.

Situations also arise where two (or more) peoples are affected. The continued British possession of strategic points such as Gibraltar, Malta, Cyprus, Aden, Singapore, and Hong Kong is only slowly beginning to be challenged on grounds of principle. But if to most people in all parties their possession might be a matter for reconsideration against the background of world affairs, only a small minority would demand that the sole decisive opinion should be that of the local population. Today the United States is beginning to follow the same pattern ; and the British people were not consulted as to the siting of extensive American airfields on British soil. For it is not merely small local societies or ' backward ' peoples whose normal rights may be set aside for what appear to those bearing power to be more important and valid considerations.

Every one of such cases has to be considered on its own merits and to justify itself by the production of unusual circumstances. Where the case is internal to a single country it is also possible to say that the decision must not lie with either of the claimants. Neither the city nor the farmers must take the decision about a

43

reservoir. But for many such cases there is no superior court of justice to which a judicial appeal can be made in the present imperfection of our international society. The only judges are time and public opinion, and neither have precise executive powers. In the case of Palestine the world came as near a politico-judicial decision as was possible in the conditions of the inter-war years ; for the League of Nations was a supra-national body in spite of all its imperfections and its ultimate failure. To call it a judicial decision would be wrong, for the issue was not one which could be settled along judicial lines. In fact the Arabs asked more than once that the validity of the Mandate should be submitted to the International Court at The Hague ; but the Court could not have pronounced on such an issue, any more than, in the case quoted of the valley and the reservoir, a national court could have given a legal decision between the farmers and the city. For it was inherent in the dilemma that the city had not already established 'legal' rights to the farmers' land. Nevertheless, it would be wrong to dismiss the Mandate as immoral simply because its validity was not amenable to establishment by process of law.

In the previous section the roots of Israel were described. These showed that far more was involved in Zionism than just a nineteenth-century Jewish form of nationalism. But it could be argued that this combination of religious, historical, and even mystical arguments should not necessarily have been expressed in an international and political decision. If the Balfour Declaration and the Mandate are to be justified as an exceptional case, two other questions need to be answered. The first arises out of what has just been said : did the Jewish situation at that time demand international and political treatment ? The second deals with the normal rights which were to be considered : was this the fairest way in which the Jewish situation could be met, supposing the answer to the previous question was a ' yes ' ?

It is the historical root in the first section which leads up to the answer to the first question. The happy period in which emancipation appeared to be the final solution of the Jewish problem was undoubtedly passing by the time of the first world war. Modern antisemitism had shattered the Jewish sense of security, even in western democracies. Moreover, the period of free movement across the continents was coming to an end, while some millions of the Jewish people were still living in conditions in Eastern Europe from which emigration might be the only solution. In the general world settlement to which the leaders of the nations looked forward in the years between 1914 and 1919 it was reasonable and proper to seek to provide security for the Jewish people by giving them a territory of their own, and the implementation of such an action would undoubtedly need both political and international action.

This fact would have been more easily understood by the people involved, whether Arabs or western workers in the Middle East, if the Jewish situation which needed such a remedy had also been in the same area. Unfortunately it was not. It was in Eastern Europe, and neither the Arabs nor the Middle Eastern experts and workers were familiar with the Eastern European situation, or could have been expected to understand that no solution in that area itself was practicable. This was to be a continuing problem all through the Mandatory period, when the British who served in Palestine were mainly drawn from the ranks of the Colonial Service. They saw obviously non-oriental Jews 'invading' an oriental country, and few of them had any knowledge of the impossible conditions in Eastern Europe which motivated such a migration.

It was then natural that the answer which was given to the second question: *should the Jewish problem in Eastern Europe have been offered a solution in Palestine?* should have appeared to many honourable men, Arabs, Englishmen, Americans, and others, to be a monstrosity. For it involved setting aside the rights of an old-established population for reasons with which they were not directly concerned at all. But from an historian's point of view this is, unfortunately, an extremely common feature of such conflicts between natural and special rights. To refer again to the other cases quoted, the farmers were not directly concerned with the growth of a distant city; the peoples of Gibraltar or Hong Kong were not responsible for the position of their homes in centres strategically important to maritime nations on the other side of the globe; in England or France, the peoples of East Anglia or some French province are not in any special or exceptional manner concerned with the issue between the Western and Eastern *blocs*. The Jewish-Arab dilemma is, then, not so exceptional as it at first sight appears.

Nevertheless, it is important to phrase the question aright. Today 'in Palestine' means 'among the Arabs of a separate section of the Arab world.' But in the years of decision no such separate Arab people existed. There was no separate Arab country known as Palestine ; there were no Arabs who thought of themselves as ' Palestinians.' The right phrasing of the question is: should it have been in that corner of the Arab world with which the Jews had retained a unique physical and spiritual association all through their centuries of dispersion ? Or should some new territory with which they had hitherto had no special association have been found for them ?

To deal with the last question first, it has to be said that nobody has succeeded in showing the existence of a territory elsewhere which was capable of accepting a population which might run into millions. The two suggestions which were actually made by the British Government before 1914, first El Arish, then East Africa, each envisaged a maximum population, when fully developed, of a hundred thousand. Other territories have been suggested which could be developed for even fewer. But none of them could have been considered a ' national home,' none would have ensured for its Jewish settlers a life politically and culturally independent. It is fair to say that the issue could be reduced to the alternatives of Palestine or yet another string of minority communities, differing in little from the communities which the Jews would have left behind in Europe, except that there would have been more farmers among the settlers.

Moreover, many of the suggestions proposed lands little emptier than was the Middle East, for it is still today, in spite of the presence of more than a million Jews, one of the least populated of the habitable areas of the world. In the past it supported a population several times larger than it has now, and it could do so again once the ill-effects of Arab, Mamluk, and Turkish misrule have been replaced by modern methods of irrigation, soil conservation, and social order. Nor is it unfair to add that Jews as well as Arabs were entitled to a preference, and they had made it abundantly clear that this land of their distant ancestors had an appeal for them such as no other land possessed.

Yet, in spite of all these arguments, it might still be said that the decision was wrong, if it could have been shown at the time, or even could be shown now, that the surrender of rights in this corner of the Arab world would do irreparable harm to the Arab people. But nothing like this can be shown. Even to-day, when the decision has unhappily led to the existence of more than half a million Arab refugees, it is not facts but political decisions and psychological attitudes which prevent their resettlement. Factually there is both room and money, and those among whom they settled would profit from their activities. The Arab world is bristling with real problems, social, economic, political, and religious, but among these real problems the presence of a Jewish community in a corner of the Middle East is of very minor significance. Today it is true that Jordan is cut off from the sea, and that land communications between Egypt and Asia are interrupted. But neither of these difficulties are due to natural causes. They are the result of the Arab refusal to make peace with Israel and could be remedied tomorrow if the Arabs willed it.

In no way would the Arab world be better off if there were Arab rule in the area between the Jordan and the Mediterranean. Palestine would, indeed, have remained an Arab country, or rather part of an Arab country. It would be, like most other Arab countries, a country of wealthy landlords and impoverished, debt-ridden peasants. Its deserts would still be deserts, its ruins, ruins. The ruling families would be squabbling for power and absorbing its profits. They would be bullying the Christian powers over the rights they would concede in Holy Places, although on paper at least they would have given generous rights to the Jewish and Christian minorities. And the young effendis, honest, attractive, idealistic, and well educated, would be struggling against odds to efface corruption, to overcome the stagnation of fatalism, and to live up to the picture of a free democratic society as it existed in their hearts and their imagination. The world, as well as the local authorities, Jewish and Christian, would have lost something. But the Arabs would have been masters in their own house.

It was, I believe, a right decision of the British when they issued the Balfour Declaration, and of the League of Nations when they confirmed the Mandate, to grant priority in this small corner of the Arab world to the Jewish people. But those rights were purchased at a cost, and, in one sense at least, the Arabs footed the bill. That they behaved violently and irresponsibly is true ; that the Jewish population behaved for long with great self-restraint is true ; that the Jews wished to be friends with the Arabs is true. But it is also true that today the Jews have the state they sought and the Arabs are for the most part refugees.

It is in relation to the refugees that Israel must ultimately square her account ; and the task is not easy. Nor has it been made easier by innumerable factors all calculated to fan the smouldering resentment of the ordinary Israeli and to dam the springs of generosity and of sympathy with misfortune which has normally characterised the Jewish people. For Jewish generosity never willingly stops at Jewish frontiers, as innumerable Christian refugees from Hitler's Germany could testify.

CHAPTER VII

Israel and the Arab World

THERE are three fields in which Israel is directly concerned today with the Arab population of what was once Palestine. Firstly there are her own Arab citizens, secondly there is the question of a further increase of those citizens by the repatriation of Arabs now refugees, and thirdly there is the compensation of those refugees who are, or should be, resettled in fresh homes in Arab countries.

In so far as her own citizens are concerned, the situation is still very fluid. It would be idle to give an exact picture of the facts at the moment of writing, since it would certainly have been altered by the time of publication. It is only possible to judge tendencies and developments. The first point, which is evident on the most superficial examination, has a greater importance than it is usually given. In the five years since the establishment of independence Israel's Arab population has not diminished, but has increased by well over fifty per cent. There were scarcely 100,000 Arabs in Israel at the beginning of 1949 ; today there are over 170,000. The former figure was made up in some measure of Arabic-speaking Druses and others who actually fought on the Jewish side, but the greater part consisted of those whom the rapidity of the Israeli advance, especially in Galilee, prevented from reaching the frontier. They would have fled, had they been able to. As they were unable to, their villages remain intact, their fields remain theirs, and materially they are more prosperous than they have ever been.

The increase from 100,000 to 170,000 is due to two causes. There has been a substantial return of individuals, most of whose relatives had remained in Israel ; and there has likewise been an open or secret return to villages where the majority of the population had stayed, and only a minority had fled. On the other hand, villages from which the majority had fled are now in ruins. If a few remained behind at first, they departed later, and there have been no cases of a whole village community re-establishing itself out of such a minority. In the towns the position was naturally different ; the

49

decision to depart or remain was more an individual or family affair, and a minority of the urban Arab population remains in most towns of Israel. Only one town, Nazareth, remains almost wholly Arab.

These facts at least show that Israel has been willing to see its Arab population increase, rather than sought to drive out those who survived within its borders at the conclusion of active fighting. There has been no general Arab tendency to leave the country. A few do so, but their ability to take out their capital must depend on the supply of foreign currency available, and this has never been large, or is likely to be large so long as the present economic crisis in Israel remains.

Of the Arabs who remain, the villagers are undoubtedly extremely prosperous. They have a ready market for everything they produce ; they have been helped to increase their production in various ways by the government ; and they get high prices for this production. The industrial labourer and the white-collar worker have had a more difficult task and are only gradually being absorbed into the economic life of the country. The exposed situation of northern Israel, with frontiers on three sides touching three separate countries—Lebanon, Syria, and Jordan—has led to the maintenance of a military government and exceptional security regulations after these had been abandoned in the rest of Israel. To some extent these special conditions have imposed exceptional regulations on Arab life and movement ; but again we can only speak of tendencies in a fluid situation ; and the tendency is undoubtedly towards normalisation, not towards an increase of the burden laid on Arab citizens.

Questions of wages and employment were not always easy to solve, for where an Arab was employed by an Arab, wages tended to be considerably less than the minimum demanded by a Jewish worker ; but there were also questions of level of skill and capacity. Again the tendency has all been in the direction of refusing to sanction a double standard which would lead to the creation of a class of underpaid ' helots ' excluded from opportunities of advancement. Arab wages have been raised to the Jewish level, and today Arab and Jewish Israeli are members of the same trade unions, and benefit from the same social security. The Arab industrial or white-collar worker is beginning to enjoy the prosperity of the Arab landowner and peasant.

No doubt a number of individual problems remain, and even individual injustices. Here two other factors are of importance. There is a vocal public opinion in Israel ; and there are Arab members of the Knesset—the Israeli Parliament. If anything which savours of injustice is immediately challenged by the idealists, anything savouring of a dual level economy is as immediately challenged by the Socialists and the great trade union organisation of the Histadruth. And on both scores the Arab members of the Knesset have perfect freedom to voice their complaints.

The underlying difficulty with regard to the Arab citizens of Israel does not lie in these fields. That there are problems to be solved and inequalities to be removed is natural, and nothing else could be expected ; and that all the facts show that these problems and inequalities are being gradually dealt with is reasonable ground for optimism. But optimism becomes utopianism if it is deduced from this that there is no further ground for disquiet on the Jewish or Arab side as to the future, or that Israel could accept a much larger Arab population. For the Arab citizens of Israel are in a situation which imposes on them a great psychological strain, so long as the attitude of their fellow Arabs in neighbouring states remains one of hostility and suspicion, and the problem of the Arab refugees remains unsolved. That the Arabs in Israel are probably more prosperous and have greater opportunities of expressing their grievances and seeing them righted than any similar group in any Arab country is not in itself proof that they would remain loyal citizens of Israel, should that loyalty be put to the test by a renewal of hostilities such as the Arab states, in their verbal propaganda, constantly threaten. To say this is no reflection on the Arabs themselves. Were it otherwise, then it would mean that they cared for nothing except material benefits and that their loyalty to Israel depended entirely on the profits they could extract from their citizenship. It will be at least another generation before it could be expected that they will come to value, as assets which would justify them in joining with their Jewish fellow-citizens in defence of their common country against an attack by their fellow Arabs, the political freedom, including votes for their womenkind, the educational facilities, and the religious and social welfare that the Israeli Government is gradually assuring them. And by that time it is to be hoped that Israel's relations with the Arab world will be so transformed that any advance secured by the Arabs of Israel may increase both the mutual good will and the advancement of the whole area.

It is not academic to raise this point of loyalty, for the suggestion is being made again that Israel, as a duty or even as a gesture, should readmit a substantial number of those who are now refugees. Such a suggestion must be resisted not merely by Jews in Israel or outside, but by all who care for the future peace of the Middle East. Israel is not the only country to possess among its citizens a substantial minority, and one which is bound by ties of blood and tradition to the majority in a neighbouring country. The growth of European nationalism and irredentism, the story of the succession states created by the Versailles settlement, and evidence provided by minorities outside Europe, all go to show that there are practical limitations to the size and nature of a minority which can be rightly and generously treated by the majority, and can respond in loyal and creative co-operation on a basis of truly equal citizenship.

Evidence on various aspects of the minority problem can be taken from the position of the Jews themselves in Eastern Europe. In Poland, for example, they formed just over ten per cent of the population, and this proved to be a much larger non-Polish population than the Polish state or people could digest, even apart from the antisemitism which increased as the digestive failure became more manifest. In Rumania, where the Jewish minority was proportionately less than in Poland, the failure to treat the Jews as equal citizens was even more complete, and not all the blame could be laid at the door of antisemitic prejudice. In neither of these cases was there the complicating factor of a powerful neighbour of the same blood as the minority. Such cases provide even more decisive examples. In Czechoslovakia, in spite of the real democracy and liberalism of the régime of Masaryk and Benes, a minority of Sudeten Germans, amounting to much less than ten per cent of the state, led to its total destruction, even before the outbreak of general war. In the Balkans the minorities, which are inevitable wherever the frontiers be drawn, have caused unrest and enmity ever since the Balkan states became independent. And so examples could be multiplied, all leading to the same conclusion that to ask of Israel that she substantially increase her Arab minority is no service, not merely to Israel, but to the Arab minority itself. It is to submit both sides to pressures and suspicions, psychological, economic, political, which would make happy relationships between minority and majority almost certainly impossible, and give ground for perpetual friction between Israel and her neighbours. Doubtless in a perfect world this would not be so ; but neither Jews nor Arabs are perfect.

It is pertinent to relate this evidence gathered from minorities elsewhere to the promises extended by the idealists of both sides in the years before the Arabs proclaimed that a Jewish state would be resisted by force. On each side there were promises that absolute justice and equality would be guaranteed to the minority, whether it was to the Arab minority in whatever area were allotted to a Jewish state, or to the existing Jewish community in a hypothetical Arab Palestine. There is no reason to doubt the sincerity or good will of those who made these promises. But it is unfortunately very reasonable to doubt whether with the best will in the world either side would have been able to implement them. In the proposed Jewish state there would have been 400,000 Arabs to about half a million Jews. In an Arab Palestine there would have been some 700,000 Jews to less than twice that number of Arabs. Neither state would have been viable. In the Jewish state there would have been the complex organisation of a semi-socialist western welfare community, which would have imposed upon its unfortunate Arab citizens burdens they would neither have needed nor have understood ; in an Arab Palestine, Jews would have suffered the opposite ; the leisurely pace of life, the corruption and inefficiency which have marked Arab societies, would have been to them an equally intolerable burden.

In any case, from the moment when the Arabs inside and outside Israel declared their unshakeable hostility to any Jewish state at all, they made such a solution entirely impossible. No state could accept that almost half its citizens were vowed to its destruction, and from this point of view the number of Arabs who are living in Israel is already wonderfully, even dangerously, large.

It is all the more tragic to have to accept such unpleasant facts when one is confronted with the contrasts of the Israeli countryside. On one side are the prosperous fields and villages of the Arabs who stayed. On the other are the pathetic ruins of those villages whence the Arabs fled. It is tempting to feel that all could equally have stayed, all equally been prosperous. Even had the Arab world freely accepted Israel, it is doubtful whether so large an Arab population would have remained. Those who were dissatisfied, however, could

53

have left peacefully, selling their property and taking the money with them to re-establish themselves in more congenial surroundings. It was the hostility of the Arabs which turned what might have been an orderly and profitable exodus into the present refugee tragedy.

For the sake of the Arabs, as well as for the sake of the Jews, there can be no going back to the past. Nevertheless, the past is more important than is often recognised by those whose sympathies are won by the human misery of the refugees, and who desire to help them. It has been no service to them to regard them entirely as the innocent victims of the wickedness of others, and to refuse to recognise the extent to which they are themselves the authors of their own misfortune and the only possible architects of their re-establishment. For sympathy of this kind has but confirmed them in their refusal to acknowledge that the past cannot be undone and weakened such determination as they might have had to seek new homes and occupations among their Arab brethren. Only of a minority of the refugees is it certain that they were driven from their homes by armed opponents, or fled when all possibilities of further resistance on their part had become impossible. The tragic fact is that, though they outnumbered the Jews by two to one and at the beginning at any rate were as well armed, few of them made any attempt to defend their homes, and the activities of Jewish forces did not play the major part in bringing about the present situation.

In most cases where a war has resulted in a vast civilian refugee problem the beginning has been the flight of civilians, mostly women, children, and old people, from homes which had been destroyed by military action, or which were in the direct line of an advancing enemy army. Such refugees fled, concerned only to save their lives and not knowing what the future held. The majority of the Arabs have become refugees in a very different manner.[1] It was their own leaders, Palestinian or other, who told them to quit their homes for a few weeks while the Jews were driven into the sea ; once that had happened they could return not merely to their own property, but to take also what had belonged to the Jews. These did not flee because they were defeated or in personal danger. They departed, men of military age as well as the rest of their families, in anticipation of a triumphant and profitable return, since no Arab

[1] It is perhaps necessary to state that none of the facts in this and the succeeding paragraphs have been taken from Jewish sources. They have been taken from the accounts of Gentile eye-witnesses, many of whom could be classified as ' pro-Arab ' in sentiment.

believed that the Jews would be able to resist them. When it is realised that this opinion was shared by many British soldiers on the spot, it is not surprising that the Arabs also were deceived as to Jewish powers of resistance.

A second category fled because they were, or thought themselves to be, in danger of massacre, did they fall into Jewish hands. This was particularly true after the murder by terrorists of the population of a village a few miles west of Jerusalem, Deir Yassin. But here also the actual facts need to be understood. The terrorists who destroyed Deir Yassin acted on the belief—a belief genuinely shocking to the immense majority of Jews in the country—that the Arabs should be treated in the way in which they had always boasted that they would treat the Jews. They believed that the Arabs should be taught that ' two could play at that game '; and it has to be accepted unhappily as true not only that Arabs made such boasts, but that there had been a number of cases where Arabs had caught small Jewish groups and had treated them even worse than that ; for I have never heard it said that the women of Deir Yassin were raped before they were murdered, or that the naked bodies of men and women were sexually mutilated and then photographed for public sale. Arabs had been guilty of both these atrocities. It was not the massacre, but the use of the massacre in propaganda broadcasts of the Arab military command which caused a panic flight of other villagers, *and the broadcasts were framed to achieve that purpose.* They were not framed in order to strengthen Arab resistance, but to persuade those who had not already done so to leave their homes—always, of course, in expectation of a rapid and triumphant return. Only towards the end of the fighting did Arabs flee because they feared that the Arab armies would not defeat the Jews and that the Jews would exact vengeance for the atrocities they had committed.

There is a third category which did flee as the result of the destruction of their homes in military operations, or because they found themselves in the middle of the fighting. During the battle for the control of the roads during the winter and spring of 1947-48, a number of Arab villages, whence attacks had been made on the roads, were destroyed by Jewish forces. In later operations, in both south and north, especially when Jewish forces advanced beyond the lines laid down for the Jewish state in the United Nations plan, Arab civilians were caught in the fighting line and fled.

In what proportion these three categories are to be distributed it is impossible to determine, though it seems probable that the first is the largest, and it certainly included most of the leaders and wealthier members of the population. There were no omnipresent neutral observers who could have provided the information. As it is impossible to allot shares of blame on the basis of established facts, it might be argued that the whole sorry story should be allowed to sink into oblivion ; and indeed the sooner it can be forgotten the better. It is, however, mentioned here only for two practical reasons which are still relevant to the future. In the first place there is the United Nations resolution of December 19, 1948, which is still referred to in every decision taken about the future of the refugees. This resolution demands ' that refugees wishing to return home and live at peace with their neighbours should be permitted to do so at the earliest practicable date, and that compensation should be paid for property of those choosing not to return and for loss of or damage to property which under principles of international law or in equity should be made good by governments or authorities responsible.' (Clause 11 of Resolution 194 [III] of the United Nations.) Behind the resolution was the opinion of the murdered Mediator, Count Folke Bernadotte. Reaching Jerusalem in May, 1948, he had been witness only of the later phases of the Arab flight when, in appearances at least, a considerable share of responsibility seemed to lie with the advancing Jewish forces. It coloured his attitude, and in his first report he spoke of the ' innocence ' of the refugees and demanded that all who fled should be allowed to return at once, or that ' full and generous ' compensation should be paid them for what they had left behind.

It was an unhappy demand, for, with the best will in the world, Israel could not have complied with it. While fighting was still continuing, or while the Arab states were refusing to make even an armistice, she could not possibly admit to her territory a vast fifth column—for the Arabs were openly proclaiming that this is what the returning population would be. Nor could she accept that full compensation was due from her alone, and that she should assume complete responsibility for the effects of a war which the Arab states had declared and the Arab population of Palestine had almost universally supported.

The facts of the preceding pages are mentioned, in the second place, because many of the demands made on Israel to-day still assume that the refugees were 'innocent victims' driven out by Jewish ruthlessness and cruelty. Voluntary workers, friends of the Arabs, and even official pronouncements endorse the demand of the refugees themselves that they be allowed to return to their homes and, in addition, paid generous compensation for their losses. But even if the facts were true, it might still be unwise for them to return for reasons already discussed. The pages of history cannot be simply turned back for Arabs any more than for any other people. And of no people is it true that they can lose a war, especially one they had themselves declared, and then expect a complete re-establishment of their previous position.

Most of the refugees have now been five years in exile, and few of them have made any effort of their own to re-establish themselves and build up a new life for themselves. The money that has been spent on them by the United Nations and the voluntary organisations would already have sufficed to turn them into a prosperous community, had they been willing to look to the future instead of to the past. Instead, it has been spent simply on preventing them from starving or being decimated by disease in the camps from which but few have moved; it has brought them no nearer a solution of their problems.

It is only those who have shown their love and sympathy with the human suffering of the refugees by their work in innumerable projects in the refugee camps who could hope to make them face the facts of their situation and accept the very large measure of responsibility for it which is theirs alone; but it is precisely among these groups that are heard most frequently the baseless charge laying the whole blame for their plight upon the Jews and the impracticable demand that they be allowed to return to their erstwhile homes. In the spring of 1951 the Churches of East and West met under the auspices of the International Missionary Council and the World Council of Churches to discuss the tragic position of the refugees. Though it is said that at the conference itself there were occasional references to the Arab share of responsibility, they were so ill-received by the Arabs present, themselves Christians, that no word on this subject was allowed to appear in the report issued by the conference. And yet it has always been fundamental in the Christian approach to any other case of similar human misery that little good will come until the victim faces his own faults first. At Beirut everything was presented as the fault of somebody else—in this case the Christian nations of the West. Not even the Arab powers who encouraged their Palestinian brethren to fight were included as having any share of responsibility whatever for the consequences. And when outstanding Christian leaders take such an attitude, is it surprising that the mass of the refugees themselves are only too willing to echo it ?

Like the refugees, the Arab states have also refused to recognise their responsibility for the present position of those whom they inspired to leave their homes with specious promises. On the contrary, they have been actively concerned to preserve them in their misery as a powerful propaganda weapon against Israel. They proclaimed them to the world as victims not of themselves but of the cruelty and wanton ruthlessness of the Jews ; and in this they have likewise been abetted by many sympathisers in the Christian West.

The ultimate tragedy of this attitude from the Arab side, whether of the states or the victims, is that it has made almost impossible any constructive attitude on the part of Israel, the only partner in the whole episode who has declared her willingness to take the full share that can be shown to be hers of the burden of their re-establishment. So long as the thesis of entire Jewish responsibility is put forward, Israel is bound to oppose it, and she is right to do so, for the entire responsibility is not hers. So long as the demand be for total or even partial repatriation, she is likewise forced into opposition, even though she has accepted a substantial number and is still accepting individuals who can show that the bulk of their families is still among her citizens. The normal attitude of the Israeli is commiseration with their plight, and neither hostility nor indifference ; and this attitude is reflected in many official declarations of her willingness to pay compensation. But she rightly insists that such compensation must help towards the resettlement of the refugees and not be dissipated in continued sterile relief. She is releasing bank accounts which have long been blocked, she has made contributions to the resettlement budget of the United Nations. She cannot complete the honouring of her accepted obligations until attitudes over which she has no control have changed.

All this is the beginning of statesmanship in the young state ; but the path ahead will be neither easy nor comfortable. For no power has found the Arab world in its present mood easy to deal with ; and gratitude is a rare occurrence in political affairs, as the British also have discovered. Compensation paid by Israel, however generous, would be at best but a first step towards the creation of conditions in which relations could move towards normalcy.

The attitude of the Churches and the United Nations on the question of responsibility cannot be dismissed as of trifling importance ; for Israel should be capable of playing a very important rôle in the Middle East, and this is only possible if the breach between her and the Arab States is healed. Anything which tends to give support to the present Arab contention that Israel is a criminal intruder with whom no relations are possible is hindering the healing of the breach.

The Middle East has given example after example in recent years, and will doubtless provide still further evidence in the future, of its suspicion and resentment towards the West, and of its unwillingness to be involved in world conflict. Geographically, Israel shares the dilemma and psychologically she shares the disquiet of the Arab world. She is far more dependent than they are on American help, and to that extent more committed to conformity with the policies and opinions of the West. But she desperately desires to retain all possible independence of action, and there her interests are identical with those of her Arab neighbours. They are, in fact, natural allies.

Moreover, whatever the origins of previous Zionist immigrations, Israel to-day is herself largely eastern in population. To the number of those who had spent most of their lives, or indeed had known several generations, on the soil of Palestine has to be added an increasing proportion of Israelis whose families have lived for centuries as minorities within the Arab or Muslim world. Both groups are accustomed to the conditions of the Middle East. They know its soil and climate, they are familiar with its opportunities and difficulties. They are no longer strangers to its way of life. Israel today is a country which is neither eastern nor western, but both. She contains within herself the possibility of understanding both and of interpreting each to the other. What Israel might have to offer her Middle Eastern neighbours need not come with the dangerous strings of western imperialism, since it would come from a neighbour less strong than themselves and sharing their exposed position in a world full of menace for smaller powers. What Israel might have to receive from her neighbours would, on the one hand, be of economic advantage, whether it was oil or agricultural products, but, on the other hand, it would be of far greater political and spiritual advantage. For they alone could accept her as one of themselves, a Middle Eastern power, seeking a precarious security amidst the dangers of world hostility and conflict.

It is impossible for the Arab world to continue indefinitely its present condition of unstable government, corrupt wealth, demagogy, poverty, and ignorance, with a small group of young educated Arabs fighting a losing battle with great courage against hopeless odds. In this period of the world's history such a situation leads only to dictatorship or a communist revolution, or both ; and apart from whether one's sympathies are with this or that side of the Iron Curtain, it is difficult to see that present-day communism has anything positive to offer the Arab world. Its individualism, its ' old-fashioned ' courtesies, its tradition of local democracy, even its affection for a slow-moving rhythm of life, none of these would survive in a contemporary communist state. China is large enough and strong enough to develop its own form of communist society, if she so desires. The Arab world is not.

The rescue of the Arab countries from their material and spiritual disorder must be primarily their own affair, and the extent to which the West can help is limited by Arab pride and suspicion. Israel certainly can do nothing. But in an Arab world which was moving forward towards a juster society, she could play a part. To suggest that it is her destiny to *lead* the Middle East into a better way of life is to exaggerate to the point of absurdity. But to suggest that the inter-action of an eastern-western Israel with the rest of the Middle East would increase the general progress and security of the region is neither exaggerated nor absurd.

What stands between her and this possibility, so desirable for her own development ? The fact that only a few are beginning to share with her the understanding of those five roots discussed in previous pages. They *are* her roots ; they *are* the justification for her presence on the Middle Eastern scene ; they are infinitely more important than the legality or the impropriety of the Balfour Declaration. It is they and not British bayonets or the decisions of the League and the United Nations which give to her a solid basis for her hopes, an anchor in her perils. But she shares the acceptance of them with no one. And, in conventional political terms, she is confronted with an impasse. For history is capable of many inter-pretations, as well as many misrepresentations. Each one of her roots could be twisted, misrepresented, judged irrelevant, contradicted by a malicious enemy, as it could be sneered out of court by the mere fact that to put forward such claims at all marks her as unique. And yet they are her title-deeds.

I believe that she must put them forward, stated with all the scholarship, the objectivity, the moderation, of which her greatest scholars are capable, put them forward without arrogance and without exaggeration, but above all put them forward with clear recognition of the debt of honour which they entail, and the clear statement of acceptance of that debt. It is certain that many Christians, many Muslims, will sneer at an action so naïve, so unusual. But the facts are, in reality, so interwoven with the past of both Christianity and Islam that there will be some, on the Christian side at any rate, but I hope on the Muslim also, who will know that in fact she is speaking the truth and will acknowledge it.

Such an action would not of itself, of course, constitute a whole political programme ; but it would give to concrete proposals a new dignity. She has, indeed, already the dignity of the courage with which she defended herself against apparently overwhelming odds. No denial of this would be involved ; for the one is rooted in the other.

The young state could not have a more difficult field in which to win her spurs as a ' good neighbour ' in the comity of nations ; and yet she cannot avoid the challenge and choose an easier object for her first essays. More intangible issues apart, she cannot achieve economic security, or devote her whole strength to the immense tasks which she has undertaken, if she is ringed round with enemies and forced into an artificial economy by the closure of her natural markets and sources of supply. The refugees across her borders are a perpetual menace, a perpetual reminder ; the Arab states make her the focus of a policy which in all its aspects is unreal and unhelpful. For at present it is only by sharing its sterile enmities that the Arab League holds together. Yet she can do what, at present at least, no western state with a past record of ' imperialism ' can do. But to do it, she will need all the help and encouragement which the rest of the world can give her. For it is not in her interest alone, but in the interests of all, that the Arab world with its instability and corruption, its foolish vanities and its real possibilities, its abject poverty and its potential prosperity, should turn over a new leaf and develop in modern form the charm and culture, the humanity and tolerance, which once put Europe to shame.

NOTE

While the book was in proof the tragic incident in the Jordan village of Qibya focused world attention on the problems of the Jordan-Israel frontier along the narrow waist of Israel between Tel Aviv and Hadera. The incident itself was revolting, and it was a pity that Israel was too slow to condemn it unreservedly. But the indignation of the Great Powers and of prominent Christians contained a painful element of unjustified self-righteousness. Too many massacres of innocent people have been justified in recent years by the cant phrases of 'military necessity' or 'punitive measures.'

The basic problem, the problem which Israel must ultimately face, is the hopelessly unsatisfactory nature of the present frontier, drawn along the armistice line, with certain rectifications conceded by King Abdullah in Israel's favour. The Arab rural economy of the area was almost entirely based on the cultivation by a single village of lands in both the hills and the plain. Now the plain lands are in Israel; and the villagers are reduced to destitution in their own homes, if their village was in the hills, as was most common; but if their village was in the plains, they are not only destitute, but homeless within sight of their erstwhile homes. Such a situation is bound to be explosive. On paper it would appear that the obvious solution is for the villages and their lands to be reunited one side of the frontier or the other. But, if that be advocated, we must in fairness look at the consequences from Israel's point of view, bearing in mind the present hostility of the Arabs. Along much of this frontier the total breadth of Israel is often not more than ten miles, and along this narrow belt go the essential road and rail communications joining northern and southern Israel.

The right solution is going to need great courage and imagination. And it is not going to be achieved except by confidence and co-operation on both sides. What it should be, I do not know. I am sure it cannot be achieved by both sides insisting that they cannot yield an inch, but equally it cannot result from concessions and surrenders by one side only. It would help if outsiders would work for that atmosphere which would enable the two countries involved to exhibit the required mutual confidence and courage. At present they too often exacerbate the issue by the violence of their partisanship.

CHAPTER VIII

Jerusalem

THERE is a second issue which is of capital importance in Israel's relations with the world. In the long run it is perhaps even more significant than her relations with her Arab neighbours. It is comprehended in the one word *Jerusalem*.

Today the city is partitioned between Israel and Jordan by an almost arbitrary line from north to south. It leaves isolated within Arab territory the great complex of buildings of the Hebrew University on Mount Scopus. It shuts the Jews off from access to the Wailing Wall and the ancient cemetery on the Mount of Olives. It separates the middle-class Arabs from their beautiful homes in the new western suburbs of the city, now all in Jewish occupation. And it breaks the traditional road from Jerusalem to near-by Bethlehem. For the Christians especially, the partition line in Jerusalem, and the straggling frontier drawn across the middle of the country, mean extra difficulties ; for though the Holy Places are almost all within the Arab sector, the Christian churches and congregations, their possessions and sources of income, are in most cases on both sides of the frontiers, and the result is inevitable difficulty and loss.

From every standpoint the partition of Jerusalem is an offence and an inconvenience. There is only one thing to be said in its favour. But, to me, it is decisive. *It truly represents, and at the deepest spiritual as well as political level, the actual facts.* For Jerusalem through the centuries has contained within itself that disturbing quality of exposing our shams and evasions, and confronting us, if we are willing to see it, with the reality about ourselves. That, and no sacred sites or buildings, gives to this austere city among the mountains the strange quality which is felt by all who in any way give their lives to it. There was truth in the statement of Sir Ronald Storrs, the first British Governor of Jerusalem, that ' after Jerusalem there can be no promotion.'

The attempt to exempt the city from the divisions which rent the land and to give it some artificially compacted international administration inevitably failed. For Jerusalem cannot be turned into a city set apart for the pious only, whether of one faith or of three. Its strange capacity to judge our actions and our professions is set within the framework of the normal life of normal men with the market, the money changer, the *bourgeois,* the peasant. Perhaps it is just because this is so that it has this strange quality. For here it is not man but God that judges the three monotheistic religions which claim to worship Him, to live under His guidance, and to exhibit His ways to men. And God made the world for ordinary men to inhabit and to control. It has had this quality since the voices of the prophets of Israel were first heard in its streets ; and to those who see a pattern in history it is no accident that Christianity and Islam have also been brought to stand before this same silent tribunal—the tribunal where ordinary citizens (who include, of course, clergy, religious teachers, monks, and such-like) show in their ordinary lives the true meaning to them of their religious professions.

I was often asked on Zionist platforms in earlier days whether I did not recognise the primacy of the Jewish claim to the possession of Jerusalem ; and I could only reply that whereas I believed that the Jewish people justifiably asked of the nations the right to return to the land of Israel, there was no political authority which could give them the right to the possession of Jerusalem. That they could only win for themselves by their conduct. For Jerusalem has borne for millennia the name of the City of Peace, and it is God's peace not man's that the name enshrines. Man has never been able to give it peace ; and in terms of human history there is no city in the world to which the name has been less applicable, whether its masters have professed Judaism, Christianity, or Islam. Even the materialist would have to admit historically that, if there be a God, for three thousand years He has judged in Jerusalem the religions which profess to worship Him, and if there be no God, there is nowhere where the claims of religion have been so challenged by the actions of those who claim to be religious.

Only those who are spiritually dead, whether they be Jews, Christians, or Muslims, can face without shame their record as it is transmuted by the mysterious quality of this city ; and only the utterly superficial could suggest that an artificial international administration could meet its soul-searching challenge. This is, of course, not all the picture. To each of the three religions God is a God of mercy ; and this also that strange word, Jerusalem, expresses. For it has also been, and is, a word of hope and encouragement, as real and creative as the sombre aspects of its history are real and (in the old sense of ' judging ') discerning.

The chequered political career of the city as the capital of an independent or autonomous Jewish state came to its end in the terrible war with Rome and the destruction of its Temple by Titus. The graphic accounts of Josephus give us an appalling picture of the horrors of its siege and capture. But what is most appalling in that story is the hideous mutual violence between different Jewish sects and groupings, their mutual hatreds and slaughter, their complete inability to unite even to face the common enemy without. The legendary withdrawal in a coffin of the rabbinic leader, Johanan ben Zakkai, contains a sinister parable. For the Jerusalem which he left was spiritually but a coffin, and it is an extraordinary fact that in the unique story of the part played by the Jewish community still living in Israel between the first century C.E. and the nineteenth, the actual city of Jerusalem has but minor significance. Of all that has been recounted in previous pages of *The Fourth Root of Israel* (p. 21f.), the scene is Galilee, especially Tiberias and Safed, apart from the first decade when the academy of Johanan was in the maritime plain.

The community which arose in Jerusalem during the Middle Ages, and has continued without a break until today, has been distinguished rather for a pious quietism than for any creative activity. It shows little parallel to the intense activity of the northern city of Safed, and it certainly had far less influence on the life of Jews in other countries ; for it produced no leaders of the calibre of Caro and Luria. Moreover the very fact that it lived in the holiest city of Jewish thought and longing had an unhappy effect upon its membership, since it could make an unlimited appeal to charity. For many centuries it was kept alive only by the collection and distribution of charitable funds, known as Halukkah, from all over the Jewish world. That this was so was not primarily the fault of the Jews of Jerusalem themselves. In the stagnant life of the city there were no opportunities by which they could have made themselves economically independent and, in addition, raised the considerable sums which were constantly needed for the bribery of officials. Nevertheless the many accounts which we have of the collection and distribution of Halukkah, while they emphasise the affection in which Jerusalem was held by Jews everywhere, often reflect also a less noble quality among those who collected and received these gifts. It became an unhappy fact that by the beginning of the nineteenth century the Jewish community of Jerusalem was notable for its narrowness, intolerance, and corruption rather than for its piety.

In the nineteenth century effort to secure an economic base for Jewish life, associated first with philanthropists such as Sir Moses Montefiore and later with the beginnings of Zionism, only a small percentage of Jerusalem Jews played a distinguished rôle. Most of them were ready to continue an existence of pious quietism and dependence, and few were prepared to forget their ancient quarrels and divisions. Today it is from within the orthodoxy of Jerusalem that the most fervent Jewish enemies of the state of Israel are to be found ; and, if these be but a small minority, of greater moral significance is the small part played by the orthodox piety of Jerusalem in building the moral foundations for the new society of Israel. The many yeshivas of all kinds which are to be found in the city reflect the closed societies of the Eastern European ghettoes rather than the new and open society, with all its responsibilities and opportunities, which is growing up around them. The orthodoxy of Jerusalem has yet to show that it can make a creative contribution to the problems confronting contemporary Jewry.

The Christian story follows not dissimilar lines. After the separation of the two religions Jerusalem rapidly lost importance. Its bishop was but a suffragan of the Archbishop of Cæsarea, and the centres of Christian interest grew in Alexandria, Rome, and throughout the Empire. No great scholars came from Jerusalem. It only became important again when Constantine, under the inspiration of his mother, Helena, made it a centre of pilgrimage for the whole Christian world by building splendid shrines over what he believed to be the sites of the Crucifixion and the Resurrection. Whether, in fact, he had identified the right sites it seems impossible that we shall ever discover. We are not likely to find evidence which was unknown to the then bishop and Christians of the city. All that we can say is that since the fourth century those he accepted have been venerated as the sites of those central events in the foundation of the Christian faith, and have acquired sanctity by the continuous devotion with which they have been saturated.

Gradually the whole of the Holy Land became covered with

Christian churches, and in the fifth century a special patriarchate of Jerusalem was established, of which the existing Greek Orthodox Patriarchate is the successor. Its patriarchal and theological history is undistinguished, and few of its patriarchs figure in general Christian history.

It is not to theology or statesmanship that it owes its special position, but to its unique place in the history of Christian unity and disunity. All Christians alike accept the significance of the life and death of Jesus of Nazareth, so that all alike feel a special veneration for the city. When in the fifth century schisms, which were to be permanent, divided the eastern Church, clergy of all the Churches were still allowed to conduct worship in the central shrines of Christendom ; and right through the period of the Arab caliphate we know that Nestorians, Monophysites, and Chalcedonians (Orthodox) shared in their use. To this day in the church of the Holy Sepulchre this situation still exists, and at its altars will be found Greek Orthodox, Latins (Roman Catholics), Armenians, Copts, and Jacobites, while Abyssinians dwell on part of its roofs. What is even more remarkable is that the congeries of buildings of which it forms the centre contain, in addition to the convents of many churches, two Muslim mosques. Only the post-reformation Churches have made no claims to a place within its shrines.

The unity of Christendom is likewise exemplified by the stream of pilgrims which have visited the Holy Places since the fourth century. Of these more will be said later ; for it is not only Christian pilgrims who venerate Jerusalem. As a city of pilgrimage it plays at least an equally fundamental rôle in the Jewish story ; and if that of Islam is less striking it still remains true that it has been visited all through the centuries by pious Muslims of many countries and continents.

Jerusalem has, thus, its place in the story of Christian unity. It is a profound pity that we cannot stop with this statement. But it has played an equally unique place in the story of Christian disunity, and for precisely the same reason. For, just as there is no other city in which Jews, Christians, and Muslims have been so intermingled, so there is no other city in which so many Christian memories are brought together, memories which each Church has sought to safeguard by devotions according to its own rites and usages, conducted by its own clergy, and under its own control.

67

The tragic aspects of this devotion open with the Crusades. The final separation between the Churches of East and West, between Rome and Constantinople, took place less than fifty years before the crusading armies reached Jerusalem. At the time when the city fell to Godfrey of Bouillon, the patriarch, who naturally belonged to the eastern Church, was either dead or out of the country. The crusaders appointed a new patriarch from the western Church. Nevertheless there is evidence that the use of the shrines continued to be granted to all the eastern Churches during the period. But when the crusaders lost Jerusalem, a new situation arose. An eastern patriarch assumed office, the schismatic eastern Churches continued the enjoyment of their traditional rights ; but now the western Church had no status whatever in any holy place ; and this at a time when the stream of western pilgrims was continually increasing, and when interest in the Holy Land had been immensely stimulated by the number of western Christians, of all countries and classes, who could speak of Jerusalem from personal experience.

It was at this moment that the fatal step was taken by the western (Latin) Church of buying directly from the Muslim governors rights in specially important shrines which were actually in the possession of other Churches. This was made possible by the fact that while the *use* of the Churches was granted to the different Christian bodies, their *legal ownership* rested always, right up to modern times, with the Muslim power ruling in Jerusalem.

The weapons used in the struggle between the Churches were such as to bring lasting dishonour on the combatants While the lesser Churches were ruthlessly squeezed out, once they ceased to have sufficient money to bribe the Muslim officials, the main combatants—the Franciscans as representatives of the Latins, and the Patriarch and Brotherhood of the Holy Sepulchre as representatives of the Orthodox Church—used every weapon available from bribery and political pressure to fraud, force, and murder. Few issues can have been so obscured by forgery, few rights so vitiated by force, as those which turn round these, the supposedly holiest shrines of Christendom; and even today there is little sign of a change of heart. To the Muslim rulers, whether Mamluk or Turk, every claim meant merely a fresh opportunity to extort money and to receive bribes. They were therefore careful always to word the privileges they sold to one side or another in such a way that the precise right involved was never stated clearly ; and the door was always open for the other side, by a supreme effort to raise sufficient cash, to upset their rivals. As time went on a substantial proportion of the revenues of both sides were wasted in the struggle ; and when to this are added the bribes and payments necessary to exist at all, the profit which the possession of these shrines brought to the local governors and even higher authorities can easily be realised. From time to time Muslim fanatics destroyed, or sought to destroy, them ; but more worldly rulers were never prepared to see so important a source of revenue disappear—especially when to the mutual bribes and payments of the quarrelling Churches is added the substantial revenue from the thousands of sincere and devoted pilgrims who century after century made the perilous journey to Jerusalem.

As we read the story in the many ' Voyages to the Holy Land ' of pilgrims of past centuries, we find, in addition to the long tale of bribery and corruption, an equally sad story of the mutual hatred of the Churches, of the delight which they took in frustrating and disturbing each other's worship, of violence and even murder at the most sacred moments of Holy Week, of willing alliance with the Muslims to vent their spite upon some other Christian body. That we also read of saintliness and goodness, charity and generosity, we should expect. What is shocking is that the other side is so frequently represented.

It must not be thought that the immense sums by which the Churches bought privileges and ' protection ' from the Sultan or the local pasha secured for the Christians of Jerusalem a life of ease and comfort. The reverse is true. The local Muslim population vented its fanaticism on Christians and Christian buildings whenever it had the opportunity ; and even the rulers who profited from their presence were ever ready to humiliate and oppress them. The lives of Christians, and especially of the Latin Franciscans, were often lives of great heroism and endurance, as we can see, for example, from the records of two seventeenth-century Franciscans, Bernardin Surius and Eugène Roger ; and there is no more foolish statement among the mass of bias and tendentiousness with which every issue concerning the Holy Land is besmirched than that which pretends that Jews and Christians lived in friendship and security under

69

Muslim rule until the wicked Zionists destroyed a situation of idyllic harmony and mutual benevolence.

The Muslim picture historically offers scarcely stronger arguments for regarding Jerusalem exclusively as a centre of religious inspiration. The city was never the central shrine of Islam, which is Mecca. It owes its position as the third holy city of Islam to its associations with the two older monotheisms. It was the site of the Jewish Temple which caused Muhammad to select it as the scene of his ascent to the heavens; and it was the presence of the Christian church of the Holy Sepulchre and the Christian pilgrims at Easter which created the two other main Muslim associations with Jerusalem. For the magnificent Dome of the Rock, built in the seventh century by Abdul-Malik on the site of Muhammad's ascension, was designed to surpass the damaged but still imposing remains of Constantine's great churches of the Crucifixion and Resurrection; while the Muslim festival of Nebi Musa was planned at some period after the crusades to balance the stream of Christian pilgrims and the solemnities of the Easter festival with a comparable Muslim ceremony. It is significant that its date is fixed by the Christian and not the Muslim calendar, so that it shall always coincide with the coming of the Christian pilgrims. The tomb of Moses on the Jericho road, where the pilgrimage culminates, is itself not older than the Middle Ages, and rests only on medieval legend. Even more recent is the Muslim legend of the tomb of David on Mount Zion, which served as a pretext to rob the Franciscans of their central convent at Jerusalem in the sixteenth century. In terms of theological thought the Muslim story repeats that of post-biblical Judaism and post-apostolic Christianity. Jerusalem has never been of more than minor importance in its development.

Of course, from each religion a great many names of noble and pious men and women could be quoted on the opposite page of the ledger, men in great positions like the Patriarch Sophronius, who surrendered the city to the Arabs, or the Caliph Umar, who received it from him; men in modern times like Chief Rabbi Kook or the Mufti Kamil el Husseini, elder brother and predecessor of the notorious Haj Amin. And together with such men there have been thousands of simple Jews, Christians, and Muslims in all centuries, scholars, teachers, clergy, and laity, to whom the religious inspiration of Jerusalem was real, and who in their lives reflected its message.

To these citizens of the city must be added the pilgrims,

especially the Jewish and Christian pilgrims, since to the Muslim Jerusalem was not the centre of his devotion even though the great shrines of the Haram ash-Sharif had a special holiness. Moreover, for the Jew and the Christian there were not only special sites, but the whole land herself and the whole city in which so many memories were enshrined, and from which such deep spiritual inspiration was drawn.

It is from the pilgrims that consideration naturally passes to that other power which flows from Jerusalem, the power which does not condemn but uplifts, which does not judge, but sustains, the power in which the grey stones of the city itself pass into the deep stream of religious inspiration which has sustained Jews and Christians throughout the centuries and given in each religion that conviction of the significance of historical facts which is common to Judaism and Christianity and separates them, on the one side, from mystery religion and magic, and, on the other, from the Greek picture of history as an endless and meaningless repetition. In this day of scepticism the recognition of this power may go no further than a vague statement, but one which is often made: *there is something about Jerusalem* . . . ! The Jewish picture of a future in which the Word of the Lord shall proceed from Jerusalem may be divested of theological implications, but even here there is the undefined aroma of a *something more* such as inspired the epigram during the dark days of 1948 that even the Left Winger, the ' Mapamnik,' if he could not acknowledge God *de jure,* recognised Him *de facto.* For to both the religious and the non-religious there is the common factor of recognition that it is Jerusalem which does something to them, not they who have from their own consciousness created a picture of Jerusalem. And the three-thousand-year-old city can afford to wait and not to press its children to accept a definition which would force them into the intellectual dishonesty of agreement with a creed which they reject in their hearts. For the influence is there factually, not in some mystery of religious imagination, *factually* in terms of every-day facts ; for it was not politics or imperialism, or hatred of Arabs, or just defiance, which chalked passages from the psalms on the lorries carrying food to the beleagured city ; and it is not vote-catching or imperialism which infuses the same mysticism of the city into the speeches of Ben-Gurion or the appeals of other Zionist orators.

Nor is it simply ecclesiastical politics, but something deeper, if

71

vaguer, which moves the Christian demand for some special status for the city. I recognise this fact, even though I believe the demand to be wrong, and the 'practical argument' of the inconvenience of the present partition to be an attempt to evade the simple truth according to Christian doctrine, that the effects of sin *are* inconvenient. There is nothing surprising in the fact that the sins of the Churches in Jerusalem have produced an inconvenient situation for them; the remarkable fact is that they have not produced something much more drastic! But, as Jews, Christians, and Muslims agree, God is merciful!

By the very fact of its political partition Jerusalem has given the three religions which in their different ways venerate it a second chance. Because the partition is political and beyond their control they have not been able to gloss it over with an ecclesiastical administration whose " unity " would be artificial, unreal, and ecclesiastical. Jerusalem is not an ecclesiastical city, even though it is a religious centre ; and the present partition serves to emphasise the fact that the city itself is not primarily a city of religious buildings and interests, but one where ordinary men and ordinary governments carry on their daily life. It is *they* who must decide its future. It is with *them* that ecclesiastical interests must negotiate for special rights and privileges ; but even that they should do with the knowledge that every concession which makes a distinction between ecclesiastical and secular life increases and does not diminish the barrier between religious bodies and religious influence. It is between *them* that the city is partitioned until *they* have discovered the will to make it one city again, and by that fact itself made real its name as the city of peace. It is therefore among *them*, the ordinary men and women of Jerusalem, Jew or Arab, Jew or Christian or Muslim, and not with governments and chancelleries abroad, that Church and Synagogue and Mosque must seek to make peace and brotherhood. For only so will that peace be real in the sight of the God whom they alike worship.

From this standpoint, that it is God and not man who has determined that the quality of Jerusalem depends ultimately on political rather than on ecclesiastical man, there is a great deal of encouragement to be drawn from the way in which Israel has sought to meet her responsibilities. During the period of the siege, there is little to be said in favour of the attitude of the Churches ;

and a great deal of the anti-Jewish propaganda which some of them circulated in the west was biased to the extent of complete untruthfulness. Now the note is very different, and from all the Churches comes the same report of the helpfulness and good will which the Israeli authorities are showing to any requests made to them. There are still thorny questions, especially concerning property, which are outstanding ; and there are real problems to be met. But there is no sign on the side of the Israelis of a blank refusal to meet them—though, of course, Israel's bureaucrats are just as imperfect, and usually less experienced, than the bureaucrats of any other human society.

Nothing good will come of the religious implications of the city until the Churches realise that there is no short cut to what they ask. The unity of Jerusalem cannot be achieved by political bargaining ; it can result only from a conversion of the spirit. There is not a pulpit in Christendom from which the phrase that " ye cannot serve God and Mammon " has not been quoted in its application to human compromise. Now they must apply it to themselves. Their difficulties are real ; but their solution comes only along the long and hard road of seeking the peace of the city. As the Churches contain both Arab and Jewish Christians, they have not to go outside their own doors to begin their task ; and it is encouraging to note that some have already begun it.

The real and the deepest danger confronting Israel on this issue lies with those chauvinists, political or religious, who dream of a military conquest of the whole city as an alternative to the unity which comes naturally as the expression of united hearts. Israel is not alone in having her chauvinists, and the follies of materialism and ignorance are not peculiar to her alone. Did they gain their purpose, they would inevitably find that they had gained but Dead Sea fruit, for they could not prevail against that spirit which is the city's and not theirs. But it must also be said that nowhere in its long history has Jerusalem *prevented* evil men wreaking evil in its name, as the massacres of the war with Rome bear witness, and the massacres which followed the crusaders' capture of the city " in the name of Christ " remind us. It lies in the hands of men, of the voters who support or refuse to support, this or that programme put to them in the normal terms of political propaganda.

So long as Israel, in the normal development of her political

73

democracy, continues the line which she is at present following, seeks to do justly with her religious minorities, Christian or Muslim, and accepts or yields such " rectifications " of the frontier through the city as may become possible, so long is she being loyal to the real city of Jerusalem, and it is her capital in spirit as well as in fact.

But because Jerusalem is divided the solution does not lie with Israel alone. The other half of the city with its shrines and homes belongs to the Arab and Muslim state of Jordan. In so far as the Christians are concerned, by all reports they have no complaints to make. But Jordan possesses important Jewish Holy Places, and to these Jews have no access. The ancient Jewish quarter in the old city has no longer any Jewish population. The Wailing Wall cannot be visited by Jews ; nor can the great cemetery on the lower slopes of the Mount of Olives. Before true peace comes to Jerusalem there are relations to be built up between Israel and Jordan, between Judaism and Islam, and these cannot be built up from the side of Israel alone. It is no part of this work to treat in detail of these issues from the Arab and the Islamic side ; not because they are not important, but rather just because they would merit treatment of equal length.

Nevertheless Islam has to be brought into the picture as well as Judaism and Christianity. To-day Israel is treating her Muslim Arab subjects well. There are still many problems to be settled in relation to them, there are still injustices to be removed. Yet the Muslim Arabs of Israel have their own religious courts, their own schools, and they certainly enjoy religious freedom. But Islam has not responded. No Jew may visit the Wailing Wall. The ancient synagogues of the Jewish quarter lie in ruins, destroyed largely by shell-fire directed from the Haram ash-Sharif itself. It is idle to pretend that the whole solution of the problem of Jerusalem lies in the hands of Israel. The divided city accuses Islam also ; and there is as yet no sign that Islam is concerned to take any step to meet the accusation.

To speak of a religious and international administration of Jerusalem must involve bringing all these different queries into consideration. Past history and present realities deny the claim of any of the three religions to have precedence over the normal inhabitants of the city in the determining of its future. Nevertheless it remains true that there is a relationship between the three monotheisms of the world and the city of Jerusalem which is unique. There is no other city in which they meet in a similar way. In any other centre one will be host, however courteous, and the others guests, however welcome. In Jerusalem each exists by its own right, and because of its own tradition, and by this very fact some relationship between them is inevitable.

To place the government of the city in their hands is an utterly inappropriate recognition of their position ; it is to perpetuate the weakest aspect of their rights and the least favourable of their traditions. It would be much nearer the spiritual realities which, at their best, they embody, to create in Jerusalem a centre where they could meet in free fellowship and voluntary discussion. There is in the past of each some element of indebtedness to the others, there are in the beliefs of each some elements which they share with the others, there are in the positive affirmations of each truths which they hold in common with the others in the presence of the indifference or materialism of the present age. These are the fields in which the unique relations between the three religions might be productive of unique results ; quiet, " academic " study and research in these fields would be far more likely to issue in an increase of fellowship and understanding than would partnership in ecclesiastical government. Out of such relationships might flow influences into the political conflicts and political divisions which at present divide both ordinary citizens and religious bodies alike, which would have far more real significance than any enforced inter-nationalisation. For one thing is certain, the city itself, with its millennial tradition, would not become a city of peace by anything less than a concord resting firmly on reality itself.

CHAPTER IX

Israel in the Contemporary World

THAT she had a unique relationship with the Arab world and with the city of Jerusalem would be enough to give the little state of Israel an unusual significance in the contemporary situation. The problem of Jerusalem appears to be returning to the agenda of political assemblies ; but, even if it does not, it is well to remember that it has not been forgotten by the Churches and others, and it would need but little to bring it back into the foreground. The integration of the Arab world into the community of nations becomes every year a more acute problem, not only because of oil or because of the relation of the Middle East to the strategic issues between East and West, but because of its own internal conflicts. An unstable society in a situation where all the nations are increasingly affected by the maladies of any, is a perpetual menace to others as well as to itself ; and Arab society today is basically unstable. Its contrasts of wealth and poverty, of education and ignorance, of crowded refugee camps, nomadism, and immense economic potentialities, of arrogant pretension and political evasiveness, all mark it as one of the chief danger spots in a world of conflicting ideologies. But a unique relationship with Jerusalem and the Arab world are not Israel's only contacts with the contemporary situation.

In two other matters, both of comparable world significance, she is involved in equally unusual ways. Nazi persecution and the massacre of six million Jews make her exceptionally sensitive, and give her exceptional moral claims, in any decisions affecting Germany ; and the origin of her population as well as the existence of Mapam as a Marxist socialist party which is still not part of the network of Communist parties owing allegiance to Moscow, give her a special place in the issue between western society and the societies ' behind the Iron Curtain.'

It is of the utmost importance to note that these four great issues concern Israel just as a matter of fact ; they concern Israel

76

because they cannot help doing so. Israel is concerned with them, not of her own choice, but by the imposition of the facts. It is not idealists, dreaming of a messianic ' mission of Israel,' who have drawn her attention to them, and attempted to arouse interest in them among a population basically concerned with its own affairs. They are of the warp and woof of the normal activities of the ministers and ambassadors of Israel ; and they are the inevitable concern of every thinking Israeli.

When all that can be said has been said about the general responsibility of western twentieth-century society for the two world wars which this generation has witnessed, it still remains true that there was a very special responsibility on Germany for their outbreak ; and that this responsibility was shared widely by ' the Germans.' The vast majority of the people enthusiastically supported their government in the declaration of war, and that support was ultimately alienated by the fact, not that their government had done evil, but that it had led them to defeat. In other words, there was little general sign either in 1918 or in 1945 that ' the Germans ' had repented and desired to turn over a new leaf. Again it is not an issue which can be left simply to idealists and dreamers ; it involves the whole western world in one of its most difficult contemporary decisions. And it involves the world at the point where the politician and the moralist face the same issues : can a nation repent ; and, if so, how does a nation repent ? That is the moralist's formulation ; but the politician deals with exactly the same issue when he asks : can a nation see the faults in its past behaviour, and, if so, how does it change its habits ?

In either formulation it is an issue which is not strange to the history of Israel. For it was the preoccupation of all the prophets from Samuel to Malachi. Nor is it strange to the writer as an Englishman. For it is but another form of the questions which arise in the British change of attitude from the imperialism of the past, from the concept of ' the white man's burden ' as formulated by Disraeli or Kipling, to the new relations with Indian, African, Persian, and Egyptian which we are now seeking—and being forced —to develop.

It is evident that a nation can change, and history has shown a number of examples of its happening. Perhaps one of the most startling is the change in the Scandinavians from the savage and ruthless destroyers, who wrought havoc from one end of the coast of Europe to the other a thousand years ago, to the sedate and peaceable people which they have been for the last few centuries. But the Scandinavian change took centuries, and the change in the British attitude to empire during the last decades does not involve any such violent turning from a past of horror as would need to be the case with a nation whose current generation has witnessed the cold-blooded massacre of untold millions—' untold,' for we must remember that the total number of victims of the Nazis, including Germans, Poles, Russians, and such groups as the gipsies may more than double the figure known for the Jews alone. How can such a nation change, and in a single generation ?

There is no evidence of anything which could be called national repentance in Germany. That the government has accepted a very limited financial responsibility for some measure of compensation for the actual material expenses involved in resettling the survivors of her victims can be considered laudable, though of limited significance. But the courageous voices of some of her statesmen and churchmen do not seem to have produced any notable effect. Nor does it seem that attempts at re-education have had more than a very limited result. It has been effective only with those who would in any case have been likely not to succumb to the propaganda of Nazism. A voluntary Jewish organisation, such as the World Jewish Congress or less extensive bodies, can satisfy its conscience by passing resolutions of protest—in fact it might be said without unkindness that Jewish politics until the establishment of the state of Israel consisted largely in an unbroken flow of protests—but the state of Israel is in the situation where, as a member of the United Nations, her particular attitude and her particular reason for distrust and even hatred of Germany has to be weighed in world scales and as part of a total world commitment. She has to ask with a new accent: can a nation repent, and if so, how does a nation repent ? and her answer is valid for more than her private sorrows. The very fact that one can speak of the murder of six million human beings as ' her private sorrows ' is a measure of the problem which confronts her. Factually the statement is, I believe, unhappily true. The world has, very willingly, forgotten, and resents being reminded of the horrors of the period of war. But morally the statement is monstrous. The deliberate murder of a people is no private sorrow to that people, but a sin which blackens the whole face of humanity.

Very naturally that is how Jewish organisations take it. On the day on which this is written there are reports that a large meeting at Tel Aviv of artists, writers, and other intellectuals, attacked the very idea of negotiating with murderers. The same bulletin of the J.T.A. carries a summary of an eight-point programme agreed at a conference of the American Jewish Committee as to what actions Germany must take in order to make moral and material amends for her crime against Jewry. Speaking with every respect, the attitude of the intellectuals at Tel Aviv and of the American Jewish Committee reflect the child's rather than the adult's relationship to life. In their different ways each makes demands whose fulfilment is exceedingly difficult—but it is someone else who has to sort out and solve the difficulties. Each makes its selection of the facts, but ignores the total situation. The American Jewish Committee demands ' the elimination of all Nazi and neo-Nazi organisations.' I have no doubt that every German democrat would be delighted to oblige : but how do you do it ? The intellectuals, in their moral indignation, ignore the facts that Israel desperately needs what Germany is prepared to send, and that the receipt of it does not involve accepting a limited material offer as effacing an unlimited and unpayable moral debt.

For centuries the whole life of the Jewish people has worn this adolescent garb in its relations with the nations. For nowhere could they take action on their own initiative. Everywhere the best they could hope for was the benevolent attention of a ' grown-up,' who actually had the power to do these things. The same thing has been true in terms of political thought. The Jew has been forced to be the perpetual theorist, the builder of imaginary worlds in which justice reigned ; the inspiration and initiator of reforms which others had to carry out. Western emancipation for a brief moment released a small section of the Jewish people from this enforced immaturity ; and during that period Jews showed without hesitation or difficulty that it was *enforced* and not inherent. Allowed to climb the barricades, they climbed them ; allowed to undertake the responsibilities of democratic statesmanship, they acquitted themselves admirably. Allowed to vote, they voted thoughtfully and responsibly. But now for the first time they are concerned with their own barricades, their own statesmanship, their own candidates to vote for. *Like the Germans, they must be given time to adjust ;* and as they see the problems involved in their own adjustment, they will see more clearly their line as an adult nation in this bitter and searching question: how does a nation repent ; how does a nation change its way of living, and renew its moral concepts ?

It is not the first time that the Jewish people has faced such questions, and solved them. The changes from the prophetic outlook to the Pharisaic in the last centuries B.C.E., and the change from the nationalist to the rabbinic in the first three centuries C.E., provide as striking examples of *planned* changes as are afforded in the life of any nation. The word *planned* is important. The change in the Scandinavian people already referred to took place over centuries, and as the result of circumstances. The more rapid change in British attitude in recent decades has had a strong element of the external compulsion of events. The only compulsion in the two Jewish cases mentioned was the inner compulsion of the Jewish will to survive.

It is these facts which could lend realism to Israel's contribution on the subject of the future of Germany. She knows from her own history that planned change is possible, and that, wisely planned, it produces results. Obviously imitation is not the issue. It is impossible just to say : this is how we did it, go and do it the same way ; but it is possible to say that under such and such circumstances such and such a line was creative for such and such reasons. Given the present circumstances, such and such might prove equally creative. It is not my business to define the matter more closely, and to say in advance exactly what Israel's examples should be. I do not know.

On the other hand, the old statement that the onlooker sees most of the game contains elements of truth ; and the onlooker can sometimes say whether in practice Israel seems to be moving in the right direction, in a wider perspective than is easily obtained by an actual actor in the game. From such a standpoint if, on the one hand, it is evident that Israel is not perfect, and that her every action is not of world significance, on the other the general picture is not discouraging. It will take time for Israel to gather up and interweave into her political life the innumerable strands of her long history ; and the attitude of the Religious Bloc has not always helped the ordinary Israeli to distinguish what is fundamental from what is secondary. But I do not remember exclaiming: 'Oh dear, Oh dear!' at the statements of Mr. Sharett or Mr. Eban at the Councils of the United Nations, or the philosophising of Mr. Ben-Gurion from Jerusalem. On these issues Israel is feeling her way slowly to an 'adult' attitude, and she must have time to remember that she is basically an adult three thousand, not three, years old !

*   *   *

In the present world conflict of ideologies her position is somewhat different. It is not that she has any particular claims to make, but that, just as in the issues between Europe and Asia. she has a peculiar population composition. The United States of America for many years proudly proclaimed herself a melting pot where many different traditions and outlooks were fused into a new unity with its own characteristics. Israel also is a melting pot, but with different ingredients, and one in which no single group can aspire to the primacy which was for so long enjoyed by the Anglo-Saxon element in the U.S.A. The older aliyoth may have a common Russian and eastern European background, and feel themselves the aristocrats of the new state. But their sabra children have not carried over a Russian tradition comparable to that of the Anglo-Saxon tradition carried on by the aristocrats of the New England States. It is their birth in Israel not their background in Europe which makes them consider themselves the successors to the claim of 'aristocrats.'

So long as the relations between the Soviet-led society and the Western world are carried on in terms of armaments and the moves and counter-moves of what is so falsely called 'real-politik,' so long Israel is but one of the small Middle Eastern Powers which stand shivering on the brink of a swirling tide of passion which can offer them no service or satisfaction, but which threatens all the time to rise and engulf them. Indeed it is not the whole truth even to say that she is merely 'one of the small Middle Eastern Powers'; for all over the world, in Europe as well as in Asia, stand these smaller Powers whose influence in terms of guns is nothing, in terms of geographical situation is but an embarrassment, but whose cultural contribution to the world is irreplaceable. To-day they can but wait for the more powerful nations to come to their senses—or precipitate a catastrophe of which all alike would be victims.

But even today these follies of giant maladjusted children do not, happily, occupy the whole canvas, and tomorrow perhaps the situation will be reversed, and adult argument and discussion will take priority over guns, propaganda, and infant tantrums. Then, indeed, Israel has her contribution to make ; for she has unusual, if not unique, experience of all sides of the argument ; and her own social structure and experiments are pertinent to wider issues.

It is appallingly superficial to think of Marx and Marxism merely in terms of Russian hostility to the capitalistic West. In spite of his typically Victorian materialism, and the errors in his economic and political forecasts, Marx remains one of the great creative and formative thinkers of the modern world ; and no society benefits from entirely ignoring his contributions, or from outlawing his ponderous literary monuments. The political world picture has forced an identification of interest in Marx with subversive Communist plotting ; and, of course, this has often been the case. Israel is unusual in possessing a Marxist party in Mapam which is not compulsorily subordinate to contemporary Russian interpretations. For myself I find listening to the political argumentation of my Mapam friends somewhat like watching a ballet dancer on a tightrope—fascinating, thrilling, but something which I have no desire to copy, and which does not seem quite real ! And in the present tensions, Mapam's unreal attitude to Israel's intimate relationship with America deprives it of the serious political contribution it might make. But the relationship between its philosophy and its admirable economic work in the communal settlements of the Kibbutz Arzi of Hashomer Hatzair remains a real one, just as is the relationship between the Russian Communist Party and creative developments in Russian society.

The transfer of the world situation from armaments to arguments would not immediately produce a release of tension. That also is shown by what is happening in Israel, where the issue has split communal settlements which had sought to avoid identification with one particular ideology rather than another. Marxism does not breed tolerance. But to divide a settlement by a vote still remains preferable to dividing a world by atomic war.

In Israel the argument between Marxist and non-Marxist socialism, and between both and free enterprise, is acrimonious and continuous ; but it is still argument, carried on in circumstances which make a recourse to civil war at least unlikely ; and it is argument whose shrill notes must from time to time give way to tasks which all alike recognise to have priority in the common interest of all. And so it becomes argument from which the bystander can learn much.

Coupled with this variety of social structure, is the variety of population origin, which is still far from being a ' wasting asset ' as more population enters the country. It comes with experience of all the contestants on the world's stage, from east and west, from capitalist and socialist societies, from both sides of the Iron Curtain, from America, Europe, and Asia. While there may be as big an output of 'hot air ' in Jerusalem as anywhere else, yet there is also something more : no other country can show quite so varied and so lively an experience, or possesses so much ingrained talent to analyse and examine. This is not a rose-coloured statement that Israel is a land whose peasants and politicians are natural philosophers, who weigh their words carefully before they speak. The press of the country would certainly not support such a picture, but it still remains a statement of fact ; and comparisons must be made, not with some ideal republic of a Greek philosopher, but with the level of political discussion elsewhere in the contemporary world.

*   *   *

It is not enough to say simply that Israel has this and this problem, which presents this and this opportunity. For an even more important issue is how such opportunities as may arise can be exploited by a small power of very limited influence. I am sure that the answer does not consist in the activity which is often described as ' the mission of Israel,' and which consists in enunciating the great messages of the ancient prophets. There is not a high moral principle with which the world is not already familiar and of which it is not heartily sick. The language of morality has been so debased by constant misuse that words like righteousness and peace have become void of all positive content.

It is at this point that it is relevant to turn back to earlier history. These great words were originally made current in the utterances of the Hebrew prophets. Then they burst on their audiences not only with unexpected novelty, but also with incomparable literary inspiration. And yet they had singularly little effect on the life of the people who heard them. Christianity seeking a social gospel, and progressive Judaism looking for an alternative to the discipline of orthodoxy, ignore this unhappy reverse to the picture ; but the story of the contemporary history of the kingdoms of Judah and Israel makes it painfully clear. That which changed the life of the Jewish people was Torah, not prophetism ; that is to say, the embodiment of eternal principles in concrete practices, not in exalted generalisations. To apply a modern phrase to an ancient religion, the Judaism which ensured Jewish survival was supremely the religion of the ' know-how.'

The prophets denounced idolatry: the Pharisees developed the congregational worship of the synagogue which had been evolved during the Babylonian exile. The prophets proclaimed that the day should come when all men should know the Lord: the Pharisees introduced schools into every Jewish community, and their rabbinic successors explored deeply into the nature of popular education. The prophets proclaimed that justice should run down like rivers: the rabbis examined the nature of evidence and how to improve the technique of law courts. The prophets summoned all men to do righteously: the rabbis studied the wording of contracts. The list could be indefinitely extended ; but almost the whole work of centuries of rabbinic Judaism could be summarised in the words: how do we put this into practice ?

The tragic conservatism of the last centuries of orthodoxy must not blind us to the greatness of its creative work. Decline inevitably followed the substitution of ' what do the commentaries say that we should do ' for ' how does experience to-day show that we should secure this result.' But so much of the blame for the tragic change lies on Christian persecution and the wanton and deliberate destruction of Jewish centres of learning throughout Europe, that certainly no Christian writer can do more than honestly record the change and utter no condemnation.

Judaism is the religion of the ' know-how,' and it has bred in the Jewish people a perpetual analytic interest in how things work, an interest which is not confined to those who accept orthodoxy or even admit the reality of any religious experience. It has made the Jews remarkable as interpreters in every field of culture ; it has made inevitable the reaction of a Jewish musician who reads a score, or a Jewish critic who sees a picture, to want to know *how* it can be interpreted.

It is this general characteristic which needs today to be transferred to the novel field of political experience—novel because political experiment was denied to the Jew during the long centuries of dispersion and the ghetto.

In her own affairs she has shown, from the very beginning of Zionist resettlement, many examples of the survival of this gift for ' know-how.' The most obvious, and in some ways the most interesting, is the variety of forms which her agricultural pioneering has assumed, and the perpetual change and development which is to be traced in the adaptation of these forms to life. Other examples could be taken from her trade union movement and the many activities of the Histadruth. During the mandatory era she evolved —often to the legitimate embarrassment of the British—a most complex state within a state, and carried by the voluntary acquiescence of the Yishuv many public burdens usually requiring the endorsement and compulsion of law and legal enforcement. She has shown remarkable adaptability in the tremendous problems of the years since the establishment of the state. Now she needs to show the same practical ingenuity and freshness of vision in the problems which confront her as a state among states.

In all the four great problems with which Israel is vitally connected, it is *how* the first steps on the road to sanity are to be taken which is the vital issue ; and it is in her contribution to the solution of this question that she will prove her assertion that she has a right to stand as a state among states. If she accepts the privileges and responsibilities nurtured by those five roots in her past which have already been described, then she will show that the tree which springs from them is still capable of bearing fruit.

It may sound paradoxical, but it is nevertheless true, that Israel cannot afford to accept the conventional definition of politics as ' the art of the possible.' Not merely might the cynic well remark that the outstanding examples in modern life of this political principle had consisted merely of ' putting the art before the corpse ' —we have only to think of Munich, the Palestine White Paper of 1939, or of the Yalta and Potsdam Agreements—but Israel, as a matter of practical necessity, is perpetually concerned with the impossible. In other words, she has no foundation on which she can expect her voice to be heard other than that she is trying to

85

build up her political experience from a foundation of morality ; and the ever present pressure of the Arab problem makes this no easy task for her. That is one reason why, whether the Arab states reject it or despise it, she needs to proclaim as a political affirmation, what are her real roots, and to pledge herself to seek to justify her future existence by raising it to the level of the grandeur of her past.

So long as support for Israel rests on the uncertainties of the clash of interests of other nations, so long will she suffer from a basic insecurity. Will the new administration in the U.S.A. be as friendly as the late one ? Will necessities of Middle Eastern defence lead to a stiffer attitude in this nation or in that ? She cannot help being concerned with such issues ; she cannot avoid seeking to meet their successive challenges by skilful negotiation. All that is of the routine of her political life. But if there be no more than that, then she will never escape from the dangers of a small state with but a small voice in a small corner of the world—a pitiful ending to a long and noble story.

PART THREE

The Diaspora

The diaspora of today is uncertain of itself, bewildered, deeply divided. The century of emancipation has ended in disillusion and disappointment. Prophets of woe proclaim the dissolution of Jewish life save within the walls of a new ghetto beside the Mediterranean. It is time for those Jews who have lived, and still desire to live, in intimate association with the non-Jewish world around them to realise how essential has been their contribution to the whole life and spirit of the Jewish people, how deeply integrated it is into the meaning of Jewish history, and, as the first essay in Part Four will show (chapter XIII), how magnificently they have carried, alone and of their own resources, the banner of Jewry through critical centuries of that history.

Many of their uncertainties are not specifically Jewish. They are shared by all who prize communities of distinctive cultures above the lumpen-proletariat produced by our mass media of propaganda, entertainment, and politics. In so far as Jewry is concerned, it is the diaspora which can save the Jewish people's distinctive contribution, and not Israel, at any rate where the immediate future is concerned.

CHAPTER X

The Jewish Community in Gentile Society[1]

THE key to Jewish history is to be found, not in any single factor, but in the tensions and interplay between two influences which, at first sight, might well seem to be contradictory. The one is the ethical monotheism which developed slowly into a national religion over the centuries of experience which lie between the days of Abraham and those of ' the men of the Great Synagogue.' The other is the Jewish will to survive as a people. For this determined that, of the many migrants and conquerors who swept up and down the Eastern Mediterranean sea-board, it should have been those whom we call Hebrews, Israelites, or Jews who survived. And because they used to the full the opportunities which their central position in the ancient world afforded, they experienced to the full the strange destiny which that position involved.

Of itself ethical monotheism could not be held to be the natural basis for the survival as a separate unit of a single people. We have only to contrast Jewish experience with that of Christendom or Islam to see the relevance of such a statement. And, of itself, a national will to survive carries with it no universal implications, but rather suggests that a constant opposition to the pressure of its environment would be a basic condition of survival. Again, we have only to think of such people as the Bretons or the Basques to see how natural such an attitude would be.

The difference in Jewish destiny lies in part in the determinism of geography. Given the will to survive of a people living on a bridge between greater and more powerful civilisations, and inhabiting a homeland narrow and not all fertile, it was predictable both that such a people should be self-confident enough to receive

[1] Presidential Address to the Jewish Historical Society of England for the session 1950-51.

90

constant influences from abroad and that it should itself accept as part of its destiny that many of its children should live in a foreign environment. But it lies still more in the nature of the voluntary experience of the people and the content which they deliberately gave to the revelation which they believed themselves to have received. For ethical monotheism developed within the Jewish society not as a philosophic system or a personal creed, but as the challenge to a particular way of life in which the whole people, from ruler to peasant, from priest to emigrant, was personally involved. It was a challenge so profound and so far-reaching that Jewry could not afford to neglect any contribution which the experiences of other peoples might offer, nor could it avoid the implications of its experience on the life and destinies of the smallest and remotest of its migrant groups. Hence the story of the Jewish people is the story of a constant interaction between the centre and the periphery, an interaction in which giving and receiving proceeded in both directions. To speak in modern terms, it is a story of constant interplay between Israel and the diaspora, and the experience and contribution of both are equally fundamental, equally essential to the picture as a whole.

For this reason it is false to ask that Jews should choose between the concepts of nationalism and assimilation, that they should determine whether they survive as a religion or as a nation, or that, today, they should accept *either* the dominance of Israel *or* the independence of the diaspora. For Jewish history has always embraced within its scope both of the alternatives offered, and while each can be dangerous in isolation, it is by the interaction of the two that health has been maintained.

From the very beginning it has been impossible for Israel to consider her religious tradition to be her private affair. Monotheism in any form must be held by its adherents to be universal in its implication ; and the explanation of the rabbis that the Law was given in the desert to emphasise that it was offered equally to all nations is balanced by the historic fact that the peoples of the Euphrates and the Nile, the cultures of Hammurabi and Ikhnaton, contributed to the spiritual experiences which Abraham transformed and to the code which Moses proclaimed. And if the migrations of Jews were the vehicle by which the monotheism of Israel exercised its influence on the nations, they were likewise the source from which Israel herself enriched her own experience.

91

Because of this active interplay between centre and periphery it is impossible to comprehend the whole of Jewish experience in emigration under the single phrase of ' galuth ' or exile, and thereby to imply that the eyes of diaspora Jewry were turned only inward on the homeland, and that their minds were filled only with the thought of return. The thought of exile and return has, indeed, nearly always been present in some measure because so much of the migration of the Jews has been forced and unhappy. But it has very rarely filled the whole canvas, and even forced migrations have been fruitful in experiences which have enriched the whole subsequent history of Jewry, and these experiences have been made possible only by the fact of exile and the presence of a foreign environment.

This paradox is amply displayed by the exile to Babylon which terminated the independent history of the kingdom of Judah. It was certainly forced, and the minds of the exiles were certainly filled with the longing to return. Now, in view of the nature of the religion of Judah at the time, it might have been expected that the exiles would have done no more than create some pale replica of the Temple worship at Jerusalem, jealously guarding their past rituals and conforming, as far as they could, to the religious customs of the metropolis. Such an expectation is not fanciful, for little more than a hundred years later the Jewish community in Elephantine, in Egypt, a community of voluntary emigrants rather than exiles, did precisely that and set up in that city their own temple worship, a worship which the priests of the restored temple of Jerusalem, not unnaturally, refused to recognise. But the Babylonian Jews seem to have accepted at once that no centre was to be found for their communal and spiritual life in some copy of the religious activities of the homeland. Instead of creating a copied temple, they evolved new forms of religious expression appropriate to their situation, and so brought into existence the synagogue, devoted to congregational worship and to the study of their sacred books. It was these exiles who made of Judaism a religion at once democratic and intellectual, and of the Jews a people of the Book.

Looking back, we may, perhaps, say that in Jerusalem itself these developments, had they come at all, would have come much more slowly. A visible kingship as the natural source of contemporary legal developments, the Temple ritual as the highest

92

expression of religious devotion, and history as something still unfolding rather than something complete to be recorded and preserved, all these would have led to a very different development in the story. Had the return meant the restoration of a new monarchy and a new sovereign state, the Babylonian experiment might have been no more than a brief historical anecdote. As it was, the returned community continued the Babylonian experience and built upon it the whole structure of historic Judaism.

The two centuries which followed the return were centuries of quiet development. As the community grew in strength and numbers there began that voluntary emigration which was to create by the beginning of the Christian era the great Alexandrian Jewish community and others in all the main cities of the Eastern Mediterranean, while pioneers had pushed even further afield to both east and west.

Up to the time of the destruction of the Temple it can be said that the eyes of those Jews who lived outside Israel were turned outward to the Hellenistic world around them. Though they formed but one of the many nationalities which mingled in every Mediterranean city, the religious inheritance which they brought with them effectively distinguished them from all others. The normal tendency in that period of religious eclecticism and national mingling was to find that gods differed only in names. When Rome met Greece it found that Jupiter was clearly Zeus. When both met Egypt they identified Zeus-Jupiter with Ammon. Stranger identifications were possible. The many-breasted fertility goddess of Ephesus could become the chaste huntress Diana, and the images, doubtless, sold as well as before. Like gods and goddesses, mysteries and esoteric rites could pass through similar identifications and absorb into their bands of initiates members of all the races who thronged the cosmopolitan cities.

The Jews alone were forced to stand apart, apart but not uninterested. For their religion was not a 'mystery' which they could proclaim to be of significance only to themselves. Its implications of universalism, which had first become understood in the prophetic period by the few who had insight, were now generally accepted by the whole people. Their God was the God of the whole earth and His was the only true worship for man. But this was not all. He had Himself laid down a code of ethical conduct for men to observe, and so revealed His will for all men. To hold such a faith was inevitably to communicate it, if only by example. But, in fact, the Jews did more. The whole of the Scriptures had by this time been translated into Greek by the Jewish scholars of Alexandria, and contained ample material to interest the Hellenistic world. The ritual laws might leave Gentiles uninterested, or, more dangerously, appear, as Paul was to find, an initiation into a new mystery religion ; but the monotheism of the prophets and the combination of homely wisdom with deep piety in the Wisdom literature could be powerful attractions. Nor must we omit the influence of the living Jewish communities. The readiness with which Julius Caesar gave them such concessions as made their loyalty to their religion compatible with loyalty to Rome is proof enough that Jews were felt to be good citizens. Jewish communities by their very presence drew Gentiles to study the nature of their communal life, a study which did not always lead to the contempt of a Juvenal or the misunderstandings of a Tacitus.

Indeed, it was natural that the Greeks, with their intellectual curiosity, and the Romans, with their puritan background, should have been interested in their Jewish neighbours. Every Jewish community became the centre of some degree of missionary effort ; and the vagueness with which the rabbis defined the Noachic commandments is itself evidence that they were attempting to find solutions for a variety of situations resulting from such activities.

We may assume that in an ordinary community, composed as it was likely to have been of merchants, business men, and artisans, it was the strong ethical emphasis and the puritanism of Jewish life which was the attracting influence. But in Alexandria more was possible, and Jewish scholars put forward their revealed religion as the ultimate philosophy, the goal of reason sought by the Greeks, revealed to men by the ultimate Power in the universe itself. Men like Philo offered their Greek friends the reconciliation of religion and reason by their skilful combination of the revealed Torah with the Divine Wisdom which was the source of its revelation. The vast majority of Jewish literature in Greek must have perished. But in what remains we can see the elaborate apologetic which was offered to the Gentile world, and it is now generally recognised that the missionary activities of the Jewish communities were far more extensive and far more successful than used to be believed. The quotation, frequently repeated, that a proselyte is as harmful to Israel as a scab to the skin cannot be held to dispose of the issue.

Roman-Christian law, the frequent canons of Church councils, as well as much literary evidence right down to the time of the Carolingian renaissance and even later, all testify to the attractive power of Judaism as revealed in the lives of the scattered Jewish communities. But it is not only in Christian sources that the evidence is to be found. The classic conversion of the Khazars and the story of Helena of Adiabene are but the most familiar examples of a missionary activity to the north, east, and south of Palestine which endured over a millennium and has left traces up to this day.

Little of this expansion from the diaspora communities was due to the activities of missionaries of the type with which we become familiar in Christian history. It is true that the family of Helena is said to have been converted through the zeal and energy of a single Jewish merchant, Ananias of an Assyrian town, Charax Spasini ; but normally it was the presence of a whole Jewish community which exercised the influence. Some of these communities were primarily caravan stations, and it is the caravan routes of Jewish traders which are responsible for the survival into modern times of traces of Judaism as far afield as West Africa, and which brought into being Jewish communities as widely separated as the North African berbers, the black Jews of India, the falashas of Abyssinia and the Chinese Jews of Kai Feng Fu.

Vast as this expansion was, in terms of both area and numbers, it is insignificant compared with the results of a different method by which ideas born and nurtured within the Jewish community, and spread by the Jewish diaspora, expanded into the world. For Christianity and Islam are both religions born out of a Jewish background, both expressions in different ways of beliefs and practices which first saw the light within the Jewish community. The link between monotheism and righteous living, with whatever differences in theology, was as fundamental to the Christian Church as to the Jewish Synagogue ; and it is increasingly recognised how much the early theologians of Islam supplemented the inadequacies of Muhammad's knowledge by direct application to Jewish scholars. They not only drew from them the framework of Muslim conceptions of worship, but were also deeply indebted to the Talmudists for the methods of interpretation, and the evolution of principles of codification, whereby the scattered pronouncements of Muhammad were welded into the complex system of Sharia law.

During this long period it may be said that the gaze of diaspora

Jews was turned almost wholly outward. They expressed and transmitted to their environment a tradition and way of life which they had received ; they did not seek to modify or to add to it out of their contacts and experience. To this statement there are two important exceptions—Alexandria and Babylon.

The Judaism evolved at Alexandria wore a philosophic dress, and by the use of allegory and symbolism softened the sharp edge of the Biblical text to make something more acceptable to a Greek environment. This Hellenisation had a powerful influence on the nascent Christian Church, but it was wholly rejected by the scholars of Jerusalem and Galilee. They were prepared to make those minor accommodations with the world around them which invested with a Jewish religious dress customs and beliefs of their neighbours which were not in themselves offensive. The Christian Church did much the same when it transformed the spirits of fountain and spring into Christian saints. But more they would not do, and almost a millennium was to pass before the Greek inheritance passed into Jewry through the Islamic environment of Saadia and Maimonides.

If the Alexandrian synthesis was rejected, the connections between Palestine and Babylon became closer and closer, until Babylon for almost half a millennium could occupy the centre in the story almost as authoritatively as Jerusalem. This relationship was unique alike in quality and duration. It was symbolised by such stories as that Shemaiah and Abtalion, leaders of Palestinian Jewry at the beginning of the Herodian period, were not merely of Babylonian stock, but actually descended from Sennacherib ; and it was expressed historically in the Babylonian origin of the elder Hillel, the ancestor of the Palestinian patriarchs. As the power of Palestinian Jewry waned with the increasing Christianisation of the country after Constantine, the effective leadership of the whole Jewish world passed to Babylon, and remained there as long as the great rabbinic schools in that country endured. When they passed away, such authority in the hands of a single diaspora Jewry passed likewise, never to be repeated. Thenceforward Judaism itself, like the Jewish people, lived dispersed, and its influence radiated from a dozen simultaneous or successive centres. Babylon had marked a necessary transition from the normal condition in which a people live united in a single country to this unique dispersion, and so made possible the effective survival both of Jewry and of Judaism. It had confirmed and strengthened the conception of a people whose religious life centred in a Book, and had made that life so self-contained that every ghetto synagogue could be an equally real centre of Jewish thoughts and hopes, spiritually secure from external influence or pressure.

The period which followed cannot be defined by exact dates. It was the result of processes which only gradually became operative. The interplay of influences did not stop everywhere at the same time ; the nature of the relationships between Jewry and the environing world did not change everywhere simultaneously. All mutual influences between Judaism and Christianity had ceased centuries before those between Judaism and Islam became operative. But gradually the characteristic of the period, that Jewish communities lived isolated by their religious barriers and physical restrictions and humiliations, came to be true of the whole Jewish world. It was to continue in western Europe until emancipation, in eastern Europe almost until the massacres of Hitler, while in Islamic lands it still survives today.

In spite of the restrictions under which Jewish life was lived, two outstanding examples of the old pattern of the influence of diaspora Jewries occurred during the period. In the days of the Abbasid caliphate at Baghdad, in Egypt under the Ayyubids, and in the western caliphate in Spain, Jews at last accepted the Greek contribution which they had rejected in its Alexandrian guise, and enriched Judaism both philosophically and culturally from the store-house of Hellenistic-Arab metaphysics, scholarship, and poetry. The other example is of the radiation outwards of Jewish thought. From the Christian Hebraists and scholastic philosophers of the Middle Ages, through the cabbalists of the renaissance and the Protestant sects of the seventeenth century, to the great Talmudists like Selden, Spencer, or Surenhuis, there re-enter the Christian world influences, not trifling if not fundamental, mediated by the contacts of Jewish contemporaries with individual Christians.

The central phenomenon of this period, however, does not lie in the religio-cultural fields in which we have previously traced the interplay of influences between the Jewish emigration and its centre on one hand, and its Gentile environment on the other. Jewish experience now enters a new field over a large area of the dispersion.

In Islamic lands Jews were neither the only religious minority, nor the only depressed class, and as the tide of Muslim culture receded they shared in the universal stagnation which gradually infested the whole Islamic world. But within the area of western Christendom Jewish immigrants emerged as an economic class.

The belief that Jews have always been skilful dealers in financial affairs has no basis in history. Anecdotic though it may be, it is at least worth recalling that the earliest recorded European Jewish money-lender lies at the bottom of a well into which his Christian debtor pushed him on the only occasion of which we have evidence that he sought to collect a debt. This argues little financial skill, but is, even so, not the whole story. He shares that watery grave with his no more skilful Christian partner. One may at least say that one element of truth lies at the bottom of that well ! It is, I think, equally fantastic to follow scholars like Sombart in the search for some subtle feature in Judaism itself which, a thousand years after its formulation, was to discover the Jews suddenly to an astonished world as possessed of an inherent financial genius.

The truth is not less interesting, but much more prosaic. It lies neither in their racial, nor in their religious, inheritance, but is a consequence of their social status as restricted immigrants, compelled to seek a living on the margin of the occupations already monopolised by older residents. In a stagnant society such a situation means a life next door to beggary. In a developing society it offers unlimited, if dangerous, opportunities ; and it is worth noting that it is in Europe and the western world that this development took place, and that it has no parallel in Jewish life under Islam. At the moment I am not concerned as to whether, from the Jewish point of view, the European development was desirable or not. I am simply concerned, as an historian, to get the true picture of the experience of diaspora Jewry.

The passage of a sufficient number of Jews into dealing in money for it to be characterised as a Jewish occupation, arose naturally out of the fact that many Jews were merchants, and this in turn was a natural consequence of their position in Roman and later society. In medieval Europe they were never the only money-lenders, and rarely the most important. The oft-repeated statement that ' the Church forbad usury ' proves that no Christians were usurers only to the extent that the statement that ' the Church forbad adultery ' would prove that all adulterers were Muhammadans. The papacy itself was the money-lender and financial monopolist of medieval Europe with the largest resources, and not the most savoury reputation. Nevertheless Jews occupied a particular niche in the money market, and it is that which is relevant. In the development of European agriculture Jews played a particular part by lending to the lesser landowners and farmers, who were among their main clients, money between seed-time and harvest, and this filled a dangerous gap in the agricultural economy of the time. They also played a part, if unwillingly, in the development of public revenues. These classes owed military service, but no financial dues in peace time. Because Jews were the exclusive property of their prince, the debtors of the Jews contributed willy-nilly to the revenues of the prince. He fixed their rate of interest by reference to the emptiness of his coffers, and whenever he was short of money simply collected such of the debts owed to his Jews as he needed, or else extracted so much money from his Jews that they were compelled to call in their loans. In either case the main beneficiary, in the long run, was the prince, and a century of the occupation left any Jewry which had been compelled to indulge in it in a state of exhaustion.

But the interesting point about this aspect of diaspora life is its apparently inexhaustible ingenuity. As one chapter closed another opened. The Jewries of western Europe were ruined or expelled by the fourteenth century. In 1344 Casimir the Great, one of the most brilliant rulers of Poland, confirmed and extended the ancient charter of Polish Jewry, and invited Jews to his kingdom as merchants and intermediaries, two classes which the Polish stratified society of landowners and peasants could not produce of itself. In a century Jewish numbers are calculated to have swelled from 50,000 to half a million ; and for some two hundred years the Jewish community, stable and self-governing, was a hive of intellectual, and public and private economic, activity. But the inherent instability of the Polish constitution led to the ruin of the country, and to a decline of the Jewish position in the seventeenth century ; and the centre of the picture shifts again.

Expelled from the Iberian peninsular at the end of the fifteenth century, or slipping out of the country as Marrano refugees during the succeeding period, Spanish Jews found a new field of activity in the colonial and levantine trades which were growing rapidly in western Europe. Their friendly relations with Islam gave them almost a monopoly to the east, while their knowledge of Spanish and Portuguese assured them an important place in that to the west. In both they were pioneers, bringing enormous wealth into their new centres of Antwerp, Amsterdam, Hamburg, Bordeaux, and London.

In the eighteenth century it was the turn of the Jews of Germany. After the end of the thirty years' war Germany entered a slow period of reconstruction, and towards the end of the seventeenth century the situation clarified itself into a struggle of innumerable princes to undermine the still medieval constitutions of their states and to establish themselves as toy Louis Quatorze's, living in luxurious palaces, surrounded by magnificent courts, and enjoying absolute authority over their subjects. The only impediment to the realisation of this fashionable ambition was that from the Emperor downwards all were in debt, their countries were still too poor for them to increase taxes, their royal demesnes were either pawned or in ruins, and their medieval constitutions had an uncomfortable capacity for enquiring too strictly into the need for any financial resources which the princes might demand.

Within a few decades the only method of resolving the dilemma had been universally adopted. From emperor to bishop, every prince and princeling had his court Jew. The court Jew was prepared to take over the work of the incompetent, often hereditary, officials who grew rich out of providing necessities for the army, and the prince found that food and clothing, fodder and ammunition actually reached his forces. He was prepared to take over the customs, and the prince found revenue actually reached his coffers ; the royal demesnes, and he found himself a prosperous landowner ; the concessions for salt, mining or industrial development, and he found that he, as well as the concessionnaire, actually drew a profit from the enterprises. Did he wish to make war or peace, acquire a throne for his son, a husband for his daughter, an electoral hat for himself, jewels for his wife, a palace larger than his neighbour's for his court, for all there was the same answer. He needed a court Jew. Of these curiously competent, and usually honest officials, there were whole dynasties. Some single merchants managed, themselves, to be court Jew to half a dozen different princelings at the same time ; sometimes whole families with sons and sons-in-law, brothers and cousins, who with their domestics might make up a household of a hundred persons, together shared the privileged position of residence in some otherwise forbidden city, and managed between them all the prince's affairs, created factories, developed trade, improved the financial system, and, among many abuses and not a few absurdities, laid the foundations of the modern economy of Germany. It was the period known as baroque, with its swirling wealth of stucco detail, its façades, its glitter, its pomp and violence. And in Jewish history it is the most baroque episode one could find, with its sudden rises to fortune, its sudden falls, its crazy magnificence reared on a structure of still crazier debts, and its usual end in ruin, if not in disgrace. For there was one principle common to all princes, that the unfortunate court Jew need not be paid back what he lent ; and indeed, did a prince die, it was a matter of principle for his successor or for the estates of his principality to make a counter-claim larger than the debt actually owed. The Rothschilds were more fortunate than their predecessors. By the time that they succeeded to the line of the Oppenheimers, the Wertheims, the Arons, the Liebmanns, the Lehmanns, and a dozen other dynasties, the profession had become safe, and emancipation gave a security their predecessors had never known.

As the colourful court Jew passes, to be succeeded by the banker, the centre of pioneering activity changes again. This time it is to be found in Moldavia, the northern province of the principality of Rumania. Moldavian Jews entered the country from Poland, to escape the disorders attendant on the partitions of the end of the eighteenth century, or from Russia, to escape the harsh rule of Nicholas I. Their numbers rose from 12,000 in 1803 to 120,000 in 1840. They came as penniless refugees to a country which general poverty and public incompetence had reduced almost to a desert. The peasants and many of the landowners were illiterate, there was no general trade, and no commercial class. In 1859, when Rumania was recognised as a European constitutional principality, its foreign trade stood at 210 million gold francs ; the country was covered by a network of busy market towns, and western industrial goods had become familiar even in the cottages of the peasants. Almost the whole of this development was of Jewish creation ; the population of the market towns was in some cases 100 per cent Jewish ; they held by mortgage a substantial portion of the estates of the landowners ; and the buying and selling which went on in the villages was almost exclusively in their hands. In fact, the economic foundations of modern Rumania were primarily laid by Jewish immigrants and their immediate descendants.

At the end of the eighteenth century a wholly new phase opens, that of the emancipation of the small, but prosperous and important, western Jewries. On the surface this might be said to have split Jewry into two, since the immense majority of the people, both in eastern Europe and in Africa and Asia, remained in the depressed social and economic conditions of the previous millennium. But this is not so. In spite of all the differences of outlook which undoubtedly existed, the ease with which, in fact, Jews could pass individually from the eastern into the western society reveals that the underlying unity of their long history had not yet been broken. Nor had its basic quality altered. There is still the same dual vision, outward and inward, the same interchange of influences both within Jewry, and outward between Jewry and the environing Gentile world. Nevertheless, the differences inherent in the new situation and in the new opportunities cannot be minimised.

The central fact that emerges is that for the first time since the destruction of Jerusalem, the protective shell within which Jewry grew and developed its own peculiar characteristics had been broken. Outwardly it was broken by the falling of the ghetto walls and the admission of Jews, individually, into full participation in the Gentile society around them. Inwardly it was broken by the inability of Jewish orthodoxy, hardened by the tragedies of the preceding centuries, to regain that flexibility of its youth which had enabled it to cope successfully with the equally severe shock of the destruction of the Temple and the state seventeen hundred years earlier. On that occasion the crisis brought unity out of diversity. This time it broke up the unity into competing interpretations of Jewish destiny. It is interesting that the court Jews, living at the centre of that flux of religious, political, and scientific empiricism which makes the period a fascinating epoch in western history, were wholly untouched by this environment. They satisfied their religious instincts by financing magnificent new editions of the Talmud, and by enriching with costly baroque ornament the traditional appurtenances of their synagogues. The new leaders of western Jewry had no such easy escape from their environment.

In the new period economic activity, important as it undoubtedly remains, passes into the third place in our interest. For, paradoxical as it may seem, the first place must be given to the emergence of the Jewish people as a political entity. By this I do not mean that it became nationalistic or Zionist. Indeed the reverse is obviously true. Jewry for many decades after emancipation was passionately assimilationist. What I mean is that the expectations of Napoleon, for example, were not realised. He emancipated individuals and looked to their becoming Frenchmen. In a measure they did ; but they did not forget that they were Jews, however much they appeared to etiolate their Jewish inheritance. They remained conscious of being members of a separate community, and it was as communities that they made demands in the political field, both for themselves and for their brethren in less fortunate lands. In some respects the Jewish story of the period is paralleled, in England for example, by that of the Roman Catholics, and so could appear to reinforce the idea that Jewry is a purely religious entity. But in some respects it has equally close affinities both with the social strivings of the labour movement, and the nationalist strivings of other minorities. No ordinary definition of religion could cover most of the work of the Alliance Israélite Universelle, the Anglo-Jewish Association, of Ort, or of Ica. Jewry, in fact, had become a political entity of which the main stream was strongly anti-nationalistic.

The second place in this new period of Jewish history must be given to the individual Jew, now differentiated from his all-embracing Jewish environment, and seen for and by himself as a free citizen of one of the western societies. Whole volumes have been written on the Jewish contributions to every department of nineteenth century western life, scientific, cultural, social, and political, and in the main these volumes record the activities of individuals, sometimes only remotely connected with contemporary Jewish communal life. And yet they are justifiably called *Jewish* contributions. For, though they were expressed in a different field of action, they were expressions of the characteristics which we have already encountered in Jewish history. In the first place there was the ready adaptability to the opportunities offered by the non-Jewish environment ; and, in the second place, there was the contribution, in new terms, to that environment of ideas and experiences already rooted in the Jewish past. The one gave Europe a whole galaxy of statesmen, scholars, scientists, and technicians ; the other determined the immense Jewish contribution to social and political reform. The struggle for justice, fundamental in Jewish thought and sharpened by Jewish experience, expressed itself as naturally in the participation of individual Jews in the whole liberal and working-class movement, as it did in the battle of Jewish communities for better conditions for their less fortunate brethren. And the result was the same as when a similar phenomenon had arisen in the religious field, and had led to the ' hiving off ' of Christianity and Islam. Many such Jews merged themselves completely into the field of their struggle and left the Jewish community to become leaders of liberal, radical, and socialist parties.

Not less fascinating or far-reaching were the consequences of the inward gaze of diaspora Jewry. The influence of the new Gentile environment on a religious core whose task for centuries had been conservation and not sensitivity was inevitably tremendous. Some of the new pressures were frankly iconoclastic, but most of them were sincere and genuine attempts to effect a synthesis between the new experience and the ancient tradition. Movements such as that of the Me'assefim, or the distinguished group of German Jewish scholars associated at Berlin, Koenigsberg, and Breslau in the development of Jüdische Wissenschaft, or the Haskala, or the French scholars grouped around the Société des Etudes Juives, all in their different ways sought to enrich the spiritual and cultural world of Jewry by studies and interpretations in which minds trained in the philosophies of Kant and Hegel, or Soloviev, and in the scholarship of Berlin and the Sorbonne, were brought to bear on Judaism and Jewish history. But the result was inevitably the breaking up of the old unity, for not all Jews were prepared to recognise that reinterpretation was necessary. Reform movements came into existence, and, in particular, as the Jewry of America waxed in numbers and importance it took on forms owing more and more to the American Protestant environment.

Before the century closed two new developments ushered in the modern period. One was the rebirth, in new forms, of antisemitism. The other was the emergence of a nationalist programme out of a combination of the political activity of the emancipated communities, the pressure of its new experience on the core of Judaism, and the external pressure of the antisemitic movement. With this new phase the next chapter is concerned. Here it is time rather to sum up the results of this survey of the long history which has preceded it.

The first point which I would make is that I have been dealing throughout with one aspect only of the picture, or rather looking at the picture from one view point only—that of the Jewish community in Gentile society. To make up the whole it would be necessary to survey the Jewish scene from the inside also, to trace the influence of the land of Israel on the changing fortunes of the emigrant communities, and the development within Jewry, and out of the Jewish environment itself, of religious movements, such as Karaism or Chassidism, and, above all, rabbinism. But while these different approaches would be needed to make the picture complete, I do not believe they would alter or modify that which emerges from our present study.

The two other approaches would emphasise what is normal in Jewish history. They would show the motherland exercising its influence on the affections of her distant sons, a source of pride in prosperity, of inspiration in distress. They would show Jewish history, as the centuries wore on, enriched and developed from native sources and broadening with the experience of the centuries. It is in the standpoint which I have been treating in the previous pages that the high-lights are on the unusual aspects of the picture.

All nations influence their neighbours and are influenced by them. All great cultural nations can trace their cultures to many sources ; and all nations whose sons have colonised and emigrated have been influenced by the fresh experiences of the pioneers. But that experience in Jewish history, while akin in kind, is most exceptional in degree. It would be difficult to produce a parallel to the closeness and intensity of the mutual influence between motherland, migrant, and environment. It would be difficult to show such rich streams flowing into the central pool of experience from such varied, distant, and, at times, temporary experiences ; and it would be difficult to find an influence spreading from a centre as pervasive, as omni-competent, as the rabbinic Judaism born in Galilee and hammered out to its full form in Babylon.

It would likewise be difficult to find an emigration so rich in influence on its foreign environment. The creation of the world's two other monotheisms would alone stamp the Jewish experience as unique. But the contribution to European economy is, at the least, most unusual. First merchants in the Dark Ages. That is nothing special ; they shared the function with Greeks, Byzantines, and other Mediterranean peoples. But then, as the other merchants, *qua* Christians, were absorbed, or, *qua* Muslims, were excluded, their rôle becomes more exceptional. Their position as private princely property marks them off still further. And from that stems the closing of two gaps, first in agriculture—and we should not forget that the mortgage by which so many of us ' own ' our houses is a product of a system evolved for Jewish loans to farmers and landowners seven or eight hundred years ago—and then in public revenues. From the princely point of view it was a shortsighted policy. Their Jews are soon sucked dry. But, penniless, they move eastwards and create a new economy in Poland. Poland sinks under the burden of her constitutional incompetence. Within a generation other Jews are richly engaged in pioneering the ocean trade to east and west. The episode of the court Jews in Germany and the creation of the Rumanian economy are perhaps the two most extraordinary episodes of this long series. Of all it is true to say that they showed an astonishing general level of competence ; and I suspect that it is equally true to say that, relative to the standards of their time and the risks of their enterprises, these Jewish adventurers were more than ' indifferent honest.'

The economic story of the Jews of Europe would be enough to mark their story as remarkable. But not less remarkable is the contribution to European culture and politics from the nineteenth-century emancipation. I am not going to try and delve into reasons, a happy region of usually subjective speculation. I am content as an historian to record. But we can, at least, make an estimate of the character of Jewish history in the light of these experiences. If we take a narrow nationalistic view we shall regret the foreign influences enshrined in the heart of Judaism, and see in the Jewish contribution to foreign societies only loss, and gifts piteously rewarded by persecution and denigration. If we take the view that no nation lives to itself, save to stagnate, then the colours change completely. The Jewish contribution, stemming alike from their religion and their dispersion, is a magnificent record ; but what is significant for us is the intimacy with which the Jewish communities in Gentile society are integrated into the Jewish whole. Without them it is not an exaggeration to say that there is no Jewish history. For that history is made up of the continuous and creative interaction between centre and periphery, and an interplay, as extensive as circumstances permitted, between that whole and its non-Jewish environment. The Jewish emigrant community is seen as from one standpoint an exile community, constantly related, whether as giver

106

or recipient, to a centre, and, from the other standpoint, as itself the centre from which there is a constant radiation out to its environment, whether that radiation expresses itself in religious, cultural, or economic terms.

When we consider more closely the nature of the contribution made to the Gentile environment, then any Gentile like myself cannot but express the deepest shame and horror at the suffering inflicted on the Jew over so many centuries. The Jewish contribution, whether to Christendom or to Rumanian economy, has been accepted without gratitude and repaid with contumely and blows, and, in our own days and our own civilisation, with mass extermination. But we must see this destiny in perspective. On the sombre tapestry of the still brief history of human civilisations it is Jewish survival, not Jewish suffering, which stamps the story of the Jewish people as unusual, if not unique. From the Christian monasteries and villages destroyed by the Northmen, to the Mediterranean city civilisation overwhelmed first by the barbarians, then by the Arabs, from the caravan cities destroyed by Genghis Khan or Tamerlane to the ancient societies of Mexico and Peru destroyed by the Spaniards, from the Armenian in Turkey to the negro slave in America, the pages of human history are stained with blood. But they record few survivals such as that of the Jewish people, and that survival they owed in large measure to the lively dynamic of the interplay between the diaspora communities and their centre on the one hand and their Gentile environment on the other.

CHAPTER XI

The Nineteenth Century and After

FOR two thousand five hundred years Jewish communities which were voluntary or involuntary exiles from their homeland have played a vital and dynamic part in the shaping of Jewish history, drawing in and digesting from their Gentile environment experiences which have permanently enriched Jewry itself. And, at the same time, in the measure which was possible, these communities have exercised an influence outward on the non-Jewish life about them. Such has been the pattern up to modern times and a study of the contemporary scene, with this experience as guide, can be of value in interpreting the present situation, confusing as it appears, and assessing the lines along which it is most likely fruitfully to develop.

The events which have determined the present situation of the Jews cluster around the year 1880. In 1877 appeared the first socialist paper among the Jews in Russia, and this was followed by the creation of the first Jewish political party, the Bund, which, in its turn led to the foundation of the Russian Social-Democratic Party, the nursery of Soviet Communism. In 1878 the Congress of Berlin made the first serious attempt to solve the problem of eastern European Jewry along western European lines, by ordering, though without success, the Rumanian Government to grant citizenship to its Jews. In 1879, when Bismarck broke with the National Liberals, antisemitism first appeared as a political weapon, admirably suited to the exploitation of a modern, politically ignorant, but politically powerful proletariat. In 1881, when the Tsar Alexander II was assassinated, the Russian Government made a scapegoat of the Jews, and the great exodus to the west began. In 1882 the first of the still existing Zionist settlements in Palestine was founded at Rishon le-Zion.

In the half century which preceded these events the gaze of diaspora Jewry in its ardour for assimilation was almost wholly turned outward to the Gentile world around it. Emancipated Jews, and Jews hoping for emancipation alike, absorbed all that they could reach of European culture and civilisation. It was a period of considerable confusion, for the shell of the ghetto had broken and at the same time, the protective shell around the orthodoxy which had been their 'portable homeland' for so many centuries had broken also. And yet it was a period of great optimism, in which no problem appeared too difficult to solve, no utopia too distant to reach. But from 1880 the outlines tend somewhat to harden again. The rebirth of ancient prejudices in the new antisemitic movement, and the immense displacement resulting from the flight from Russia, compelled Jews everywhere to give more thought to their own affairs, to strengthen their communal organisations, and to reassert their inter-communal loyalties. But the increased need to take thought to their own affairs could neither shut the door on the pressure of the outside world, nor could it stem the inevitable radiation outwards from the diaspora Jewries to their Gentile environment. Jewry entered upon a period in which it was self-conscious but not united, and in which the world became increasingly conscious of it, and yet viewed it with strongly contradictory feelings.

In some respects the nineteenth-century situation repeats that of the Roman period, when Jews could move freely in a civilisation which exercised a powerful attraction for them, and when they were restricted by no ghetto walls. And it is therefore interesting that the century witnessed a repetition of the phenomenon which resulted from the contact of Judaism with Greco-Roman society. Then a new religion was born, historically speaking, out of Jewish monotheism and the Greco-Roman longing for salvation. In the nineteenth century it was not the ethical monotheism of Judaism but the passion for social righteousness, produced alike by its prophets and its experiences, which provided the spark ; and the milieu was not the pessimism of Hellenistic society but the optimism of the disfranchised, as they saw political power within their grasp. Consequently, the result was not a new religion, but the new political creed of socialism. But, allowing for the differences, there are close parallels in the two stories. Both produced bitter controversy within the community ; both were rejected by the majority of Jews and became primarily Gentile in membership, character, and outlook ; but both drew numbers of individual Jews into a change of allegiance, and both attracted such Jews in all parts of the Jewish world. The connection with Jewry is, of course, closer in the case of Christianity, when it is evidently possible to say that without Judaism it could not have come into existence. But, while it would be quite untrue to say the same of socialism, it is certainly true that without the Jewish contribution it would have become a very different movement. And in saying this, we must think not only of the dominant figure of Karl Marx, but of the rôle played by the Jewish Bund in Russia and Poland in the creation of a Russian Socialist Party, and of the many Jews who rose to prominence in central and eastern European socialist parties. This was largely because it was much easier to find men capable of executive and administrative activity among Jews, who were by tradition literate and accustomed to intellectual work, than among the non-Jewish proletariat, of whom only a minority had had any access to formal education. In consequence there were usually more Jews in positions of leadership than their proportion among the rank and file. But the presence of Jewish socialist leaders accentuated the malaise in relation to the ' Jewish question ' among all those who were determined to defend the existing order against socialist ideas.

In reality there was never a period in which it was less correct to speak of a single ' Jewish question ' ; for the dominant note of the whole period from 1880 onwards is the close reflection within Jewry of the deepening confusion of the world around them. There could be no single problem, because Jews were completely divided within their communities, both as to their own position, politically and religiously, and as to their relationship to their environment. And, as there were no ghetto walls, all their divisions could have immediate repercussions on their Gentile neighbours.

Only in the organisation of succour for the vast number of refugees from Tsarist Russia was there a semblance of unity ; but, as the settlement of the refugees began to provoke social and political repercussions, even that unity disappeared. Free now to make political demands for themselves, large bodies of Jews began increasingly to reject the old leadership and the old ideas of assimilation ; and the increasing difficulties of their situation lent urgency to their demands. The days of leisurely philanthropy, of paternal education, of back-stage diplomacy, associated with the outstanding work of men like Sir Moses Montefiore and Adolphe Crémieux, and organisations such as the Alliance Israélite Universelle and the Anglo-Jewish Association, could no longer meet the new demands, any more than the old synagogue funds for the relief of captives or the care of the needy could meet the clamant needs of hundreds of thousands of destitute and uprooted refugees. As the first world war accentuated both the problem and the apparent possibility of a solution, these different developments began to crystallise into the vast network of activities of the Joint Distribution Committee, and the strident voices of the Zionist Organisation and the World Jewish Congress.

The Jewry of the world between the wars saw a new phenomenon in Jewish history, the complete isolation of a large Jewish population in the U.S.S.R. from all contact with the rest of the Jewish world. The Jewry of the U.S.S.R. itself also manifested an unhappy phenomenon which, if not wholly new, reached unique proportions. Within the unity of Jewry there had always been divisions, and these divisions had sometimes led to great bitterness. But there was no precedent for the violence with which, in the early decades of the Russian revolution, the rank and file of Russian Jewry, particularly those who were religious minded, or had previously been affiliated to Zionism, were harried and persecuted by the officially organised body of Jewish Communists, the Yevsektsia. The traditional view of the relations between Church and Synagogue during the second century C.E. might appear to offer a parallel ; but, in fact, once the exaggerations of the traditional picture are corrected, the mutual hostility between Jews and Jewish-Christians at that time was trifling compared with the situation in the Soviet Union.

In the rest of Jewry the keynote of the twentieth century, and particularly of the decades between the wars, has been Jewish pressure on its Gentile environment in the political and social fields, and, in all fields, Jewish reflection from its environment of the confused and changing temper of the times. In previous centuries it had always been possible to speak in terms of a core of Jewry which was self-sufficient, homogeneous, and strong, even if this core was, geographically, dispersed through a thousand communities. By the twentieth century this had ceased to be true. Even apart from Russian Jewry, there was no universally acknowledged core, no single definition of the Jewish position which would be universally accepted by Jews, or universally recognised as adequate by Gentiles. The word ' dispersion ' had come to describe the heart as well as the bodies of the Jewish people.

In this disintegration what was most significant and, at the same time, natural in the total picture of diaspora Jewry was that each of the conflicting solutions put forward was, in its different way, a solution drawn not from the Jewish tradition, but from the Gentile environment. The hall-mark of Gentilism was stamped on every one of them.

At one end was the group which based its claims on the assumption that in a situation of complete emancipation the only basis for the separate survival of a Jewish minority which the non-Jewish world could not question was as a religious community. Outside the synagogue they proclaimed and practised a complete assimilation. The social interests natural to Jews they found catered for in participation in the voluntary activities, the politics, and social life of their non-Jewish neighbours. Politically they completely identified themselves with their citizenship. They saw no bond between the Jewish people save that which personal acceptance of a religious definition provided, and so they accepted as Jews only those who proclaimed that they were religious, and that their religion was Judaism. For them emancipation, as it had been achieved in the western liberal world in the nineteenth century, had solved the ' Jewish problem,' at any rate in so far as demands on the non-Jew were concerned. They sought only to extend the same solution to all Jewry within a framework of universal democracy. It was not their fault that the framework never came into existence, and that it had gaps even in their own societies. But they would never face the fact that the world of which they dreamed had been still-born. While, therefore, the abuse which was heaped upon their heads by Zionist and nationally minded Jews was often unmerited, and while the contributions which they made to the well-being of Jewry by their close relations with their Gentile environment were as often unfairly belittled, the majority of Jews were right who saw in such a choice no solution which was universally valid, or even universally desirable.

Yet even this group, which clung to Judaism as the sheet-anchor of their position, made a profound compromise with Gentilism. For the whole conception that religion is a matter of individual choice which carries no social or political imperative, is a product of seventeenth- and eighteenth-century Europe, exhausted by nearly half a century of religious wars which had ended in a stalemate. Europe proclaimed tolerance, only half-heartedly, and because neither side had won. And toleration of the idea that religion was a matter only for individual choice did not become effective until the paganism of Rousseau and the classical tradition, linked to the apparent victories of a màterialistic science had, in fact, turned it into indifference. To ease their political conscience, this section of Jewry accepted a definition of religion as a sectional interest in a water-tight compartment, a definition which had never previously been accepted by the Jewish tradition.

The same hall-mark of ' Gentilism ' lies also on many synagogues, whether orthodox or reform, whose members were most passionately concerned with the political assertion of their Jewishness. From early in the nineteenth century western orthodox synagogues had been increasingly influenced by the concept of ' proper behaviour in church,' and so tidied up their own worship— to their loss perhaps more than to their gain. For it made of the orthodox synagogue in the west a religious building which was opened when required for communal services, and in which decorum was more important than life ; and what was gained in ' reverence ' was lost in vitality—just as it had been in the non-Roman Catholic churches. For only the Roman Catholic Church in western Christendom continued to make feel at home within the walls of its churches, at any hour of the day, the working woman coming home from shopping, the children in the midst of their play, and the sorrowing in their loneliness.

Reform and liberal Judaism were even more conspicuously involved in the pressure of their environment. The synagogue passed through all the phases of ' liberalism ' of the Protestant Churches, and, like them, suffered from the difficulty that it is much easier to agree as to what to discard than to find a common mind as to how, positively, to rebuild a faith which will express creatively the reality of an ancient religious tradition in a totally new environment. Reform synagogues, like liberal Protestant churches, multiplied their organisations to cover their spiritual uncertainty and, if they could not mediate God to their adherents, could at least fill their time with improving activities which might divert their attention from the gnawing spiritual vacuum within the lonely heart of modern man. A Young Men's Hebrew Association paralleled a Young Men's Christian Association, and, especially in America, there was no difficulty in a pulpit exchange between liberal Christians who were hazy about the divinity of Christ or the doctrine of the atonement, and liberal Jews who could transform the stern crudities of Torah into the soothing phrases of the ' mission of Judaism.'

113

When we pass from consideration of the religious sphere to the social and political, the dominance of the outside pressure becomes even more pronounced, and the Jewish surrender more complete. For, whether in the negative field of defence, or in the positive activities of the World Jewish Congress and the World Zionist Organisation, the universal cry was: 'we Jews are just like other men ; give us what all other men have or want.' It may seem exaggerated to make this claim about organisations which appeared passionately to be championing 'Jewish' rights, and it is obviously not the whole of the story, especially in relation to Zionism. But the fact is there, and even where it does not embrace the whole picture it dominates it.

If we consider the story of Jewish defence from the time when it passes out of the area of purely religious apologetic, that is from the end of the eighteenth century onwards, we can see the process of 'gentilisation' steadily increasing its pressure. The literature of the emancipation period concentrates on presenting the nobility of Jewish ethics, on claiming the high standards which Jews would impose on themselves in return for the gift of citizenship, and on insistence of the value to society of the contributions of the Jewish genius. It is a far cry from this to the oft-repeated phrase of contemporary apologetic—I have used it myself—' are not Jews entitled to their criminals as much as any other people ?' But it is not in that extreme form that the change is most significant. It is rather in the denial in every field that there is anything identifiably Jewish in the wide variety of individuals, types and outlooks to be found in any Jewish community. Of course there is an element of truth in the statement. But there is also an element of exaggeration so gross as to be an untruth. For, apart entirely from any common stamp which might be thought to have resulted from two thousand and more years of Judaism, the suggestion that the peculiarities of Jewish history, with its restraints, its sufferings, and its fears, had left no common impress, however differently worn by individuals, on those who passed through it, removed Jews not merely into the ranks of Gentiles, but clean through their ranks into the region of the fabulous and the apocryphal. For any other people certainly would bear, for a number of generations, the stamp of so unusual an experience.

In no organisation is 'gentilism' more rampant than in the World Jewish Congress. Born out of the Comité des Délégations

Juives which formed itself at Versailles to oppose the assimilationist tendencies of the older generation of western Jewry, it has from the beginning been an expression, Jewish only in the formal sense, of contemporary nationalism. The vehemence and one-sidedness of its propaganda, the exaggerations of its claims, the techniques of pressure and publicity in which it indulges, are all familiar enough in the contemporary scene. To say this is not necessarily to say that there was no place for such an organisation, or to condemn all its works as valueless. Only those will legitimately do so who likewise condemn the whole development of modern nationalism. But, on the other hand, those who see in modern nationalism much to regret, those who approve it as a cultural necessity to avoid the dead level of cosmopolitanism but deplore its invasion of the political field, these will find nothing in the World Jewish Congress to distinguish it from its contemporaries. But again it may be considered as representative of a phase which the modern world imposed on Jewry. The rights for which it asks are rights which ought to be conceded, wherever Jews suffer inequality before the law. The freedom which Jews possess to express themselves is legitimately used to protest where Jews have no such freedom. Nor could it be avoided that when a common problem beset Jews of many countries they should combine to solve it. Indeed, when a writer who is himself a Gentile describes a Jewish body as gentilised, it is obvious that he would be condemning himself if he regarded that as synonymous with complete condemnation. But it is equally evident that if comparable activites seem to him regrettable when practised by Gentiles, there is nothing which changes their quality when they are practised by Jews!

Finally there is the ' gentilism ' of the Zionist Organisation itself. That it would be a gross caricature to describe it as wholly ' gentilised ' is evident ; and its ' Jewish ' features will be discussed in the reckoning of the positive side of the balance-sheet. But from its inception as an organised political movement Zionism has been riddled with gentilism at all levels. Its political programme, its emphasis on the right of Jews to be ' just like other nations,' its propaganda and political pressures would often justify the witticism that ' Jews are just like other people only more so.' For even before external circumstances excused, if they did not justify, the violence of the one-sided abuse hurled from Zionist platforms on anyone, Jew or Gentile, suspected of being an opponent, the Zionist move-

115

ment in its absolute refusal to consider any point of view except its own had become the most violent of all the violent nationalisms which marked the inter-war years. And the final mark of gentilism was set by revisionism and its outcome in terrorism.

Though usually in less violent and extreme forms, this gentilism marked also the Jewish National Home itself. The political structure of the Yishuv, with its multitude of shrilly abusive political parties, owes everything to the Eastern European background of the majority, and nothing to any Jewish values. But the Gentile world is not merely a world of secularism, or of tub-thumping nationalism. It is also a world of great scientific and social achievement. And what was of deeper significance was that the whole experience which enabled the Yishuv to build up a modern state with a complex and scientific foundation in agriculture, education, industry, as well as in its whole social structure, arose out of the diaspora experience of individual Jews, and their access to every aspect of modern European and American life.

If, then, we were to concentrate the essence of the experience through which the Jewish people had passed in the last fifty years, into a single paragraph, it could be expressed only in the paradox that Israel today is the quintessence of Jewish secular experience in the diaspora, and that the only firm foundation for continued Jewish life in that diaspora is a reborn Judaism.

CHAPTER XII

The Future of the Diaspora

THE emergence of a state of Israel has modified everything in the world picture of Jewry, save the fundamental fact that Jewish history rests on a permanent tension between two apparently contradictory ideas—the universalism inherent in its monotheistic religion, and the separatism involved in its will to survive. The state of Israel has such deep implications on every aspect of Jewish life and thought that there is nothing surprising if wild and unwise statements have been made about it on all sides. The early utterances of Israel's statesmen and Zionist leaders as to the withering of the diaspora should no more be remembered against them than the equally unbalanced statements which have come from anti-Zionist sources in that diaspora. Only if it were a matter of secondary importance could one expect every one to see clearly its implications from the very beginning. As it is, they will provide an admirable subject for a Ph.D. thesis in fifty years' time, and can best be left until then.

The really significant point about the present situation, and the real basis for discussion about its possible development, is that in a most unexpected manner Israel and the diaspora begin this new relationship from a point where they start level. Those who see in the development of the last years merely human events may feel that this also is very lucky ; those who see a deeper purpose at work will admire also this admirable attention to detail. For the two not merely start level, but they start in a condition where each is fluid. There have been periods in Jewish history where the one side or the other was clearly pre-eminent ; there have been periods when the re-establishment of Israel would have meant merely the extension to that country of a pattern of life already fully worked out under diaspora conditions. Such would, for example, have been the case had the Turkish concession to the Duke of Naxos led to the establishment of an autonomous Israel. It would have been patterned on medieval orthodoxy and mysticism, and would almost certainly have shared the decline of all countries under Turkish

117

rule in the subsequent centuries. Had a Jewish state been established early in the nineteenth century, when the powers were uncertain what to do with Syria after the defeat of Mehmet Ali, it would have been an appanage of the nineteenth-century ideas of the not yet born Alliance Israélite Universelle and the Anglo-Jewish Association.

On the other hand, there have been periods when it was well that Israel was not in a position to dominate the diaspora. It was very fortunate for Jewish survival that the scattered Jewish communities in the Roman empire were largely uninfluenced by the wave of chauvinistic nationalism which swept the province of Judæa in the first century of the common era. Jewry suffered enough when that nationalism perished in the conflagration of Jerusalem. Had there been similar disasters in Corinth and Rome, Alexandria and Ephesus, Marseilles and Damascus, the result might well have been fatal. No Jewish people would have survived intact. Of other periods one may say that it would have been doubtful if the rabbis of the Holy Land would have accepted with pleasure the great flowering of Jewish culture in the western caliphate and in Fatimid Egypt; and certainly in the post-emancipation period a direct conflict between the givers and recipients of Halukkah would have been disastrous.

To-day neither side is in a position to dominate the other; each needs the other; and both are fluid, since in their present situations neither is strong enough to bear alone the responsibility of future development. The result is that the equality with which they start is largely a negative equality, especially in the field which ultimately counts most, the spiritual field. The gambols of the Religious Bloc in Israeli politics have ensured that, even had there been any previous doubt that this was so, the orthodoxy of Israel is not the pattern on which Jewish life in the diaspora will recover its stability and creativity. On the other hand, the progressive Judaism of the United States and elsewhere is so clearly an emergence from a particular diaspora situation that we have had the curious spectacle of American Zionism having for years been led by progressive rabbis, none of whom have dreamed of establishing religious congregations in Israel. And in any case both orthodox and progressive Judaism are minority movements in Jewish life.

But the equality is not merely negative. It is also gloriously positive. In a discussion on charity in Baba Bathra (9a) Rabbi Assi

(I do not know if it was Assi I or Assi II) remarked that 'charity is equivalent to all the other precepts combined.' Now it is certainly true that whatever may be said of the present state of Judaism, neither the Jews of Israel nor the Jews of any country of the diaspora have betrayed their Jewish inheritance in this field The ingathering of the exiles has been a task which has demanded immense sacrifices. The demands made on the Israeli in terms of standard of living, social as well as material, have been enormous ; and the demands on Jews elsewhere have been stupendous. A Christian can but stand amazed at the Jewish conception of what giving means—and still more amazed at the common Jewish feeling on both sides that not enough has been done. And again, for those who see more than the effects of political chauvinism or social desperation in the emergence of Israel, there is a fascinating point of detail to be observed. The kind of diaspora which was available during these formative decades is exactly that which could most serve the needs of the time. A diaspora which had been a temple of orthodoxy would have spent its time debating whether it could serve a Yishuv, many of whose most valuable experiments were not merely not religiously conducted, but were opposed to orthodoxy. A diaspora which was well knit and contented would have been concerned only—as were some non-Zionist supporters of Israel—with the experiment as a new and extended method of relieving the wants of the needy and the persecuted. What was needed was exactly what the diaspora had become during the twentieth century—a diaspora uncertain of itself and hesitant about its future, but a diaspora which had become prosperous and capable of giving the enormous sums which would be needed if Israel was to be re-established. At no other period of Jewish history has the phrase of Rabbi Assi so perfectly described the real Jewishness which was needed of the Jews of America, Britain, South Africa, and elsewhere.

Israel and the diaspora do not merely start equal ; they start with the most intimate and all-embracing mutual dependence. The very fact that a state of Israel exists to which any Jew can go and in which he can become a citizen, has radically altered the nature of the diaspora, even for the most fanatical adherent to the American Council for Judaism. For previously one of the bonds of Jewish life was the absence of alternatives. A Jew could not but live as a member of a minority, with no more security than his minority position offered him ; and if he felt insecure where he was, he could only change his position for another where a similar insecurity could arise. Now he can go to Israel ; and consequently, if he stays where he is, there is a quality of individual choice in his action which was previously lacking. Israel is equally dependent on the diaspora. As was said at the end of the previous chapter, the whole of the life built up in Israel, from her religion to her latest technical devices, is built up from diaspora material ; and the continuation of Israel for many a long day to come will be dependent on diaspora investment and donation. If, then, we are to discuss the future of the diaspora, we must always keep Israel in the corner of our eye. She is never wholly out of the picture.

It is easy to plan or to forecast the future of the diaspora on the basis of one or two favourite foundations on which most prophetic structures are reared. If we will use an adequate supply either of *must* or of *if only,* we can prophesy for world Jewry any future we may choose. It is less easy, if more profitable, to eschew absolutely these insidious narcotics.

One thing is certain. No ' must ' or ' if only ' will affect all Jews in the diaspora. There will always be a flow from minority Jewries into their environment, and this for three reasons. It is an inevitable implication of the strain of universalism, and as such it is part of the ' Jewish mission.' At a time when the centre is weak, as the religious organisation of Jewry is weak to-day, there will always be some whose main interest, even though inspired by their Jewish inheritance, will find better fulfilment in a sympathetic Gentile environment than in their local Jewish community. And there will always be the indifferent and the climber, those who have no interest in any communal loyalty, and those who desire to follow only what is socially acceptable to their neighbours.

The future of the diaspora does not depend on reaching and retaining all these elements within Jewry, and it is to be noted that these elements contain some of the best representatives of the Jewish tradition as well as some of the worst. The future depends on the quality and size of the core—but even so, very few of that core are amenable to the dictates of the prophetic ' must,' or will change their ways on the basis of ' if only.' We must accept that what happens will be untidy, illogical, full of contradictions, for those are the characteristics of a lively and dynamic group which is held together more by inner vitality than outside compulsion. Nevertheless, there are two generalisations which can be made. From the standpoint of the Gentile world the obvious and acceptable basis of a Jewish community within its borders is religious ; and a minority community will always be subject to certain cohesive forces which do not affect a majority. What will decide the future will be bound up with the Jewish definition of ' religion,' and the nature of the pressures to which Jews as a minority are submitted. Those, as it were, are the positive and negative poles between which the future will be built.

Everyone will hope that, in terms of persecution or exclusion, the negative pole will be continuously weakened. But, if that happens, then Jewish life will disintegrate unless the positive pole is comparably strengthened, that is to say, increases its power of attraction for Jews as they are, and in relation to their actual environment. It is no good drawing a perfect blue-print of all Jews learning Hebrew, making themselves experts in Jewish history, and becoming devout synagogue-goers. But there is a wide gap between making such demands and accepting as inevitable the indefinite continuation of the present position.

To say that the ultimate basis of Jewish life in the diaspora is as a religious community, does not mean that it is as a theologically minded community ; for the essence of traditional Judaism has been its refusal to recognise a distinction between the ecclesiastical and the secular. The tragedy of post-emancipation Jewish life was the stripping of the community and its synagogue of Jewish concern for the ordinary lives of its members. This, in turn, was due to the fact that orthodoxy, as it had become fixed in ghetto conditions, had ceased to be relevant to the majority of problems with which an emancipated Jew was faced. It became an ecclesiastical department of life ; and in a century where all such ecclesiastical controls were weakening, the synagogue, like the churches, lost influence. The ex-religious Jew, like his ex-religious Christian neighbour, fell into the way of accepting any standard which was at the moment in vogue in his neighbourhood.

The problem of the future presents itself in exactly the same terms to both to-day. When we reflect on our present world situation, most thinking people are painfully aware that the brave new world which was expected to materialise out of our scientific conquests has not happened. Materialism and the sciences have alike failed us. Today we are not only exposed to destruction from

121

the forces we have created, but we face the fact that modern man is increasingly conscious that he is caught up in a whirl of life which gives him little satisfaction and leaves him lonely and lacking all inner peace and harmony. This situation affects Jews as much as anyone else ; but to move society on to a happier position needs, not huge programmes, but quiet work at the ' grass roots.' Nevertheless, the position is more hopeful than it has been for many decades, because the consciousness of the need for change is becoming steadily more widespread. It has, of course, a definitely religious, indeed theological, side, but that is discussed in the following chapter ; for it is not exclusively religious, at any rate in the terms in which that word has been interpreted by all for the last hundred years.

It is a permanent feature of diaspora life that it feeds into the Jewish centre influences which it has received from outside. The most striking example of this in the contemporary situation is the extension of the pastoral duties of the rabbi and the expansion of the synagogue building as a social centre. Both have been most highly developed in progressive congregations in America ; and both owe an enormous amount to the Protestant congregations with which American Jews are familiar in their environment.

It would be a great mistake to consider this development merely a product of reformism which the conservative and the orthodox should shun. For the developments which have led to it are developments common to all Jewish life, and not merely to those dissatisfied with the traditional values of Judaism. In the old days of the ghetto community and of universal acceptance of the orthodox tradition among Jews, even by those Jews whose private lives were at variance with it, there was a sharp distinction between the tasks which the rabbi and the Protestant priest or minister were called upon to perform. In the ghetto the synagogue and its administration had so obviously a central place in communal affairs that they needed no positive attractions to draw men to them. The rabbi himself had no administrative duties ; he was required only to be a man learned in the interpretation of the Law ; and as the Law provided the main intellectual interest of the community, the rabbi's superior learning in this field gave him his authority.

Emancipation radically changed this situation by making any positive relation with the synagogue a voluntary affair and by opening up to Jewish eyes new fields of culture in which the rabbi had no automatic authority. All this meant that the rabbi needed to go out to his flock as friend and counsellor, and that the synagogue needed to develop activities related not merely to the Jewish tradition, but to the interests created by the non-Jewish environment.

Today there is a certain emptiness behind the magnificence of many progressive congregations with their multifarious activities and their often lovely buildings ; but I do not believe that this should cast doubt on the value of this new development in Jewish life, nor is it a development of significance to progressive Judaism only. I was interested in the remark made to me recently about the rabbi of a very orthodox and traditional synagogue in England that he was ' so good at attracting the young people.'

The centres of interest in Jewish life for a number of decades have been defence and Zionism, and in many Jewish communities these occupy far more time and require far more funds than the communal activities centring in the synagogue. Both have come under considerable fire in the last few years and, indeed, external circumstances are forcing a change of emphasis. The Zionist organisation is full of uncertainties about its future programme and activities ; and defence organisations have just been the subject of a very critical analysis in America. For some years to come the collection of funds is bound to be a primary interest of Zionists, and the needs for defence have not wholly vanished. But there is an opportunity today, which there was not a few years ago. for them both to move closer together as natural activities of one many-sided synagogal centre. For Zionism this will have the advantage that it will make easier the discovery and upbuilding of permanent and creative relations between Israel and the real core of diaspora life. And for the defence organisations the advantage will be equally great. Particularly in America, organisations such as the Anti-Defamation League have increasingly realised that their main task is positive and not negative ; it is to build healthy communal relations, not to concentrate on areas of conflict. But they seem rarely to have realised that a community building centring in the community synagogue is the one place where Jew and Gentile can meet without embarrassment to either side, since neither side has anything to conceal. In such a building Jews can concern themselves openly with all the social problems of the community of which they form a part, and help to develop its cultural and intellectual life without embarrassment. There they can invite

Gentiles to participate without fear of misunderstanding, since there is no ' propaganda ' intention ; and can participate with Gentiles to the fullest extent, since such participation raises no problem of weakening their own Jewish loyalties. Only where such a centre is in an exclusively Jewish district is such a development difficult ; and few Jewish districts are so completely and exclusively Jewish.

From an historical standpoint the development of the synagogue centre, and of the pastoral conception of the rabbinate, was the inevitable and necessary consequence of the passage from the enforced community of the ghetto to the voluntary community of emancipation. It involves no imposed ' must,' and rests on no idealistic ' if only.' It has happened because it was natural that it should happen ; it remains to exploit it to the full, and with the maximum foresight and intelligence.

A healthy Jewish community not only draws in from its environment ; it also radiates out. It is unlikely that there will be anything comparable to the situations revealed in the description of the pre-emancipation history of the diaspora ; for they depended on conditions which have passed. There are no economic advantages today out of which Jews could re-create conditions such as led to the court Jew of the eighteenth century or the Rumanian Jew of the nineteenth ; there are no experiences the Jewish tradition can mediate to the Gentile world as it once mediated the Christian religion. The radiation is likely to be less obvious, less identifiable. In recent decades Jews have been too concerned with their own affairs, and their own affairs have been too controversial for this issue to arise. For tomorrow I believe it will depend on the extent to which Jews are in the van or the rearguard of the move which humanity is bound to make, if it is to avoid destruction, towards the discovery of spiritual and social values which will be as compelling to their generation as the ortho- doxies of Christianity and Judaism were in the past. In the nineteenth and twentieth centuries Jews mirrored, and even by their critical faculties contributed to, the widespread intellectual *malaise* which accompanies a dying age ; it would be in conformity with their past if they showed themselves equally sensitive to the changing atmosphere of tomorrow, and if it brought into play a characteristic as Jewish as their critical faculties, their undying optimism.

It might, perhaps, be said that all these issues were secondary, and that a community really lives neither by radiating out nor by drawing in, and that these are but by-products of what it is itself. But, while this is obviously true, I would compare the approach of this chapter to one of those complicated games of patience which are such an admirable foreground to reflection. The ultimate objective is neatly ordered packs of cards, each in its own suit and ranged from the ace to the king. But this objective is not achieved by a direct approach. The player follows a trend here and exploits an opening there, until suddenly the game falls into place. In the same way, with the four suits of loyalty to Judaism and Jewish history, links with Israel (including knowledge of Hebrew), good relations with non-Jewish neighbours, and quiet satisfaction with being a Jew (which are our four suits), their right ordering cannot be achieved by pressure, propaganda, and direct approach. They emerge from the intelligent use of the trends and material available in the actual situation.

It might be claimed that all were ultimately comprehended in the last of the four—the quiet satisfaction of being a Jew. For only as the others are dealt with will this, the least self-conscious, the least plannable, but the most fundamental necessity, be met ; and, as it is met, the others will be found to have been met also. And in this last need is comprehended the question often asked, whether it is possible to live a ' full Jewish life ' in the diaspora.

It is a moving phrase with its memories of the colourful Jewish past—the intense life within the ghetto and orthodoxy as a living and guiding ' portable homeland '—and, linked with all these, the vivid contemporary picture of the kibbutz, the young sabra, or the heroic defence of of Jerusalem, of Kfar Etzion and many other lonely outposts. It is easy to say that surely here, and not in the streamlined western Jewries, is *the only* authentic Jewish life. It is moving, but it must not be overdone. Such pictures, each in its own way, are fully Jewish, in the sense in which life in a free Gentile environment may not be. But neither really expresses the fullness of the Jewish tradition ; for that tradition rests on the tension between universalism and separate survival. Life in the ghetto could not express the whole of Jewishness, because the ghetto Jew was deprived both of free relations with his neighbours and of that political independence which is the necessary crown to the life of a community. And life tomorrow in Israel could easily become merely a nationalism which, as the generations passed, became more purely levantine, less capable of more than local significance.

It is Israel *plus* a free diaspora, contented but not static in a relationship of mutual harmony, which alone expresses to the full the reason for the survival over so many bitter centuries of the Jewish people. The full Jewish life is in neither, if separated, but in both, if united. It is in that contentment that Jews can become ' just like other peoples.' For it gives them a place in the world which is theirs by right *and* by privilege, as is the position of the other nations who bear between them the cultures and civilisations of humanity.

PART FOUR

E Pluribus Unum

Not the least of the miracles of Jewish history lies in the fact that the longest and most bitter struggle for survival took place at a time when no Jew was a free man, when the heart and core of Israel—the portable homeland—was dispersed through a thousand communities of medieval Europe, and when there was no possible line of retreat. For in the Muslim world, shattered by successive inroads from the recesses of Asia, there was but stagnation, disorder, and decay, in the midst of which the Jewish community of the land of Israel was but a tiny fragment hanging on with grim and desperate determination, and the Jewry of the Babylonian Talmud was little more than a ghost. In this situation, politically powerless and physically utterly outnumbered, the Jewry of Europe sustained three centuries of conflict with the triumphant Church, and emerged scarred but victorious.

In the period which followed, the period of the Eastern European ghetto, Jewry was able to withdraw into a strange world of its own to heal its wounds, a world into which the religious influences of Christendom could scarcely penetrate. It was the period of 'Yiddishkeit,' whose tender memories still tug at Jewish hearts today. For three centuries a secret Israel lay hidden within a diaspora itself largely inaccessible to outside pressures, waiting until a further advance was made possible. The moment came when Russian persecution spilled Eastern European Jewry over the western world and ushered in the present epoch.

CHAPTER XIII

The Diaspora in Battle for the Heart of Israel[1]

THE CONFLICT WITH THE CHURCH IN THE MIDDLE AGES

THE conventional picture of the relations between Christians and Jews in the Middle Ages is dominated by the immense disparity in power and numbers between the two groups. Jewry appears as a tiny and dispersed minority, constantly the object of political and economic discrimination, of ecclesiastical hostility, and of mob violence, all of which Jews were powerless to resist. In the political and economic fields this picture is true ; and it is useless to attempt to whittle it down by exaggerating either the financial power of Jewry or the anecdotes of friendly intercourse even with ecclesiastics of the highest rank. The power of money is severely limited when its owner is not in a position to decide whether to give or to withhold it ; and no friendship with individual ecclesiastics moved the wheels of religious intolerance to reverse their direction for a single moment. Besides, the conventional picture is amply confirmed by the tragic position in which Jewry is revealed at the end of the period. Poverty-stricken, expelled from almost every country of Western Europe, their centres of culture destroyed, their numbers reduced by compulsory or semi-compulsory baptisms, carrying the burden of solidarity and of sympathy with the thousands of unwilling and suspect marranos left behind, they would prove, had no document survived of the medieval story, that their experiences in those centuries had been tragic and destructive.

But they survived. Fugitives along new roads of exile in Poland, North Africa, and the Levant, seeking new occupations among people materially less advanced and still unfamiliar with the charges

[1] Presidential address delivered before the Jewish Historical Society of England on October 25, 1949.

130

Western Europe had laid against them, yet they carried with them a Judaism which, if narrowed and hardened by its experiences, was unimpaired, and a social structure which had weathered all assaults and remained the foundation of their national survival. They survived. It was the powerful medieval Christendom they had left behind which was in ruins.

To offer some explanation of this extraordinary paradox is the purpose of this chapter. Their survival had no physical explanation. Even if they could profit from the conflicts between different authorities over their possession, and even though the dispersion of their communities often secured them advantages, yet physically they could, without difficulty, have been exterminated from Europe, especially when the brief period of their semi-monopolistic money-lending terminated in the emergence of Christian money-lenders far richer and under far more powerful protection than they had enjoyed. They could have been compulsorily baptised, and their children weaned from the older faith, while those who backslid could have been crushed in the fires of the Inquisition. The Middle Ages were not squeamish, and the massacre of heretics provoked little humanitarian protest. But neither of these fates befell them ; and to approach the reasons for this strange survival we must turn from the political and economic scene to the religious.

Once we turn from contemplating Christians and Jews to examining Judaism and Christianity we pass from a picture of two unequal combatants to that of two religious systems confronting each other as equals alike in the profundity and the scope of their religious thought and in the richness and variety of the way of life which they had evolved.

Both religions stem from the experiences of the Jewish people in Palestine up to the period of the Roman domination. They part company when on one side the little group which had come to accept Jesus of Nazareth as Messiah began to explore the formulation of a Christology which would render their experience comprehensible to the Hellenistic world, and in doing so were led into a wild and exaggerated attack on what they understood as ' the Law '; and when on the other side the vast majority of the Jewish people sought in that same ' Law ' a foundation to national survival which would be an effective alternative to their ruined temple and their lost autonomy.

For nearly a thousand years the two faiths developed their

experiences in isolation from each other. Judaism gradually relaxed its hold on the Greco-Roman world and turned its back on the attempts at a synthesis with Hellenism which had begun in the Wisdom Literature and reached its apogee in Philo and the Alexandrian School. It is significant that all Jewish religious documents in Greek cease within a century of the separation of the two faiths ; and the conclusion is irresistible that one element in this withdrawal was the advancing power of the Christian Church. But the life-lines from the Palestinian patriarchate, which had grown more tenuous towards the west, were being strengthened towards the east. In Babylon, free from the influences of both Christendom and the Roman Empire, rabbinic Judaism came to its full stature, and assumed an all-embracing authority over the life of the nation. For Jewry remained a nation, unquestionably a single people, strung out across the inhabited world from China to the Atlantic in a thousand autonomous communities, each of which followed a pattern which all would have found familiar, a pattern voluntarily preserved under its own religious and civil magistrates. None doubted their membership of a single people ; and all were identifiable from outside by the single name of ' Jews.'

The rich Old Testament conception of God is too unsystematically presented in the Bible to be called a ' doctrine.' But in its ready, and indeed unconscious, acceptance of those paradoxes which so puzzled the Greek mind, paradoxes between the finite and the infinite, between a presence which was universal and a local manifestation, between being and becoming, and between eternity and time, it provided an adequate background and foundation to the interests and speculations of the rabbis. They felt no need to probe or to define ; and it remained, unchallenged and unchanged, the background throughout the whole period of the growth of rabbinic Judaism. In place of theology the rabbis concentrated on the tasks of biblical exegesis, and of the ordering of common life according to the will of God, revealed in Torah and interpreted under divine guidance to each succeeding generation. They recognised no clerical caste and, apart from the transitional value of the Palestinian patriarchate, evolved no ecclesiastical hierarchy. Except in Babylon itself their communal affairs were subjected to no hereditary aristocracy, nor any authority based on birth. Though shadowy princes of the house of David enjoyed a dignity of affection and tradition, and the descendants of the cohanim possessed the exclusive right to pronounce a particular benediction, these distinctions were of the accidents, not the substance, of their history. There existed in their communities no distinction of status between a clergy and a laity. They strove rather towards the ideal of an educated democracy, based on an elaborately detailed pattern of social and religious conduct, and a strict code of social and personal morality, firmly cemented by a programme of universal literacy.

The growth of the Christian Church presents a picture equally rich and fascinating in its totality, but different in every single detail of its structure. As with Judaism, it gradually spread its broad mantle over the whole life of the peoples who acknowledged its authority and looked to it for salvation. And if, in fact, it had to meet a challenge from within more severe than that experienced by the leaders of Jewry, it must be remembered that its missionary character brought within its sway societies resting on other foundations, and that it had to adapt its political and social structure not only to its own biblical inheritance and the civilisation which it had rescued from the failing grasp of the Roman emperors, but also to the rude but dynamic traditions of the peoples of Northern and Western Europe.

In its long struggle for authority, theological uniformity had come to be the weapon on which it placed its chief reliance ; and this conception, so alien to our modern eclectic ways of thinking, was readily accepted by those who acknowledged that in orthodoxy alone lay their eternal salvation. We are no more entitled to sneer at the intensity of the credal warfares which stained the formative centuries of Christianity with rivers of blood, than we are to fling the conventional denunciations of sterility and externalism at the less deadly occupations of the rabbis who spent years in the minute discussion of the ritual of a temple which had perished centuries before. Both alike belonged to a world which few of us can understand today ; but both had their place in the upbuilding of the great European civilisation which we have inherited.

We have only to look at the innumerable volumes of the church fathers to realise that to them no subject equalled in interest and importance that of metaphysical and theological analysis and speculation. Their discussion of those other subjects which interested the rabbis received a treatment which rarely extended beyond generalisations and was often utopian and perfunctory

F

On the other hand Christendom evolved an elaborate and comprehensive ecclesiastical system, with an equivalent geographical pattern. Although it was never able to secure the same balance and uniformity of structure in the political world, with a hierarchy from emperor to baron corresponding to that from pope to diocesan bishop, this hierarchical pattern produced approximately the same effect in stabilising communal life as did the halachic foundations of rabbinic Judaism.

The basic distinction lay in the consequences of the Christian belief in the link between orthodoxy and salvation, which created and justified the prerogatives of a clerical order, independent of the political pyramid of authority, and involving a basic superiority of cleric over layman which was particularly manifested in the field of education. During the greater part of the Middle Ages the Church exercised considerable political authority by the mere fact that among clerics alone could be found a literate class capable of exercising all the functions of government from chancellor to clerk of the archives.

In spite of this ecclesiastical predominance, medieval Christendom was not an other-worldly society. It possessed a comprehensive philosophy of the State, constantly modified and developed by conciliar action and by canon law, which transformed the disparate societies of the Roman and barbarian traditions into a single Christendom, which in the richness and variety of its life exceeded anything which the world had so far known.

Up to the threshold of the Middle Ages the two systems had grown up in almost complete isolation from each other. Jewish abandonment of its Alexandrian interpreters was balanced by Christian ignorance of Hebrew. At the time of their effective meeting in the Middle Ages it might have been expected that they would have come nearer to understanding each other from the fact that Islamic scholars, intoxicated with the infinite capacity for building impressive sounding metaphysics inherent in the Aristotelian syllogism, provided, in the recovery of Greek manuscripts, a foundation alike for the rationalism of Maimonides and the scholasticism of Thomas Aquinas. But though the latter even borrowed from the former, with honourable acknowledgment of his debt, there is no evidence that Thomas Aquinas thereby acquired any closer knowledge of the nature of Judaism than did the Italian Jewish philosopher, Hillel b. Samuel of Verona (1220-1295), better appreciate the nature of Christianity by using Thomas's arguments for the immortality of the soul in order to confute the Averroistic tendencies of his Jewish contemporaries. The borrowing was superficial because, in fact, the Aristotelianism of both sides was superficial. The experience of both religions of a God who acted in history was not enriched by the pallid deity of Aristotle ; and those experiences could not be communicated through so slick and superficial a medium as the syllogism.

The two religions thus confronted each other, alike in the comprehensiveness of the authority which they exercised over their adherents, and dissimilar on every point on which it could be imagined that two monotheisms, stemming from the same root and worshipping the same God, could differ from each other. One may even say that it was their common origin which rendered them incomprehensible to each other. For neither could understand how the same ingredients could be so differently mixed. This is apparent, more than in any other field, in their amazement at each other's theology. The paradox of the God, complete in himself and at the same time active in history, shows itself in Judaism in an astonishing freedom of expression, which appeared to Christians, who did not say the same kind of things about God, the most blasphemous frivolity and deliberate irreverence. It shows itself in Christianity in the doctrine of the Trinity, which no Jew could believe was anything but tritheism, thinly veiled—if veiled at all.

So they confronted each other, with no possibility of accommodation, just because of the comprehensiveness of each. That the physically weaker group could be so comprehensive in its control of its own members it owed to two factors. Before the medieval period there had grown up within Jewry, scattered under a hundred sovereignties, the doctrine that " the law of the land is law "; and the flexibility both of the thought and the organisation of the Jewish community of this period made possible a considerable elasticity of accommodation which allowed all essentials to remain inviolate. But even more it owed its ability to survive to the medieval conception of law.

The conception which was universally accepted at that period, and had been inherited from earlier civilisations of both east and west, was not that which is now familiar to us. Laws were not regarded as the bonds which held together a wide variety of people and professions politically united under a single sceptre. Within the very wide limits which would, for example, proscribe murder, adultery, or theft, numerous separate courts of justice and even codes existed side by side within a single political society, even within a single city. Clergy, lawyers, and merchants, city burghers and manorial tenants, ethnic groups such as Flemings, Lombards, or Jews, all enjoyed the possession of their own codes and the jurisdiction of their own courts ; and the validity of this variety of privileges and customs was universally recognised, save when some particular situation or urgent need involved a clash with higher authority, or some blatant injustice aroused popular anger or the jealousy of rivals. Jewry in particular did suffer infringements of its autonomy. Aragonian kings rashly allotted seats in the synagogue to their favourites, the system of judicial autonomy varied from charter to charter, rabbinic literature was censored and destroyed. But at bottom the autonomy had to remain. For medieval man would have found the alternative improper, the alternative that Jews should be treated as Christians and enjoy the rights and duties inherent in acceptance of the orthodoxy on which salvation rested.

The two religions confronted each other as equals ; and only so can we understand that while among a small minority of Christians it might be regarded as a friendly and tolerant equality, among the majority and among those who had executive responsibility, the basic attitude of the Church to the Synagogue was fear —a fear which was reinforced on each occasion of contact by two simple factors, Jewish literacy and Jewish knowledge of Hebrew.

It was said earlier that the survival of Jewry rests on no physical foundation. Yet when we recognise that the basic attitude of the churchmen throughout the period rested on fear, we must ask again why it was that the Church did not make use of her unquestionable superiority in force to annihilate Jewry. To destroy what we fear, if we have the power to do so, is a natural urge. Why did she not make an all-out attack upon the Synagogue ?

In the first place she could not make an all-out attack on Judaism theologically. She could damn the Jews for their deicide and abuse them for their blindness. But she could not adopt the easy attitude she adopted to Islam, when she denounced Muhammad as a charlatan and the *Quran* as a sham. How could she say the same of Moses, whom she honoured equally with the

Synagogue, or of the *Torah* which, as the Old Testament, she included in her divinely inspired Scriptures ? She had to do battle on the much more slippery and subjective terrain of interpretation, and there she had to meet the infuriating Jewish knowledge both of Hebrew and of the text of the Old Testament. From the fascinating thirteenth-century anecdotes of meetings between Jews and Christians collected by Joseph ben Nathan, the Official, we can see how skilfully Jews learned to turn the Christian arguments by use of those same Scriptures which the Christians could not attack. Two slight examples will illustrate the point. Christian exegesis liked to use the passage of the Red Sea as a symbol of the passage into a new life by baptism. But, pointed out a Jew who was asked to be convinced by this argument, it was the Egyptians who had received a ' baptism ' in the water, and as a result they were drowned. The Israelites, who survived, had passed over dry. Again Christians contrasted the length of the present ' exile ' with that in Babylon. We meet this argument at the very threshold of the Middle Ages round about the year 1000, and at that time it found the Jews in a state of great depression. But in the anecdotes of Joseph, Jews have a complete if daring answer. The first exile was a punishment for the fact that some of the Jews had made wooden and stone images of false Gods. It was natural that a heavier punishment should follow when some of them had identified a man with the true God. So effectively had Jews fortified themselves against arguments based on scriptural quotation that these largely disappear in the Middle Ages from polemic works, though they still formed the basis of the conversional sermons Jews were compelled to listen to in their synagogues. But even the scriptural polemics emphasised the weakness of the Christian position. They were inevitably arguments about interpretation. They could not claim that Judaism was a false religion ; but only that Jews interpreted falsely the divine revelation they had received.

But a second impediment to an all-out attack occurred in the New Testament itself. The foundation-stone of the Christian attitude to Jews and Judaism was St. Paul's epistle to the Romans. And there it was clearly stated that some at least of the Jewish people must survive as Jews until the second coming of Christ. For only then would they be converted. The most important verses are ch. xi, 25 and 26 :

'A hardening in part hath befallen Israel, until the fullness of the Gentiles be come in ; and so shall all Israel be saved, even as it is written:
There shall come out of Zion the Deliverer ;
He shall turn away ungodliness from Jacob.'
It was therefore legitimate that Jews should be kept in subjection and humiliated ; for the sin of deicide merited such treatment ; and the spectacle of their continued sufferings reminded Christians of the truth of prophecy. But they could not be annihilated.

The sequence of events in the twelfth and thirteenth centuries illustrates the point. The Church, and by that I mean the Papacy, the bishops, and the general and local councils, was slower to express its attitude to the Jews than many princes or populaces. Privileges had been given by the one, and Jewish quarters sacked by the other, before the Church issued her rules of conduct ; and before she was ready to do so, the Popes found themselves in the rôle of protectors of the Jews against violence, whether physical or religious. Letters forbidding them to be either killed or forcibly baptised became an established tradition at the Vatican.

When the Church was ready to act, her action admirably illustrated the thesis that the foundation of her action rested on the fear of Judaism and of Jewish influence ; for it was designed firstly to prevent Christians from being in any way in subjection to Jews, or in a position where they would be submitted to Jewish influence ; and secondly to isolate the Jewish community from its Christian neighbours. The ghetto only slowly came to be a compulsory segregation ; but the badge, or different Jewish dress, was in force from the fourth Lateran Council of 1215. Throughout the whole period repeated efforts were made to break intercourse between the two communities ; for even the most godly and pious Christian might be suborned by the subtlety of the Jews. For example, a biblical scholar needed Jewish help to interpret difficult passages of the Old Testament ; and the various medieval attempts to purify and correct the text of the Vulgate all bear witness to 'Jewish influence.'

More serious was the possibility that Jews might induce the innocent into heresy ; and in her long battle with heretical movements, even in Roman times, the Church was always tempted to see the hand of Jewry. Actually in the great heresies of the Middle Ages it is difficult to distinguish exactly Jewish religious pressure.

It was not unnatural that a prince at enmity with the Church should be friendly towards the enemies of the Church ; and the fact. that Provençal or other nobles during the Albigensian period were favourable to Jews does not prove that Jews were behind the Albigensian heresy. Further, where the inquisitors and the orthodox saw the influence of the Jewish community, it might, in fact, have been the influence of the Bible. The *pasagii* in Italy and the predecessors of the levellers in England were probably influenced by the latter rather than the former.

Nevertheless, the fear and danger existed ; and when there arose in Spain a substantial Christian community of immediate Jewish origin, and the orthodoxy of these ' new Christians ' was the subject of serious doubt, the Church was not wrong in believing that Jews would do everything they could to aid these ' heretics.'

In 1240 the medieval Inquisition inspired a public disputation in Paris over the Talmud ; and from then onwards another line of attack was adopted. Unable to trace Jewish lack of faith to the Bible, or to defeat them over biblical texts, churchmen eagerly took up the question of the Talmud and rabbinic literature. Before the end of the century the Dominicans were training a school of Christian Hebraists—many were of Jewish origin—whose task it was to censor Jewish religious literature in order that Jews might be deprived of arguments against the Christian religion ; and that they might be punished for blasphemies against that religion and its Founder. Though they were instructed in the nature of the Talmud by converted Jews, Christians never grasped the distinction between *haggadah* and *halachah,* and this failure had an important influence in another battlefield.

Apart from the innumerable private discussions which must have taken place, there were from time to time public disputations which Jews were forced to attend. Their opponent, as in the famous controversy of 1240, was often a convert. In these disputations, and in the written polemics of the time, pages are filled with proofs from Midrashic and Haggadic phrases that the Talmudic scholars taught the doctrine of the Trinity, and that they accepted Jesus of Nazareth as Messiah. Still further pages are filled with denunciations of their puerilities and blasphemies. If these disputations and polemics are thought of as primarily directed to the conversion of the Jews, then they must appear fantastically ill-directed. For no Jew would have had any difficulty in answering them since he was well aware that the rabbis whose discussions fill the Talmud were neither Trinitarians nor Christians, and that in any case neither *Haggadah* nor *Midrash* was authoritative. But once we align these works with the policy of protecting Christians from Jewish influence, and recognise them as part of the campaign dictated by the fear of that influence, they become not only comprehensive, but skilful. They were admirably directed to the end of convincing the Christian firstly that, even if Jews denied it, Jewish religious literature admitted the truth of Christianity ; and secondly, or alternatively, that Judaism was a puerile and ridiculous superstition often verging on blasphemy. The greatest monument of medieval polemics, the *Pugio Fidei* (*Dagger of the Faith*) of Raymund Martini, is only comprehensible from this standpoint.

The campaign against the Talmud had more serious effects on Jewry than the ghetto or the badge. For it effectively destroyed Jewish centres of learning by the drastic expedient of burning their libraries. But even more serious were the effects on the more ignorant clergy and the populace of the inculcation from above of this general atmosphere of fear of Judaism and the Jews. It must not be thought that there was any centrally directed or conscious campaign, such as might be created with the instruments of modern propaganda ; it was rather the communication of an atmosphere, interpreted at each level in the manner of the thinking of the day. The charge of ritual murder and the ritual use of blood came from below, not from above ; and the same was true of most of the accusations which caused such widespread bloodshed in the Jewish communities. The frenzied mobs, which in city after city, country after country, sacked Jewish quarters and massacred their inhabitants, drew their force from the imaginings of men like themselves, more than from the pronouncements of popes, bishops, or councils. But it was the language of popes, bishops, councils, and theologians which made their imaginings possible. In the end a whole mythology was built up which Dr. Trachtenberg has admirably illustrated in his book, *The Devil and the Jew*. While it would be absurd to consider this popular fear of the Jews as a reasoned fear of Judaism and Jewish influence on Christian orthodoxy, it at least served the purpose of those who did possess that fear, in that it contributed to the separation of the two communities ; and it certainly made it less likely that simple men would listen to Jewish religious arguments against their faith, or fall into heresy under Jewish inspiration.

None of this is explicable on the basis that the main attitude of the Church was conversionist, and that her main objective was the winning of the Jews to the Christian faith ; and those voices which were raised against popular actions and beliefs, on the basis that they would do little to persuade Jews of the superiority of Christianity or the affection towards them of Christians, were but a tiny if cultured minority. Yet all through the Middle Ages the Church did continue a missionary activity among the Jews, apparently little conscious of the paradox in her behaviour. Special inducements were held out to conversion, and from the time of Pope Nicholas III (1277-1280) a definite scheme of preaching was laid down, and Jews were compelled to listen to sermons three times a year in which the merits of the Christian religion were expounded to them. The weakness from which such an activity, however sincerely carried out, inevitably suffered, was that the Christian preacher had nothing new to say, and that Jews had evolved answers to all the biblical points which he could raise. Hence until the time of serious persecution in Spain which followed the missions of Ferrand Martinez in 1391 and of Vincent Ferrer in 1411, and was constant in the fifteenth century, there is extraordinarily little record of conversions. At a time when there was no ' racial ' feeling and when a Jew who joined the faith of the majority was saved from the danger of violence as well as the mass of restrictions and humiliations under which his people lived, this is a remarkable fact. It is in itself a support for the thesis that the two religions confronted each other as incomprehensible equals. Yet this is probably not the whole truth ; and I do not think I can be suspected of ' Zionist ' propaganda in saying that a very important element in the Jewish ability to stand firm was the belief in a future outside the influence and jurisdiction of Christendom. Beyond was the land of Israel, and the Messianic hope played an important part in the life of medieval Jewry. An event, particularly a religious event, does not necessarily exercise less attractive power for appearing distant. If the incidence of false messiahs be any indication, it is interesting that in the earlier part of the period there were several, and they found widespread credence. In the fourtenth and fifteenth centuries none appeared ; the messianic hope had become dimmed by the hideous drudgery of later medieval life, with its incessant persecutions, and this was the period in which conversions were most numerous.

Yet even at the end of the period the mission and its converts play but a minor rôle in the story ; and the main emphases are different. It is indeed a remarkable picture which emerges, when the expulsion from Spain and Portugal closes this chapter of European and of Jewish life.

Physically the Church had won. The Jews had been deprived of their property, robbed of their learned institutions, and harried from land to land. When those of Spain took the long and hard road to exile the last great medieval Jewry was destroyed, and the Church was triumphant. In the whole of Western Europe no Jew could endanger her faith, or pervert her children.

That is the physical picture. The religious picture is a total and fantastic contradiction. The Jewish exiles rewrote in Safed among the Galilean hills the text-books of their orthodoxy and their mysticism. The Judaism of Joseph Caro and of Isaac Luria is the direct successor of the Judaism which had entered medieval Europe five hundred years earlier. It was undiminished and unaltered in any detail by the long defensive battle against Christendom. Jewish orthodoxy had indeed lost resilience and flexibility, and was to encounter its own difficulties later from movements from within the ghetto itself in Eastern Europe and, after emancipation, in Germany and the west ; but it had surrendered nothing to the Christian attack, and abandoned none of the doctrines with which it entered the apparently so unequal fray.

With the Christian Church the situation was totally different. Before Caro and Luria had finished rewriting their orthodoxy in Safed, the banner of rebellion against the whole medieval expression of the faith had been raised in Bohemia, in Germany, in England, in Holland, and in Switzerland ; and in that rebellion the unity and authority of medieval Christendom was shattered into fragments. The Reformation had deep roots in European history with which Jewry was in no way concerned. But central in the whole upheaval was the translation into the vernacular and the printing of the Bible ; and it is appropriate that in the new biblical scholarship Jewry, even if indirectly, should have had a hand. It can be traced in many fields. But nothing is more significant than the case of Martin Luther himself. As a biblical commentator he owed a great debt to the work of Nicholas of Lyra, the Franciscan scholar of the early years of the fourteenth century. And Nicholas of Lyra transcribes wholesale the interpretations of Rashi.

142

The expulsion from Spain ends a chapter in Jewish-Christian relations. When the two religions confronted each other again from the period of emancipation onwards, the situation had completely altered. Christendom and Jewry had both become less homogeneous, more diversified. Churches and scholars could differ in their attitude to Jews and Judaism ; the Churches no longer dictated the political and social destiny of Jewish communities ; states could adopt different policies ; and Jews on their side also were conscious of internal differences.

In the conflict in the early centuries of the Christian era, neither religion had yet assumed its final form. It is only in the medieval period that the two religions confronted each other as monoliths, each complete, both in its way of life and in the discipline which it exercised over its adherents.

CHAPTER XIV

The Heart of Israel in Retirement in the Diaspora :

THE LOST WORLD OF YIDDISHKEIT

IN the period from the tenth to the sixteenth centuries Jewry
had lived in the most intimate relationship with the two great
civilisations of Islam and Christianity. She had been more
influenced by the former than by the latter ; for Islam was, at the
time of her contact, more open to friendly relations, less concerned
with conversions and the assertion of an intransigent orthodoxy.
But the Islamic episode, if sweeter, was of shorter duration. The
conflict with Christianity lasted until the sixteenth century.

In the period which spanned the centuries between the Middle
Ages and modern times the centre of the Jewish world lay in
Eastern Europe, at the beginning largely under Polish rule, but from
the time of the partitions of Poland mostly in the Russian Pale of
Settlement which stretched from the Black Sea to the Baltic. But,
whether the rulers were Russian or Polish, Rumanian, Hungarian or
Austrian, Jewish life was almost unaffected by these distinctions, and
it was one Jewry which developed its own way of life throughout the
region. In 1880, just before the flight from Russia began, Ruppin
estimates that Jews in this area must have numbered six millions
and amounted to three-quarters of the whole Jewish people.

These Jews lived in compact masses such as they had not known
since the classical days of the Alexandrian community, or the
Babylonian Jewry of Talmudic times. Many lived in the smaller
towns, and these towns were often entirely Jewish creations in
which everyone save a few officials was Jewish. In the great cities
such as Warsaw, Vilna, Odessa, Kiev and many others Jews lived
in such large and compact ' ghettoes ' that it would have been
easily possible for a Jew, or still more a Jewess, to pass the whole
of life without any contact with a Gentile. The pedlars, the inn-
keepers, the travelling merchants dealing in grain, timber or other

144

local products naturally had business contacts with Gentiles. But except for business they would live entirely apart from their clients. They never dreamed of partaking of the smallest Gentile hospitality ; and no Gentile would ever enter Jewish houses.

Geographically it was, of course, just ' life in the diaspora.' But in fact the definition is almost misleading. It could rather be said that, in culture and religion, the land of Israel had been transferred to Eastern Europe. Throughout the region Jews formed over ten per cent of the population. This may sound a small percentage, even though it is larger than would have been known in any medieval Western European area, and, I suspect, larger than their percentage in the western caliphate. But that ten per cent did not mean that nine Gentiles lived around each Jew. Far from it. The immense majority of the Gentiles were peasants, living in villages where there were no Jews or possibly just one Jewish inn-keeper and one trader. The Jews lived in the market towns and in the cities. In the former they might form up to ninety-five per cent of the population, and in the latter over fifty per cent. In either case their units of residence were large enough to give an impression of an all-embracing Jewishness unique in diaspora history.

To the fact of concentration must be added another. They were surrounded, not by the keen minds of Islamic scholars and poets, or Christian theologians, but by the most primitive inhabitants of Europe where landowners were often illiterate, and where the peasantry had a standard of life hardly higher than that of their animals. Even in the towns and cities the standard of general culture was extremely low. There was nothing to tempt a Jew to be anything other than Jewish, or to seek cultural interests outside his own circle.

In this all-embracing Jewish environment there was developed a peculiar culture. Its language was Yiddish, liberally sprinkled with Hebrew words, its folk-lore was Jewish, but perhaps somewhat sprinkled with beliefs from the Gentile world around, its customs had their origin in rabbinic teaching, and were universally accepted as authoritative in every department of life, its dress was peculiar to Jews ; and it was as completely a ' Jewish ' life as any Jew could hope to live in the land of Israel itself.

It developed two typical forms of religious expression, both the product of a life which, if warm and satisfying in many respects, was also narrow, traditional, and unexciting. On the one hand rabbinism became increasingly a form of pure intellectual escapism, since the endless repetition of a narrow round of life left almost no real problems asking for new solutions, and introduced to successive generations almost no new intellectual ideas which could promote independent thought. It developed the characteristic activity of *pilpul*. But pilpul was, after all, a form of intellectual cross-word puzzle ; and could not appeal to all the members of a population whose intellectual standards could not but tend to fall amidst the environing stagnation. Hence there arose an extraordinary popular movement, squarely based on an emotional appeal, despising, or at least ignoring, the long intellectual tradition in Jewish life, and in the eighteenth century it swept through the Jewish population of Eastern Europe like a forest fire.

That movement was Chassidism ; and though we know a good deal about it today, it still presents many puzzles which (so far as I know) have not been scientifically examined. That the founder of the movement, the Baal Shem Tob, *the Besht,* would have been judged a saint by the standards of any religion is commonly accepted. But before the end of the eighteenth century it had developed hereditary dynasties of Zaddikim, wonder-working rabbis who were regarded almost as incarnations of the Divine. How such an extravagant conception as a kind of hereditary priesthood came to be accepted still appears a mystery. There had been nothing like it in Jewish life since the Patriarchate ended in the fifth century and the shadowy house of David disappeared a few hundred years later. What is just as surprising is that, while, as any one would expect, it produced a fine crop of charlatans, it also produced a very large number of men of profound spiritual insight and real gifts of spiritual leadership. Chassidism makes itself more difficult for the outsider to understand by also having developed a peculiar form of literature. A systematic account of its doctrines is unobtainable, because no such system existed. Some Zaddikim were relatively orthodox in their acceptance of Talmudic teaching ; some were, from the traditional Jewish standpoint, ignorant men. But their characteristic literary expression was the parable, the short story with a moral, the pithy saying, the unexpected paradox. In this easily memorable form of literature Chassidism excelled.

The basis of all Chassidic teaching was the conception that at the centre of religion was joy ; worship should be founded on and express joy ; social life and meeting should be filled with joy. And the source of that joy should be the realisation of the indwelling presence of God, of which the Zaddik was the supreme expression. God dwelt in all things, but in the Zaddik above all. Hence the immense reverence with which they were treated, the numerous court with which they were surrounded, the parade which was made whenever they travelled, or when they summoned their followers to particular celebrations.

Such a religion was admirably calculated to counter the gloom of the long northern winter, the primitive poverty in which most Jews lived, the narrowness and overcrowding of their homes, and the external restrictions of their existence. It possessed a highly developed technique for producing ecstasy, and there is no doubt that the Chassid in such moments believed himself to achieve that union with the divine which is the objective of the highest mysticism. But it had incorporated too many curious superstitions, it was too emotional and illogical, to survive the searchlights of a scientific age.

The life of eastern Jewry has been described, affectionately or mockingly, in innumerable Jewish novels ; it has been analysed and set down by two American anthropologists, Mark Zborowski and Elizabeth Herzog,[1] with loving skill, and it is no part of my purpose here to describe it again. My interest in it lies in two things : the curious way in which its exclusion of the outside world made it, not a series of diaspora communities but a single ' displaced land of Israel,' and the extent to which it was the nursery for contemporary Jewish life in most of its more important aspects.

To the statement that it was a single ' displaced land of Israel ' one important qualification must be made. The essential feature of Jewish life in Israel, as already suggested, is its power of communicating fresh vitality to the Jewish people. But this Eastern European world was bound inevitably by the conditions of its life to a steady but inescapable decay. If Toynbee be right in his famous evocation of civilisation from the interplay of challenge and response, it can be put in the form of saying that neither from outside nor from within was there that challenge which could lead to new and creative forms of expression. Repelled by the Gentile life on its immediate horizon, and finding complete satisfaction in the maintenance and elaboration of ancient traditions, or in the escapism of Chassidism, it ignored the new world which was arising, for both Jew and

1 *Life is With People*, International Universities Press, New York, 1952.

Gentile, beyond those immediate horizons ; and when Jews came into contact with the fresh and exciting opportunities which that new world offered, it was bound to crumble. Even if it had not perished in the death factories of Hitler, it was already being undermined from every side by the materialism, the impatience, and the economic pressure of the twentieth century, both Jewish and Gentile.

Nevertheless, before its departure from the scene, it had handed on the torch ; and though its own Jewish life might have become distorted and even degraded by the barren verbosity of pilpul, or the emotional extravagence of Chassidic revivalism, yet what it handed on was authentically Jewish, and entitles it to its honoured place in the transmission of the Jewish inheritance. For from the children of these eastern ghettoes came both the intellectual and moral vigour of the diaspora Jewry of the western world of the nineteenth and twentieth centuries, and the founders and builders of the Jewish state.

The immense majority of the Eastern European Jews who entered the western universities after their doors had been opened by emancipation turned their backs with relief, and even with contempt, on the religious practices and beliefs of their families and ancestors. They saw in them nothing but narrow and arid legalism, outworn theology, and medieval caperings ; and they contrasted them with the wide open horizons, the adventurous intellectual freedom, the political opportunities of the west as though there could be no possible question as to which was the more desirable world. In many ways, of course, there was no comparison. The new world had innumerable possibilities closed to the old ; it accepted vast responsibilities for knowledge and for conduct which the old patterned life had smothered under a closely woven web of custom. But these emigrants from a forgotten Middle Ages brought with them something infinitely precious, something more highly prized in the world which they had left than in the world which they had entered. They brought with them a passionate sense of justice and mutual responsibility which was wholly Jewish ; and which had never been completely suffocated under the mass of custom which might have appeared to cover it. In the western world they threw themselves into every liberal and radical movement of the nineteenth century, political, medical, and educational. Their place in the history of socialism has already been discussed. But even that is not all. Pilpul may appear an entirely arid perversion of the original

148

intention of the rabbis who framed the world of the Mishna and the Talmud. But those who came from a world of pilpul to a world in which acute analysis opened the doors to continual scientific discovery seem to have been well trained for the transition, if one may judge by the number who distinguished themselves in the world of chemistry, physics, economics, psychology, and many other fields of research.

This was one side of the contribution of the eastern ghettoes. It is an example of that feeding out into the Gentile world which is a recurring motif in Jewish history. But from the Jewish point of view it will seem more important that this strange world which I have called the ' displaced land of Israel ' did, in actual fact, prepare for the return to Israel herself. It is true that the origins of Herzl are obscure, but almost every other leader and thinker of Zionism came from it, from Moses Hess, whose grandfather came from Poland into Germany, to President Weizmann and Mr. Sharett who were born in Russia, and Mr. Ben-Gurion who was born in Poland. And it was within the ghetto itself that the first dreams of liberation took shape under the pens of men like Leo Pinsker and Achad Ha-Am. From Russia and Rumania came the earliest pioneers of land settlement, and the immense majority of all those who made up the Yishuv before the time of the mass immigration of oriental Jews after the establishment of the state.

There remains that third characteristic of diaspora life. It feeds out into the Gentile world, it feeds inwards into the heart of Israel, and it draws from its Gentile environment fresh experience to incorporate into Jewish life. This also has been done. Not only the majority of those Jews who compose the western communities, but the organisations which they have made typical of modern Jewish life, are both of Eastern European origin. I remember before the war hearing the report of an ' international ' Jewish student conference which had just been held, I think in Belgium. I was told that the delegates had come from eighteen different countries. I was at that time seeking to build up the connections of International Student Service with the Jewish student organisations of different countries, so I asked to see the list. I saw it, and it did not help me ; for every one of the eighteen different Jewries was ' represented ' by an exiled Polish Jewish student—and with these exiles I was already in contact!

Of Eastern European origin, and presenting too often the face

149

of the now defunct Eastern European parliamentary democracy, with its multiplicity of parties, its violence of division, its inability to understand the nature or necessity of compromise, and its tendency to protest against any one and everything on the slightest provocation, is the structure alike of the World Zionist Organisation (and so the Knesset of Israel) and the World Jewish Congress. Both grew up at the same time as eastern nationalism, and though it is superficial to deduce from that that they are merely Jewish copies of Gentile nationalist movements with no roots in Jewish history. they adopted the forms and behaviour familiar in their Eastern European environment. Even the hideous growth of terrorism in Israel has its counterpart in experience in Eastern Europe, as *The Revolt,* by Menachem Begin, makes clear.

On the surface the world of Yiddishkeit is dead ; even Yiddish itself can scarcely hope to survive, for a people cannot be expected to be at home in three languages, and Hebrew and English are indispensable to an educated Jew. The characterisic forms of Chassidism would need to be completely transformed if it is, as men like Martin Buber and other scholars wistfully desire, to make a contribution to Jewish religious life tomorrow. Nothing that reminds directly of that world which perished with Hitler's fires is likely to be visible to the ordinary Jew of tomorrow. And yet it created almost every aspect of the world in which he will live ; and without its loyalty to the Jewish tradition he would scarcely know that he was a Jew.

CHAPTER XV

The Religious Issue in Contemporary Jewry

THAT which was common to the long-drawn conflict of the Middle Ages and to the world apart of Eastern European Jewry was the recognition by all Jews that Jewry was a society based on a religious foundation. The modern conception of a nation had not been born ; neither Christendom nor Islam knew of such a thing as ' the secular state.' In none of the three societies were ordinary men necessarily more virtuous or more humane than they are today. In fact it is probable that the reverse is true ; but the relevance of religion to life was nowhere a matter of controversy ; and there was this important distinction that a man who lived an evil life knew that by the standards of his society it *was* an evil life. He might continue in his evil ways ; but to cope with his case Christianity, if not Judaism, evolved the displeasing formula of the ' death-bed conversion.'

Today all that is changed ; but I have made no secret in previous pages of my belief in the relevance of religion, and particularly of the necessity laid by facts on Israel that she found her politics openly on a basis of morality. And equally I have maintained that, however it be interpreted, the secure basis for permanence in the diaspora is the recognition of the religious element in Jewish separateness and survival. I would claim, then, that no writer on the contemporary Jewish scene can be said honestly to have faced the facts if he evades the religious issue. But if, as in the present case, the writer is a Christian, some word of explanation is not out of place. In all that I have written about Judaism I have never concealed the fact that I write from a Christian standpoint. But I have also made it clear that I write from the standpoint of one who does not accept the traditional missionary attitude of the Churches as being either right or relevant to the issue between the two faiths. In so far as the ' Old Testament ' and the Sinaitic revelation are concerned I believe the rabbinic understanding of Torah and their

151

doctrine of continuous interpretation to be true ; and I believe the Sinaitic revelation to be still valid, in spite of the emergence of the Christian Church. All this I have already put forward at various times, and particularly in a book, *God at Work,* which was published in 1952.

We are no longer living in a period in which there is a flat opposition between religion and a materialistic or deterministic attitude to the universe. There is, of course, a great deal of materialism today, but it is no longer, outside Marxist circles, the dominant philosophy of the scientist and the humanist. Today the diagnoses of openly religious thinkers like Berdayeff, Buber, or Maritain are widely read, and their opinions quoted with respect, by those who would certainly claim themselves as agnostic, if not atheist. Moreover, the very gravity of the world position, and the extent to which the scientific humanist with his discoveries is responsible for that gravity, are slowly inducing in the scientific mind a new humility, and among religious people a recognition of the immensity of their failure to make valid their religious claims in the sphere which has now become the most determinant of our future, the sphere of social and political activities. The gulf between the religious man and the scientific humanist may still be deep ; but in many places at least it has become much narrower. When the scientist asks that we align ourselves with the evolving process of the universe, and warns us that if we fail to do so we shall destroy our civilisation and possibly humanity itself, he is not speaking a very different language from the religious Christian or Jew who asks that we co-operate with a purpose which is revealed in history, and that if we do not we shall perish. Intellectually the two statements differ only in the fact that the religious Jew or Christian, by using the terms ' co-operate ' and ' purpose ' affirms the existence of a ' Thou ' who responds to his ' I.' He accepts an evolving process because he sees a God at work in history. But if the intellectual difference is slight, the difference in terms of consequence is great, and it is there that the gulf exists. For the humanist leaves man unaided to achieve this alignment ; and, in spite of all his past failures to do so, believes that he can achieve it. The religious Jew or Christian believes that man is asked to co-operate with One more powerful and more understanding than himself.

In any other circumstances, if a man who knew that he was facing an exceedingly difficult task were to be offered the co-operation of a power claimed to be greater than his own, and vitally concerned with his success, he would leap to accept the offer Why then does the scientific humanist refuse even to experiment with what the Church and Synagogue offer ? Here is the crux of the situation. And the answer is tragically clear, and equally applicable to both religions. At the superficial level the scientist can point to the failure of Church and Synagogue (especially of the former, for the Synagogue represents but a small minority in western society) to implement their claims in action. But at a much deeper level the scientist can claim that the expressed views of the two religions exhibit to them a set of values and a series af affirmations which they must so decisively reject that what is left is largely irrelevant both to what they have discovered of the nature of the universe, and to what they understand of the nature of man and his institutions. The co-operation which is offered is, therefore, no real co-operation.

I have said elsewhere that, in so far as Christianity is concerned, the scientists are far more justified in their attitude than the Churches, and that there can be no fruitful co-operation between the two until the Churches have faced the need for a much deeper theological rethinking of their position than they have yet undertaken. But here I am concerned with Judaism, and am bound to say that there is no field in which the epigram is truer that ' Jews are just like other people, only more so.' For the dilemma affects both orthodox and progressive Judaism more violently than it does the Churches. In the nineteenth century, when Darwinism and its offshoots provided the main field of conflict, this was not true, and Judaism rallied more quickly than did Christianity. But in the twentieth century the situation has radically altered.

Antisemites have constantly reviled the Jews for being parasites. In the fields in which the charge is usually made it is almost wholly untrue, and usually it is meaningless. But there is one field in which Jewry can be called parasitic—that of theology. Apart from its beginnings, almost the whole development of rabbinic Judaism took place within the monotheistic environment which was provided for it by Christendom or Islam. Judaism could accept monotheism from that environment, and found no need to develop its own arguments in favour of it. To say that Judaism has no theology does not mean that Jews who accept their religion are uncertain whether it demands belief in one God or not. What is meant is that in seeking to speak to those Jews who do not accept their religion, the religious Jews, both orthodox and progressive, are hampered by the fact that the one presents a complex practice and the other noble ethical principles which have their sanction in the existence of God ; but if the unbeliever denies that such a God exists, their arguments are left suspended in mid-air. It is not a case today of producing a Jewish twentieth-century version of ' Paley's Evidences of Christianity.' One may readily accept today that it is impossible to *prove* in a scientific way that God exists. But it is still possible to show that it is *reasonable* to believe in a God, that such a belief is not necessarily in conflict with our scientific knowledge ; and it is also profitable to discuss, in relation to both science and contemporary philosophy, the divine nature and our means of apprehending it. It is possible to examine the prophetic and rabbinic conceptions of the divine attributes in such a way that a sceptic or a doubter can see their relation both to the divine nature and the divine activity. All these issues, and many more, are the common subjects of Christian religious literature ; in Jewish literature they are extremely rare.

Jewish religious leaders, and the Jewish religious colleges, still assume that they are living in the world in which it was axiomatic that there was a God, that He was One, and that He was at work in history. Within this field provided for them, Jews interested themselves in the nature of His activities and of the human response to them. They found no need to reaffirm, or to strengthen, the foundation on which such interests ultimately rested, that a God *did* exist, and that He *was* concerned with human life and history. With the exception of the medieval Jewish philosophers working within the Muslim-Arab culture, they regarded such speculations as unnecessary ; and even where they admitted such a field of interest to be desirable, they held it to be no concern of religion. The position could not be better put than it is by Rabbi Dr. Epstein, Principal of Jews' College, London:

> God is a reality ; how exactly He is to be apprehended is a philosophic, not a religious problem, which, strictly speaking does not concern Judaism. The unity of God is axiomatic ; and that excludes whatever tends to obscure the sublime conception of God as the One and Only Being ; the dualism of the Parsee, the demiurge of the Gnostics, the trinitarianism of the Christian. But precise intellectual definition is a task left to philosophy. Judaism affirms the divine attributes of Mercy, Justice, and Love without attempting to explain the relation

154

of the attributes to the being of God. Revelation is a fact ; yet the *modus operandi* of this divine communication with man does not trouble Judaism.[1]

When I was in Palestine in 1946, I found it quite commonly assumed that not to believe in all the *mitzvoth* as proclaimed by the orthodox was automatically not to believe in the existence of God. Atheism was held to be an inevitable concomitant of non-acceptance of orthodoxy, and the best alternative offered was some vague conception of ' the Holy,' as proclaimed by a German theologian, Professor Otto, in the '20s. The idea of God was not rejected on philosophic grounds, or in terms of an alternative philosophy, and this was the inevitable consequence of the fact that it was not presented in these terms by those who professed to be religious. In America, a few months later, I found a comparable situation among the progressive Jews. If we read the work of such liberal Jewish thinkers as Claude Montefiore, Israel Mattuck, or Leo Baeck, we shall find a theological emphasis running all through their books. But neither in England nor on the Continent are there facilities for training liberal rabbis. The great liberal seminaries are in the United States, and it would be difficult to detect any adequate theological training in the curricula of the now united Hebrew Union College and The Jewish Institute of Religion. That there is a growing realisation of this lack is suggested by the publication of such books as *The Meaning of God in Modern Jewish Religion*, by Mordecai Kaplan,[2] *The Way to God*, by Maxwell Silver,[3] *Judaism and Modern Man*, by Will Herberg,[4] or *Man is not Alone*, by Abraham Joshua Heschel[5] ; but the output of such books is small and, except in the last, there is still a tentative note in them which shows the extent to which their authors have felt themselves to be pioneers.

In Israel itself the position is even more serious ; for there the orthodox minority is claiming for itself an exclusive prerogative which not even the Roman Catholic Church claims in countries in which it is itself a minority among other Christian bodies. It recognises no place among Jews for those who believe in God but cannot accept its interpretations of His demands upon men. It is one of the curious anomalies of the present situation that almost

1 *Judaism*, by Rabbi I. Epstein, B.A., Ph.D., D. Litt. Epworth Press, 1939.
2 Behrman's Jewish Book House, New York, 1937.
3 Philosophical Library, New York, 1950.
4 Farrar, Strauss, and Young, New York, 1951.
5 Jewish Publication Society of America, 1951.

every outstanding leader of the Zionist Organisation of America has been a reform rabbi ; and yet there is no place for any kind of progressive Judaism in Israel. On the day on which this was written I read a statement from the President of the Union of American Hebrew Congregations (the association of progressive synagogues) admitting that the Union had, as yet, no intention of trying to establish progressive congregations in Israel, though it was exploring the situation. This would be more satisfactory if it were not certain that there are many Israelis, especially perhaps among those who have come from Germany or western countries, who are not atheists, but who cannot accept the discipline of orthodoxy. It is, I believe, true that it would be impossible simply to copy the forms of English or American liberalism in Israel. They are forms adapted to the life in which they have organically arisen ; and it would be no help for the progressives to copy the mistake of the orthodox in failing to distinguish between Israel and the diaspora. But they are not even free to evolve and organise their own forms of worship, or to build up their own synagogues, and for these to enjoy the same recognition by the state as is given to the orthodox.

I believe that the basic reasons for the present situation are to be found, as I have just said, in the failure of the orthodox Jews of Israel to realise either the extent to which the establishment of a state of Israel involved reversion to pre-mishnaic conditions, or the historical fact that rabbinic Judaism, as it has been handed down in the orthodox tradition, was a product of the artificial life, not merely of the diaspora, but of the ghetto.

In the days before the fall of Jerusalem there had always been many simultaneous interpretations of the Jewish religion ; and even if there were bitter controversies between their various adherents, there was no period in which any single interpretation claimed and exercised exclusive sway over Jewish religious life. Pharisees, Sadducees, Essenes, Zealots, and others existed side by side. Even Jewish Christians had a place within the synagogue during the first fifty years of Christian history. A single normative Judaism came into existence only after Jewish independence had been lost. It was a substitute for the more obvious and normal link of political identity, and as such preserved both Jewry and Judaism. But the paramount need for religious unity, and ultimately uniformity, rested only on this unique situation, and was only justified by it. Moreover, the uniformity had already ceased to exist a hundred years before Israel was re-established. Within the Jewish religion there had again grown up differing interpretations and practices, all of which were identifiable from outside as being 'Jewish.' I find no evidence that when the state was declared the orthodox minority ever considered seriously the question as to what claims they were normally entitled to make in regard to the very large number of Jews who were not orthodox. It was assumed from the beginning that they should seek to force them, at any rate, to an external conformity. In consequence they started their life within the new state not by an appeal to those who accepted their authority to observe, under these new and glorious conditions, an even stricter loyalty to their tradition, but by pressure in the political field to enforce upon the whole country observances which had a spiritual significance only for a minority, and which, to the rest, were a burden without spiritual value.

The issue of the relation of orthodoxy to other religious interpretations of Judaism and Jewish history could not arise during the period in which orthodox Judaism had obtained its monopoly of interpretation. There was consequently no obvious authority to which to turn for an insight into this fundamental problem. But it is reasonable to argue that the position would be very different today had the orthodox postponed any political pressure until they had cleared their own minds as to the way in which they should seek to win those outside their ranks.

Such an argument brings to the front the second failure, the non-recognition of the extent to which orthodoxy had itself become a religion of the diaspora and the ghetto.

The multiplication of *mitzvoth* rested on two foundations, the need to 'make a fence about the Torah,' and, historically, the gradual diminution of the fields in which new and independent action remained possible to a Jewish community. Minds which intellectually were capable of debating the major political and social issues of their day were restricted in their practical life to the problems of a tiny and narrow existence. Inevitably they sought an outlet in the ever more detailed elaboration of the sphere which was still open to them. Like a miniaturist with but a tiny piece of parchment, they delighted to cover every portion of the available surface with the most exquisite and detailed work. From the right motive of seeking action in conformity with the will of God for every detail of daily life, they became so concerned with the details that these

157

came to assume a wholly disproportionate place when suddenly the available field of activity was widened to cover the whole life of a nation. It is legitimate to blame Christian persecution and intolerance for the extent to which orthodoxy had lost its suppleness and its wide horizons ; but the blame does not help to solve the practical problem created when a scale of religious activity evolved over centuries for the restricted existence of a ghetto is suddenly forced by political pressure on the life of a free nation.

The problem has been made more acute, and the situation more bitter, by the fact that the scale of orthodox interests has left them voiceless on the major moral issues confronting Israel—and they are many. I cannot think of any action of the orthodox *bloc* in the Knesset which recalled the moral grandeur or political realism of the prophets of ancient Israel. It would be difficult, I believe, to find anything to distinguish the political manœuvres of that *bloc* from the manœuvres of any other group which claimed no such high sanction for its appetite for power.

The same consequences have followed the fact that the long centuries of ghetto life imposed a canon on interpretation. The whole dynamic conception of a law perpetually reinterpreted in accordance with the needs of successive generations foundered amid the shoals of attributing permanently continuing authority to past interpretations, and to methods of interpretation, both of which belonged to a period which had irrevocably passed, not indeed with the establishment of a state of Israel, but a hundred and fifty years earlier with the disappearance of the ghetto. The discussions which took place about the observance of a sabbatical year illustrate the point. No reproach can be levelled against the rabbis who originally evolved such casuistry as fictitious sales, and declarations which were in themselves untrue, but which established a truth. To us they appear trickery, but in the knowledge and the needs of their times they had no alternatives available ; and indeed every field of human knowledge makes use to some extent or other of fanciful assumptions as temporary bases for the establishment of desirable deductions. But orthodoxy has refused to change its method, long after it has not merely ceased to bring positive results, but actually brings the ends involved themselves into disrepute. The issue was whether the fields of the orthodox kibbutzim should be cultivated in the sabbatical year, or whether in accordance with Leviticus xxv they should be allowed to lie fallow ; and for those orthodox who did not cultivate fields, whether they could eat of the produce of such fields. The Levitical injunction applied, of course, to land cultivated by and owned by Israelis ; and, as the need to grow the maximum food in Israel was obvious to all, two suggestions were put forward. In the previous sabbatical years before the declaration of the state the law had been evaded by a fictitious sale of the land to an Arab. This would now be a somewhat delicate proposal. The alternative proposed was to declare the land, again by a fictitious declaration, to be ownerless. Neither solution could win the slightest respect by its moral grandeur ; and the parallel demand of those who did not themselves cultivate land that food should be imported for them, at a time when Israel was desperately short of all foreign currencies, was equally unlikely to inspire admiration.

There is a saying about justice which is always communicated to newly appointed magistrates in England. They are told that it is the task of the court not merely to do justice, but so to carry out their functions that justice *is seen to be done*. It is not illegitimate to ask the same of religion ; for the character of God Himself is brought into disrepute if He is claimed to be the sanction for legal trickery or selfish pietism. The orthodox socialists came nearer to a spiritual approach in suggesting that the year should be used for intensive study of Judaism and the strengthening of Jewish values ; but they also were involved in the casuistry described above.

It is a serious matter when a method of argument is given a sanctity which cannot be recognised or accepted by anyone except those who use it ; it is more serious still when it is impossible to take the line that a group indulging in such activities is of no importance. But such is the situation both politically and spiritually. The nature of Judaism is such that there is bound to be political activity on the part of the religious element in the population ; for Judaism has no tradition of pietistic quietism such as allowed Lutherans so long to evade political action, or of other worldly asceticism such as motivated much of Christian monasticism.

That, however, is not all. It is not merely the ' nuisance value ' of the orthodox *bloc* which is involved, but something much deeper. Judaism was described in an earlier chapter as pre-eminently the religion of the ' know-how ' ; and when reform movements substi-tuted for these detailed ordinances for conduct the proclamation of lofty principles, they only emasculated the Jewish faith.

To reword a famous declaration, the only thing which any Jew, who is not completely an atheist, can say to the orthodox is: 'I hate the rules of life which you proclaim, but I will fight to the death for the belief that it is your right and duty to proclaim rules of life.'

To an historian the peculiar tragedy of the present situation is emphasised by the contrast between the artificial and unnatural life deduced by orthodoxy today from its rabbinic inheritance, and the rabbinic Judaism discovered by Christian scholars as soon as thought freed itself from the shackles of the medieval tradition. To Jean Bodin early in the sixteenth century the rabbinic religion was the most perfect achievement of the reasonable society based on natural law ; and the theme that Judaism showed natural law in action is repeated again and again in succeeding centuries. John Selden in his studies of the Jewish conception of the law court, Surenhuis with his vast Talmudic learning, Tolland and the early deists, all in different ways expressed their enthusiasm for a religion which so admirably met man's natural needs, and which exemplified so realistic an approach to life.

A profound change is discoverable in the post-emancipation nineteenth century. Contact with contemporary orthodoxy created no enthusiasm, and progressive Jewish writers were almost as loud in their condemnation as were Christian Hebraists. Interest on the part of both shifted from ' the Law ' to the prophets ; and the latter were seen, not as interpreters of Torah, but as rebels against a legalistic religion. That the prophetic voice needed to be recovered could be easily admitted ; but in the change of interest the essential Jewish link between principles and practice was too often lost ; for both progressive Jews and Christians saw Jewish practice only in terms of contemporary orthodox obscurantism. Today there is a widespread recognition among progressive Jews that the nineteenth-century enthusiasm for reform often went too far ; and that valuable elements were too easily abandoned. But if one studies such movements as Reconstructionism, it would seem that the adjustments which are proposed as remedies are largely in the direction of the restoration of the warmth and colour of ceremony. That in itself is good. But there is an uncomfortable warning available in the story of the Catholic revival of the nineteenth century in the Church of England. Undoubtedly that movement restored both colour and seemliness to Anglican services ; but the Anglo-Catholic movement itself became increasingly medievalist, and in recent decades has lost much of the social enthusiasm which marked its earlier days.

The whole of Jewish history marks out one clear line along which Judaism can recover its vitality ; the line of practice in the concrete realities of everyday life. It is not indulging in paradox to say that it is for this reason that there is a paramount need for Judaism to recover a theological interest, and to develop its own positive doctrine of God. For it is only by relating directly each development of the orthodox tradition to a dynamic picture of a Creator who desires such practice that the gold in orthodoxy can be separated from the dross, and that its true development can be recovered. Only a living theology can cut through the tangled web of methods of interpretation, rabbinic authority, precedent, and casuistry by confronting each proposed result, in true prophetic spirit, with the will of a God who asks of men that they should do justice, love mercy, and walk humbly with Him.

Any statement that Judaism needs a theology, and a theology resting on its own authentically Jewish foundations and speaking with authority to the scientific humanists of our day, brings the diaspora back at once into the centre of the picture. For the task is beyond the strength, and to a large extent, even the understanding of the religious Jew of the land of Israel. For he has only secondary and indirect contact with the centres in which contemporary scientific humanism is expressing its philosophy and issuing its challenge. It is British and American Jewry which can alone share the main burden of this new interpretation, at any rate today. Tomorrow new factors may enter the picture. But at present it is in Europe and America that scientists are speaking in those terms of the ' formative process ' with which we should ' align ' ourselves which offer both a challenge and an opportunity to religious thought.

But the diaspora comes into the picture in another, and more permanent, manner also. I have called Judaism a religion of the ' know-how ' ; and the whole strength of rabbinic development has lain in its ability to see great moral principles in terms of actual practical programmes. It is because of this factor that it was able so creatively to mould Jewish life in the diaspora ; and it was out of this background that emancipated Jews in the nineteenth century made their astonishing contribution to Western European and American life, entering with enthusiasm into all schemes for political reform and for improvement in educational, medical, and social services. But there was a fundamental distinction between this life of a free Jewry, and the life of the ghetto. In the ghetto it was possible for a Jewish community to ensure that all its members accepted the same interpretation and· directive in matters of practical conduct. Norms could be established in business and social relationships and they could be given very strong sanctions. This was not possible after emancipation, when the field of activity was immensely widened, and the traditional authority of the rabbi or the codes correspondingly weakened. A ghetto rabbi had at his finger tips the appropriate answer to any of the normal questions which could arise in a ghetto community. He knew what the codes demanded in business, in education, or in health, and his verdicts were normally accepted or at least respected. He could expect to receive no such acceptance or respect when the issues involved in Jewish behaviour covered all the political, business, and social relationships of a modern nation, fields in which he usually knew less than many of his congregants. He could not lay down how a loyal Jew was to vote, what party he could or could not join, or how he should develop his business ; and the same was true of many other fields. In consequence his authority became ' ecclesiastical ' ; its area of activity was sharply distinguished from the ' secular ' ; and his exhortations had to deal in generalisations about righteousness, justice, and mercy, instead of showing specifically how these applied to a given situation. Now the same situation exists also in Israel, where the orthodox community, from its degenerate extremists to its keen and forward-looking socialists, is in the same dilemma. That the rabbi should develop a sense of pastoral responsibility for the welfare of his flock was, I believe, a right development once a Jewish community became a voluntary religious congregation. That the rabbi should have also become a professional ecclesiastic on the Christian model involved a much more radical departure from the whole Jewish tradition, and its consequences seem to be lamentable. For Christianity by its very nature must include a professional ' ministry of the word and sacraments ' ; but Judaism contains no such need. The rabbinical academies of the ancient and medieval world included Jews who were professionally competent in every occupation open to the Jewish community ; the sanhedrin which is so often proposed as a solution of the problems created by the emergence of Israel would not. It would consist of professional ecclesiastics.

Israel and the diaspora, then, stand side by side confronting this new dilemma, and with equal needs they face the problem of recovering an autonomous theology which will, in turn, reveal a new path to be followed in the search for the kind of practical directives which might be valid for contemporary Jewish life. I doubt whether theological interest will, or should, ever occupy the same place in Jewish that it has always occupied in Christian interest. I doubt whether there will ever be a ' systematic ' Jewish theology. But, whatever it is, it needs to be autonomously Jewish ; for the easy disclaimers of responsibility for intellectual examination which are expressed in the quotation on an earlier page are no longer adequate. There is no longer a monotheistic environment provided by the non-Jewish world on which Jewry can feed.

This need covers the whole of Jewish religious life ; for if it evidently brings into a single picture the orthodox of Israel and the diaspora, it also brings into a single picture both orthodox and progressive Judaism. Nor is this all ; for in both capacities it brings in the two strains of post-emancipation Jewish history which have so far been sharply divided between ' assimilationist ' and ' nationalist ' or Zionist. An understanding of the ' know-how ' in the diaspora will be feeble and one-sided if it does not make itself relevant to the problem of those who fully accept their position as free minorities within a non-Jewish society ; and, on the other hand, this whole section of Jewry will be lost if it is not given an autonomous religious faith which will provide a core and centre to its communal existence.

It is a vast programme of activity which has been no more than signposted in this chapter. To the timorous and the blinkered it could appear alternatively terrifying or unnecessary. But I am convinced that such will be the exceptions among the Jewish people, and that in the decades to come more will see it as a supreme adventure, an adventure which in its scope and scale justifies the long centuries of waiting, and is a worthy memorial to the tragedies through which this generation of Jewry has passed.

163

CHAPTER XVI

The Diaspora and Israel

IT will be evident to anyone who has read the previous pages how inextricably interwoven in Jewish history are the strands of the diaspora and Israel. This interweaving is an inevitable consequence of the paradox of universalism and separatism at the birth of the Jewish people before Mount Sinai, or even earlier at the call of Abraham. In a previous work I spoke of the history of the Jews as exhibiting ' a combination of non-cosmopolitan universalism and non-exclusive particularism.' It is Israel which prevents the universalism from degenerating into cosmopolitanism ; it is the diaspora which saves Israel from becoming arrogant or parochial in her particularism.

It is perfectly true today that the diaspora is passing through a difficult time. Those who desire to prophesy its inevitable disruption can, quite truly, point to intermarriage, to reduced synagogue attendance, to the passage of Jews from any distinctive Jewish observance to the cultural lumpen-proletariat of our time. But in all this it would be just as easy to point to the disruption of many non-Jewish cultural associations. There are fifty million Englishmen in England, but it is easy to draw a picture of their Englishry being steadily undermined by American films, ' comics ' and a dozen other signs of American penetration, and to foresee the passing of all that we knew as England. In any of the Churches the same distressing picture could be drawn—diminished church attendance, intermarriage with no care as to whether the children are given any precise religious education, a loss of distinctively Christian virtues.

In other words, Jews are in no different position from any other of the distinct cultural or cultural-religious communities of which the world has been thus far composed ; and there is no reason why our attitude to the future consequences of the present situation should differ in dealing with the Jewish aspects of the question. If we believe that all that England once stood for, all that the Church of England stands for, is doomed to pass, through its

164

inability ever to stand up to the evil trends of the cinema, the contemporary materialism or disillusion, and so on, then let us, by all means, believe the same of the Jews. But, if this is indeed the future for the diaspora communities, it will be exactly the same for Israel. There is no law by which the one will be saved and the other perish. If this is to be the future, there will be nothing to choose between Americans who remember from time to time that once they were Jews, and Levantines who also remember that once upon a time they were Jews. The process of disintegration may take one or two generations longer. That is the only possible difference. But I do not think that anyone with an historical sense would accept the evidence of a couple of generations as sufficing to disprove the previous evidence of centuries, indeed millennia. I do not believe that either nations or religions are doomed to disappear.

It may be argued that the trend ever since emancipation has been towards disintegration. This is perfectly true ; and the more complete the emancipation, the faster the signs of disintegration emerged. But there also emerged, spontaneously and simultaneously out of the total Jewish situation, a demand that an opportunity be created for a Jew simply to be a Jew, without any hyphen of English-Jew, American-Jew, and so on. In other words, emancipation gave birth not merely to assimilation but also to Zionism ; and the attempt to condemn Zionism, or such manifestations as the World Jewish Congress, on the grounds that they arose merely out of Jews aping the insurgent nationalism of the Gentiles, ignores this fact. The forms which they have taken were largely aped from the Gentiles, and I have already expressed, in a number of passages, my dislike for the stridency and intolerance of both organisations. I could not do other ; for if I dislike such stridency and intolerance when manifested by Gentiles, there is no alchemy which could make it attractive among Jews.

But, as an historian, I am bound to claim that they were needed, and that they were proper precipitations from the historical situation created by emancipation ; and in fairness it should be added that, when I complain of their ill-manners, I would have to accept their excuse, did they wish to make it, that the Jewish leaders who were more experienced in western ways gave them singularly little help in so framing their activities that they would fit better into the cadres of the highest western decorum. Indeed they did the opposite, and by their constant denigration so raised the temper of mutual discussion within Jewry that everybody began to shout at the top of his voice. The subtle pinpricks and sneers of the well-assimilated western Jews were just as malevolent as the clamour and exaggerations of the nationalists and Zionists. To this must, I believe, be added the sober fact that on every major issue since the First World War the latter have had a more realistic appreciation than the assimilationists of the total world scene within which Jewry had to live.

The nationalists, represented by the American Jewish Congress and the Comité des Délégations Juives at Versailles, were right in their insistence that the one hope for Eastern European Jewry was some kind of corporate protection and recognition, and that merely to attempt to guarantee Jews individually before the law (which appeared enough in the experienced western democracies) would be futile. In fact the minority treaties failed. This was not the fault of Jewry, and in many cases not the fault of the contemporary Gentile majority. The reasons lay deep in Eastern European history. This time it was the Zionists, with whom the nationalists were in complete agreement on the matter, who realised that even the minority treaties at their best could not solve the Jewish question ; and so fought for the full recognition of the implications of the Balfour Declaration, and the full use of the opportunities for Jewish emigration into Palestine.

It was again the nationalists who were first to warn Jewry of the dangers of Hitlerism, often very much against the wishes of the assimilationists, who wished to condemn only the antisemitic element in Hitler's policy, while disinteresting themselves entirely from his attack on democracy. Some readers may still remember this issue being fought out in England over the Mosley agitation in the 'thirties when, in my opinion, the Jewish People's Committee in the East End of London had a wiser appreciation of the threat of the British Union of Fascists than the Board of Deputies—I say this without any wish to condemn the excellent work which the Board did.

In any case it is time now that the battle of words and abuse should come to an end. Eastern European Jewry has perished ; and the emergence of Israel has to be accepted by both sides alike. For the failure or success of Israel will affect both sides alike, just as the failure or success of the diaspora will affect both sides alike.

Once each side would recognise the essential contribution of

166

the other the acerbities of each side should soften, and so the cause of offence created by each side should be removed. It is, perhaps, almost impertinent for a Gentile to labour these points ; but as my reading regularly covers Jewish material reflecting views as far removed from each other as the Agudas Israel and the American Council for Judaism, and as I read all alike as an onlooker and not as a participant, I hope it will be forgiven me.

What then are the contributions of each to the life of Jewry in the diaspora ? I do not think that it is possible to challenge the statement that the core of diaspora life is the synagogue. That which represents the irreducible minimum which justifies the separate existence of Jewry in the eyes of the Gentile majority is the religious distinctiveness of Judaism. Unless we are to revert to the ancient conception of *one State : one Church,* of which all members of the state must be members, we cannot deny the right to separate existence of those whose religious loyalties demand some form of special association. And we should remember that even medieval Europe conceded this to Jews, and medieval Islam to both Jews and Christians. The synagogue is the inescapable core around which Jewish life in the diaspora is built. This, however, cannot be taken to mean that *only* those Jews who sincerely demand recognition as a religious denomination are entitled to justify their distinctiveness while living among a Gentile majority. The Synagogue can no more insist on religious belief among those who call themselves Jews than can the Church of England insist on acceptance of its creed by all who call themselves Englishmen. For, whatever logical arguments can be adduced to justify such an insistence, the plain fact is that it does not correspond to any historical reality. There are very many who think of themselves as Jews, and who are thought of as Jews by their non-Jewish neighbours, who are not Jews by religious belief. There is no valid conception of Jewish life in the diaspora unless it covers their situation. Nevertheless, they cannot dominate it. Jews cannot rest their position in any country on their possession of a separate ' nationality.' The minority treaties failed even in the Eastern European situation to which they might have been thought to be appropriate. They could not possibly be introduced in England or the United States. But there is no reason why around the synagogue should not cluster activities which are not religious, and which reflect ' nationalism ' in its cultural forms.

Nevertheless, it is here that the emergence of the state of Israel and the consequent relationship between Jews in the diaspora and in Israel have caused the most violent divisions and the most bitter conflicts. Jews, as well as antisemites and plain puzzled Gentiles, hear the nationalist claims made and raise the issue of a dual loyalty, and much Zionist propaganda lends support to the anxieties expressed. We can readily agree that, in principle, the whole idea of all loyalties being concentrated into one single knot is untrue to fact and undesirable in conception. It is totalitarian and has no place in a democracy. A peaceful world will be a world in which the tangle of innumerable loyalties is so intimately interwoven with the universal realities of life that they cannot be untangled to align men of one geographical or political area against men of another. But we have not reached that situation yet, and there is a real issue when the claim is made that an American or British citizen, who is a Jew, owes a loyalty to Israel which creates obligations which all other American or British citizens would accept only in relation to America or Britain. The assimilationist is right when he raises his protest against such claims. But that does not settle the issue. For the assimilationist is undoubtedly wrong when he claims that, in fact, Jews are merely members of a religious denomination, like Methodists or Roman Catholics (both are world Churches) and have only the same benevolent interest in Israel that American Roman Catholics might take in the Vatican, or Methodists in the life in other countries of the Methodist Church. Both assimilationist and nationalist will fail to find the right way forward until they accept that, however unfortunate it may be, the Jewish people is a unique people, their position in the diaspora is unique, and Israel as a sovereign state is unique. This uncomfortable uniqueness has also, of course, to be accepted by the Gentile ; but it would help him if Jews themselves had a clear idea of what it involved, in responsibility as well as privilege. For in fact it presents no insoluble problem ; and it would be a happier and richer world if there were more place in it for still more unique relationships.

Where, in diaspora life, has the assimilationist to take on the burden of this uniqueness ? The answer is : in the field of religion, as Judaism interprets the word. Contrasted with the Christian tradition, that which characterises the Jewish tradition throughout its history is its basic denial of a distinction between secular and religious, and its constant overflowing of religious emphases into fields, social, intellectual and ultimately political, where, in actual fact, it would be impossible to discover any distinction between, let us say, a Baptist and a Methodist. Stephen Wise was known and loved in New York, not because he fought against injustice to Jews, but because he hated injustice wherever he saw it. And he was often being more fundamentally Jewish in his battle for causes which had nothing to do with Jews, than when he was denouncing his Jewish opponents on Zionist platforms.

Ever since emancipation Jews have been embarrassed to assert their Jewishness outside the synagogue. The orthodox have converted the Beth Din into an " ecclesiastical court," and the progressives have substituted prophetic generalisations for the extremely concrete social imperatives of Talmudic Judaism. In the long run neither will do. Judaism *is* concerned with the day to day realities of political and social life. Much of the fault undoubtedly lies on the Gentiles who, ever since Clermont Tonnerre asked the Constituent Assembly in the French Revolution *tout accorder aux Juifs comme individus, et tout leur refuser comme nation.* have been ready on the slightest pretext, or on none, to raise the cry that Jews were seeking to be a state within a state, that they were flocking into, or dominating or intriguing in, this or that political party. But it is natural and proper that one political opinion should appeal to more Jews than another, that one line of action should win widespread Jewish support, and another should not, even though no particular Jewish issue be involved on either side. Organisations like the Anti-Defamation League have found that they are concerned with *all* community relations, and not merely with Jews ; and the same experience has happened elsewhere.

For a diaspora community to recover a corporate expression of its social conscience will not be an easy task, nor will it be one which can be undertaken with no regard to the Gentile environment. Where there is organised antisemitism its recovery is rendered doubly difficult. It could well be argued that, at the present moment, all that could be expected of a Jewish community would be not to go on saying the opposite, and denying its Jewish inheritance, as those Jews did who were prepared to accept Hitler, save for his antisemitism. In South Africa, for example, the Jewish community is almost inevitably tongue-tied. If it spoke up against Apartheid, it might only put an argument in the mouths of the nationalists, who would seek to discredit their opponents on the grounds that they were but the instruments of " Jewish Communism." It is a task to be undertaken at the moment in lectures, in books, in discussion groups between Jews and Christians, and the time is not ripe for official pronouncements and corporate action. But at the heart of the issue must be a Jewish longing to express, as Jews, in the community in which they live, the extraordinarily concrete insights of their prophets and rabbis, and to express these openly and corporately as their contribution, as Jews, to the totality of their particular political situation.

The nationalist also needs to take on the burden of Jewish uniqueness, otherwise his interest in world Jewry and in Israel will inevitably degenerate into a dangerous chauvinism. The present moment is dominated by the financial needs of Israel, but this will not be the permanent basis of the relationship.

That Israel needs to absorb such immense sums of money seems to some of the opponents of nationalism evidence of the incapacity of Israel, and of the monstrous exhibitionism of the nationalists. I have not the slightest doubt that some of the money sent to Israel is wasted, as some of the money spent by every country is wasted. No one has ever claimed that the uniqueness of Jewry consists in their capacity to produce a bureaucracy which never makes a mistake. But I doubt if much is wasted ; and it is difficult for anyone living in an old-established country to realise the costs of building a new country at contemporary prices. I can illustrate the problem from my own home. I live in an eight-room house on two acres—eight dunams by Israel measures—of land. I have a two-storey barn as large as the house and a smaller barn. My land is surrounded by a wall. Before my gate runs a first-class road, and the public mains for electric light, water, and telephone. The whole property cost me just over a thousand pounds. The house was built between four and five hundred years ago, the barns are nearly as old, and the land has been cultivated in all probability for a thousand years. By today's prices the money I spent on the whole would not replace the barn. But whether the man who built the house made a profit or loss on it is no longer any concern of mine, what wages were paid to bring my land into cultivation does not affect me. To bring in the electric light, water, and telephone cost me very little. The upkeep of the road, the school, and all the other communal services makes a sizeable charge on the rates, but a mere trifle compared with the cost of making the road, building the school, and so on. To create a similar property today, and to pay my share of linking it by road to the towns and villages north, south, east, and west of Barley, and of installing all the services I enjoy, would certainly cost me between ten and twenty times what I originally paid. Now the previous owner was a small-holder, and he lived on the income he earned from the land. At a cost of a thousand pounds for the whole (actually he paid much less) it was an economic proposition. But by no possible means could he have earned from the property enough to pay for the buildings, and the clearing and fencing of the land, at present prices, let alone enough to pay his share of what it would have cost to create the whole village and its services in one generation. That a billion dollars or more have been absorbed by Israel is not surprising. It is only a beginning. But, at the same time, this extreme financial dependence on the diaspora cannot be the permanently decisive factor in relationships between the two. Its true basis must be sought elsewhere.

Some have actually suggested that the determination to build up a close relationship between Israel and the diaspora through the Zionist Organisation and its special status guaranteed by the Knesset recalls the links created by Nazi Germany with Germans elsewhere ; that it is another kind of fifth column, destructive of loyalty and decency in citizenship. The difference in power between Israel and Nazi Germany is enough to shatter any parallel between the two, and the difference in finance shatters it still further. Nazi Germany poured millions into her German colonies overseas : here it is the exact reverse. It is Israel that needs the millions.

What then is the true basis of relationship ? It is the traditional one unchanged, save by temporary necessity. The diaspora community feeds into the heart of Jewry in Israel the experience, spiritual, cultural, social, or material, which it garners in its life in the Gentile world. Israel feeds back into each diaspora community the same experience digested and transmuted by the values inherent in the Jewish way of life. So long as there is need for extensive financial assistance, and the special work for installing new immigrants with that assistance, so long is there a justification for a special Zionist Organisation having a special relationship with the state of Israel. But the true and permanent relations will be much more flexible, and they will surely need no special organisation. In fact a special organisation would be a liability rather than an asset.

Such a line of argument may seem to have swept too lightly

171

over the permanent political issue. In the world as it stands we have to recognise that situations may arise which will strain severely the loyalty of the Jews. The policy of governments which number within their citizenry Jewish communities may at any time, and for reasons which have nothing to do with antisemitism, turn in directions felt to be disfavourable to Israel. So long as a third world war menaces us, and so long as the hostility of the Arab world to Israel is unabated, this may well happen, in Britain, in the United States, or elsewhere. It is evident that, in their capacity as citizens, Jews will be perfectly entitled to argue and to advocate such alterations or modifications of national policy as seems good to them. There would be nothing shameful or treasonable in their openly avowing their anxiety lest this or that political decision should adversely affect Israel. The essential thing is that they should do it because it is their normal right to do so. The fact that there are unique aspects of Jewry does not mean that all their actions are unique ; and in this interlocked world, there is nothing unique in one or another group of citizens, for reasons which are perfectly valid and reasonable, exercising pressure in one direction or another.

Supposing the decision goes against them ? They are still in exactly the same position as other groups of citizens to whom a similar tragedy might happen. There is only one condition that a free democracy is entitled to demand of those of its citizens who cannot for conscience sake approve the national policy : that what they do they do openly. That is the legitimate demand of loyalty. Did the pacifist, instead of openly refusing service, secretly attempt to sabotage the war effort of his nation, he would rightly forfeit all sympathy, and all protection of the law. After the issue of the 1939 White Paper the Zionists, as well as the Yishuv, openly avowed their refusal to accept it. Their efforts to get immigrants into Israel were secret ; but they did not pretend they were not making them. In 1947 and 1948 British Zionists made no secret of their determination to help the Yishuv in its battle for existence, though the organisation by which British Jews reached the fighting lines were again secret, and could not be otherwise. All such situations are naturally intensely painful. In a perfect world they would not occur. In this world there is unhappily nothing unique in the fact that Jews may individually or corporately find themselves faced with such painful decisions. Naturally I hope it will never happen. Naturally the possibility of its happening aligns every Jewish community on

172

the side of peace. And more cannot be said, save to say to the non-Jew that the Jew is entitled to the same respect in the choice which he makes on a question of conscience as is accorded to the Quaker.

The true function of Israel, however, in relation to the diaspora lies not in political authority but in its transmuting into Jewish values the experince garnered by contact with the Gentile world, and so incorporating it into the heritage of Israel's own spiritual pilgrimage. And this brings one at once into the centre of the controversy about Israel as a ' Torah State.' There could be few more difficult issues for an outsider to tackle ; and yet it cannot be avoided, for it is central.

The issue has been made more complicated by the fact that those who press for the creation of a ' Torah State ' represent but a small minority of the population, and that their definition of such a state is not likely to command wide acceptance either inside or outside Israel. But is it the only definition, or indeed, the only *orthodox* definition ? To the orthodox Jew the essential quality of orthodoxy has come to lie in obedient conformity with the peculiar Jewish way of life, with shechita, strict Sabbath observance, strict observance of the rabbinic rules for marriage and divorce, and so on, as they were evolved in centuries of rabbinic dominance. He will claim that it is these special observances which maintained Judaism and the Jewish people intact during the long centuries of diaspora life. Now no one with any historical sense would deny that the separate daily living which these laws implied contributed a great deal to Jewish survival. But it is very open to question whether they are the actual reason for that survival ; and I would suggest that the exact opposite is true. What ensured Jewish survival was not those aspects of life which Jews themselves recognised as not being obligatory on Gentiles, but those basic ethical and moral principles which Jews recognised as being obligatory on all men, but found better understood within the Jewish community than elsewhere.

Jewry in the last two thousand years has been exposed to the temptations and attractions of every one of the world's great civilisations. Jews were familiar with the world of classical philosophy and science, and with the eastern world of Zoroastrianism. They lived in intimate relations with eastern and western Christendom and with every section of Islam. They were not unacquainted with the mysticisms, the philosophies, and the

173

religions of India and China. They were a people with a keen intellectual appreciation, and adventurous in character. And we are asked to believe that they resisted the seductions, spiritual and cultural, of these civilisations, as well as accepted a varying number of galling and humiliating restrictions on their freedom, because by doing 'so they might be prevented from eating pork or lobster, and could submit themselves to a number of restrictions on their freedom one day in seven, and so on. The picture makes complete nonsense. It is one thing to say that, having chosen to remain Jews, these distinctions made the daily observance of the choice easier : but it is quite another to claim fundamental religious necessity for the permanent observance of these practices in completely different conditions.

I have no idea what will be the future of present orthodox practices—just as I have no idea what changes will take place in the practice and doctrine of my own Church in the coming centuries. But I am quite sure that neither Jew nor Christian will get the right answer to the question until he has asked, and found the answer, to a previous one: what are the spiritual values which persuade a man to remain a Jew (or a Christian) *today* ?

If one could imagine that a religious Jew could, like the rabbi in the trial scene of the Dibbuk, summon his ancestors from their graves and ask them what it was that had kept them loyal to Judaism in spite of the restrictions and humiliations which that loyalty involved, I think that there would be little mention of the ' fence about the law ' in their replies. There would, instead, be a constant emphasis on the ethical standards which they had learnt to prize as Jews, and their inability to accept what they saw around them in the Gentile world. They might speak of the cruelty of killing animals for sport and how the rules of shechita preserved them from such bloodshed. They might speak of the procedure of Christian courts, of the torture sanctioned by the Inquisition and other tribunals, of the indifference to the laws of evidence and the frequent use of the death penalty in the magistrates' courts in England during the time of their early struggles for emancipation, and contrast them with their dreams of being themselves magistrates, and putting into practice what they had learnt in poring over the pages of Tractate Sanhedrin. They might speak of bishops refusing to support laws to abolish the slave trade or to protect tiny children from lives of hideous deformity and brevity in the employment of those who swept chimneys, and contrast them with the meticulous laws for the protection of servants elaborated by their ancestors.

As one can asume that the ancestors would have lived in many countries, we can imagine descriptions of idolatrous superstition contrasted with the stern simplicity of the Shema, of barbarous cruelty of man to man in Islamic as well as Christian countries, of the crass acceptance of ignorance and dirt, of cruelty between man and wife sanctioned by law. And, if they were asked: why then did you spend so much time on such little things ? On the scales of turbot, on minute regulations about the Sabbath and so on ? I think they would answer: ' my dear child, we were not saints ; we were constantly tempted to throw overboard our sensitive consciences, even our knowledge of what was right and wrong, and conform to the Gentile ways around us ; and this strict separation of daily living, this building up of habits influencing every moment of our lives, was an enormous help to us in moments of temptation. They were the setting which protected the jewel ; but we never thought that they were the jewel itself. Nor did we claim that they would, by themselves, draw attention to the jewel which they surrounded. We knew very well that sometimes some of us thought they *were* the jewel, but, as we said, we were not saints. The essential thing was that the Jewish way of life entrusted to us should not perish, and that we should bear witness to standards of righteousness in relations between men, and seek to overcome cruelty, ignorance, and superstition. These things must remain if Judaism is to remain.' And it is from considerations such as these that they would say, not in arrogance but in thankfulness and humility: ' Thank God that I was given strength to remain a Jew, and not to seek the easier path of conversion to Christianity or Islam.' And I believe that not a few of them, surveying the centuries of Jewish history, might add, as does Victor Gollancz in his recently published autobiography: ' why in the name of God did not our sages realise how much they were endangering the spiritual heritage which was ours by multiplying beyond reason acts which could become mere conformity, obscuring its spiritual splendour.'

Writing as a Christian, I should add that the foregoing paragraphs are not written just to denigrate Christianity. But I believe that the historical evidence is unchallengeable that in the field in which I have imagined the answers to be given, the field of social conduct, the Jewish tradition has shown itself much more sensitive than the Christian. There are other fields of which I would not make that claim, but they are irrelevant to the present subject.

Were I to continue the imaginary conversation, and carry it back to the Talmudic period itself, I believe it would be reasonable to suggest that much of the elaboration of laws arose naturally by a kind of intellectual escapism, out of the inability of Jews to control the whole of their lives, and so exercise their intellectual faculties on larger matters. It it easy to forget that the rabbis who started and continued the process were forced by circumstances to deal with communal life in very restricted circumstances. As I have suggested on an earlier page, they were painting a miniature, lovingly covering every tiny surface. I do not believe they would have advocated covering the vast canvas, now not merely available but obligatory for the future of Judaism, with work on such a scale.

In many ways the establishment of Israel takes Jewish history back to the period before the Mishna, when Jews followed many religious observances, had many interpretations of their faith, and yet unquestionably were Jews. It is from a situation in which men of many interpretations claim with equal right the name of Jew and belief in the God of Israel that Judaism needs to approach its task today and tomorrow. I am not saying that rabbinic observances will or should be abandoned. But I am saying that no man can say today what will be their place in the Judaism of the future until he can answer positively the question which I asked : What has kept Judaism alive until today ?

It is at this point that it becomes clear that in the permanent relationship between Israel and the diaspora there is a spiritual as well as a material thread. For the reinterpretation of Judaism can only be achieved by drawing on the total experience of the Jewish people, and the Israel of today represents but a fraction of that experience, as will indeed the Israel of the future. The position with regard to American progressive Judaism illustrates the point. There is a widespread feeling among American Jews that it cannot be transplanted to Israel as it stands. But it is a vital part of total Jewish experience, and the values which it seeks to incorporate and express certainly have a place in the rebuilding of Judaism.

The danger of contemporary life is that every movement of thought tends to develop into an organisation ; and every organisation, to be effective, develops a bureacracy. Most of what I have been describing in this chapter can neither be organised nor transmitted by paid organisers. Organisations rise and perish, play their part and are forgotten. But such relationships as have been here described belong to the spirit of a people. They are permanent and yet often indefinable ; they are potent, and yet they are often not consciously pursued as planned objectives. They are at their best when they just happen, and it is left to future historians to discover that they were there. Today Israel is passing through the stage where she is obliged to plan. Her calls upon the diaspora for financial and material help have to be organised. If the orthodox seek to repeat in the religious sphere this pattern, they are bound to fail. There is no place yet for a new sanhedrin, no material adequate to a new definite interpretation, no sufficient exploration of the noveltv of the situation to give direction. When the time is ripe, new spiritual adventures will reflect not one interpretation of Jewish history alone, but the whole of contemporary Jewish experience.

While these are, I am convinced, the true proportions of the over-all picture as seen in the perspective of Jewish history, yet each detail has its own concrete existence and is not merely a part of the whole. When we look around us from that standpoint, there are two facts in the situation of Israel whose concrete existence, if not taken into account, could alter the whole future. It has already been said that if Israel ignores the diaspora, she may well become just another Levantine state, a state whose citizens from time to time remembered that they had once been members of the world-wide Jewish community. It has also been said that Israel is a state which is neither eastern nor western but both. Today too many Israelis tend to regard the diaspora as little more than a milch cow to supply her financial needs ; and the more serious implications of this short-sightedness are accentuated by the new composition of her population. For, except in terms of charity, eastern Jews have no means of knowing what values are possessed by modern Jewish life in the western world.

Life in Israel today is turbulent and dynamic. Israelis have more problems internal and external than they can easily solve. In such a situation it is easy for the intangibles to be forgotten, or pushed away until there is more time to think about them. History unfortunately does not allow of such comfortable arrangements. It is true that at the moment the Israelis are bound to think of the diaspora mainly in terms of the funds of which they are in such dire need ; and it is equally true that, elated by the success with

177

which they achieved statehood by their own military courage, they should feel capable of solving all their other problems without help or interference from Jews abroad. But that only means that the burden of carrying forward the millennial Jewish inheritance lies more than ever on the diaspora. Nothing could be falser than the conception, which has found too frequent expression in recent years, that the appearance of Israel has made the survival of the diaspora unnecessary.

To look at the facts behind the establishment of Israel is to see how the present attitude has arisen. To the Zionist pioneer who came to the land between 1880 and the issue of the Balfour Declaration, the upbuilding of Eretz Israel was the culmination of more than thirty centuries of Jewish history. It was the ending of two thousand years of real ' exile.' He came voluntarily and of his own spiritual decision. He came with his pack weighted with Jewish traditions which (though he forgot this) the diaspora had maintained for him. He forgot it, because he thought of the diaspora mainly in terms of the pressures of its Gentile environment ; and his pack was heavy with memories of religious and political persecution, and with personal experience of the sufferings wrought by modern antisemitism. Nevertheless he came also—if unconsciously—with a feeling of relationship—even membership—with the wider world of thought and experience of the nineteenth and twentieth centuries which had been the background of his diaspora life. Though after 1917, and particularly after 1933, an element in the Jewish population came less from Zionist conviction than from the pressure of the economic and political breakdown of the post-1918 world, yet it was still true up to the war of liberation that the overwhelming majority of the Jewish population had a perspective wider than that which would have been theirs had they known only life in Eretz Israel.

The war of independence has brought into prominence the younger generation, which had naturally played a leading part in the fighting ; and the leader and spokesman of the younger generation is the native born, the *sabra,* who lacks both the wider perspective of the older generation, since he sees the world with Israel as its centre, and the memories of a world-wide Jewish tradition, since he is naturally obsessed by the problems of the present and the future, and has little time for the past. He sees a new life, a new age, just beginning, and of that new age he sees himself as at once the centre and the architect. To what an extent this can involve a reversal of all previously established values we can see from the emergence of the 'Canaanites.' They are but a tiny minority, almost a 'lunatic fringe,' but that they exist at all is a symptom. For to the Canaanite even the word 'Jew' is anathema. He not merely denies all special association with a Jewish world in 'foreign' countries, but sees no value even in the maintenance of a specifically Jewish tradition in his own. He takes the name 'Canaanite' deliberately because it means *only* 'the inhabitant of the land' without any universal implications whatever, and *all* the inhabitants of the land, not merely the Jews.

The Canaanites will, it is to be hoped, die out of themselves. But it is no use for the diaspora to shut its eyes to the significance of this new outlook of the native-born Israeli. It is there, and it cannot be changed except by time and patience. It is, in its own curious terms, the fulfilment of what is repeated annually at the Seder, when each generation is taught to identify itself with that original generation which came out of Egypt. The *sabra* is of the generation which came out of Egypt. Like his remote ancestors, he is full of newness, brashness, inexperience, impatience, and is terribly liable to get things mixed and to worship the first golden calf which he encounters. The Moses of today and tomorrow will have no easier time than the Moses of the Exodus.

Of course, there are vast masses of Jewish experience and history which can lie dormant until some future native-born graduate of the Hebrew University, seeking a subject for his Ph.D., decides to explore the unknown story of the ghettoes of Europe or the literature of antisemitism, the past practices of reform Judaism in America, or the conflicts between Zionism and assimilation in American political life, and does so with the same scholarly interest and personal detachment as he now gives to the relics of the cave men in Galilee or the sites of Byzantine settlements in the Negev. But not all the Jewish past can be so treated. Much is as vital today as it was yesterday and will be tomorrow.

If the outlook of the native-born Israeli is the first of the special problems affecting this generation, the second is the future composition of the population of Israel, native born or immigrant. The immense increase of immigration from Muslim countries means that within a generation, even if there be no further substantial increase by future immigration, eastern-born Jews will outnumber those who have known by personal experience or inheritance something of western culture and tradition, Jewish or Gentile. For the birth-rate of the oriental is much higher than that of the western Jew.

Jews who enter Israel from the Yemen, or Iraq or North Africa, come from a very different pattern of social, economic, and cultural life. The ' extended family ' of eastern life was the basis on which the whole social structure rested. The oldest male possessed an automatically accepted authority over the lives of his children and grandchildren, nephews and nieces, and possibly cousins also. This was possible in a traditional and static society, such as has been admirably described by the archæologist and anthropologist Carleton S. Coon in *Caravan*,[1] for in the mosaic pattern of Middle Eastern life the whole family would probably be engaged in approximately the same occupations. But when they migrate to Israel this pattern is shattered long before any compensating alternative can become effective. For the oldest members of the family are likely to find it most difficult to adjust themselves to new occupations. While their youngsters can quickly acquire new skills and so earn higher pay, they are more apt to be fixed in unskilled jobs, or even to be unemployable. For many occupations followed by Jews in the ghettoes of Muslim countries are meaningless, or even undesirable, in Israel. In consequence they at once lose the authority to which they are accustomed, and the whole group of immigrants becomes like a rudderless ship until its members have adapted themselves to the new pattern of the western restricted family, in which a parent takes responsibility only for his not yet adult children. Equally fundamental is the change in the status of women, who suddenly become not merely equal partners in the home, but economic rivals for employment.[2]

Such changes cannot be accepted and absorbed into a new harmony in the twinkling of an eye. In the intervening and transitional period the new nation is confronted with the danger of developing into a community with a dual standard of living and a pattern, easier to acquire than to change, by which a western aristocracy occupies a higher social and economic level, while

[1] Caravan. Henry Holt & Co., New York, 1951, or Jonathan Cape, London, 1952.
[2] An excellent study of all the problems involved in the eastern immigration is Raphael Patai's *Israel between East and West*. Jewish Publication Society of America, 1953.

easterners and their descendants, their erstwhile dignity and composure completely destroyed, are expected to fulfil all the less skilful and less remunerative posts. That they would be officially or socially degraded to the position from which the American negro is struggling to emerge is in the highest degree unlikely. The danger is the more subtle temptation that the whole people come to accept that anything ' western ' is automatically better, and that there is no field in which westerners have to learn from those coming from the eastern world. By tradition and necessity the eastern Jew has learnt to acquiesce in life's injustices ; it would be tragic if he acquiesced in the idea that he could not expect to become a leader in Israel until he had become a complete exemplar of the existing pattern of western political or economic leadership.

To a considerable extent the coming pattern of Israeli life is bound to be the product of imponderable and, indeed, incalculable, factors ; but there are certain desirable developments which can be planned, and are being planned, to meet these dangers. The eastern immigrant, like the western, will soon be succeeded by his own *sabra* ; and the *sabra* of eastern origin will have passed through the same educational system, and will have undergone the same military service as his western cousin. The fact that military service in Israel has a very carefully thought out social patterning can be of immense value. Both the educational work done in the army and the long period in which the young men and women are engaged in agricultural pioneering, will tend to create a new unity between east and west based on working together for a new Israel. Likewise, in the economic field, the unwillingness of the Histadruth to accept anything which savours of a double pattern of wages and employment will tend to help the new citizens to find the level of employment appropriate to their individual capacities. Nevertheless, the problem remains, and remains in two fields of vital importance, the religious and the political.

It has been said that the western-born *sabra* is turning his back on the European inheritance of his parents. But at least he is aware that it was theirs. The eastern-born Jew never had any access to it ; his background in the Jewish quarters of the cities and towns of the Middle East has no relevance whatever to the life he will lead in Israel. He is completely uprooted, and the more so as he can, under present conditions, perform no function which would balance his lack. Were there peaceful relations with the Arab world, he could balance his ignorance of the West with his knowledge of the East ; he could be not merely an interpreter but a mediator with Arab neighbours seeking relations, social or economic, with Israelis. He could move out from Israel into the Arab world and, speaking Arabic himself, show the Arabs that Israel was not a foreign intrusion. As he acquired positions of importance in the political field he could bring with him an invaluable experience to sweeten the daily relations between Israel and the Arab states. He would know how to present his case, he would understand the fears or reluctances on the other side, and so could help to make Israel understand the Arabs, a task just as important as making the Arabs understand Israel. But if peaceful relations are delayed too long, he will no longer be able to play this rôle. His eastern background belongs to this generation only, unless there is some motive for his native-born children to retain it.

The problem of religion is a somewhat different one ; for here the eastern-born Jew merely emphasises the already existing situation that the only knowledge which a *sabra* has of Judaism is of the religion in its traditional and ghetto form. For the eastern Jew, as for the eastern Muslim or Christian, religion was an automatic part of the total pattern of living. Its social imperatives were more significant than its spiritual or theological attractions. It determined a man's pattern of living in this world in all kinds of ways which, in the west, had come to be totally neglected even by those who retained religion for the spiritual and theological truths which it embodied. By the fact that all through Islamic dominions the ancient *millet* system prevailed, and determined a man's status by his religion and not by his nationality, the eastern Jew had his whole life and his environment determined by his Judaism, and its daily practices made a clear and visible distinction between him and his neighbours. Such a situation imposed restrictions, but within them he had freedom and control of his circumstances. All that has gone. It is not religion that distinguishes him from other Israelis, and there is no boundary within which he has freedom to live his own life and continue his traditional practices. Religious as well as economic corrosives are undermining his self-confidence and giving him a feeling of insecurity, and even inferiority, in the land of his fathers.

Western and eastern-born Israelis have, then, to work out a new life for themselves ; and while they are doing this they have also to face problems of which the diaspora has no experience. This is a fact to be remembered when we speak of the break with the past for either group. No diaspora community can forge links of Jewishness uniting Jews of Iraq and Yemen with Jews of Poland and New York. No diaspora community has among its members Christian and Muslim Arabs, nor has it to relate its policy to the presence of representatives of all the Christian Churches. But, and this is the most important distinction of all, no diaspora community has to develop relations with foreign powers, a task rendered trebly difficult for Israel by the fact that her nearest foreign powers, and those that have most influence on her own position, are the Arab states. All these are tasks for Israel, and tasks which have to be undertaken now, and not in some more convenient future. It is reasonable to say that while Israel sets herself to master these new tasks the main responsibility for maintaining the Jewish tradition must rest with the diaspora. It is in New York and London, in South Africa and South America that the assertion of the unity of Jewish history and experience must be repeated and the authenticity of Jewish life ' among the Gentiles ' maintained for some time to come. But the assertion will arouse little interest in Israel, except in so far as it is obvious that contact with the intellectual centres of the west can offer knowledge and opportunities with which the Hebrew University cannot yet compete. But even here the Israeli will tend to think that a year or two of post-graduate study abroad will give him all he needs.

Wherever it is possible the diaspora will need to work—I hope unobtrusively—to help Israel not to develop a purely Levantine outlook. From this standpoint it is unfortunate that no means have yet been found to persuade any considerable number of young men and women from the western Jewish communities to settle in the country. Much of this must be attributed to the very foolish statements made in the first flush of independence by Israeli spokesmen that no authentic Jewish life could be lived outside Israel, and that there was no security for Jews save in Israel. The last argument was particularly unfortunate. Personal safety and social security are neither the most obvious, nor the most desirable, characteristics revealed by life from Metullah to Eilat, and those who seek such objectives are happier in Hampstead or the Bronx. It is as a worthwhile adventure, calling for noble and generous service, that the proposition must be made that a young Jew should exchange the safety and security of western life for the hardships and uncertainties of Israel. For Jewish youth is no less moved by an appeal to the highest motives than the youth of any other nation, or any less indifferent to personal security and adequate financial reward.

As so many times before in Jewish history, a new situation has thrown up a new challange, with unexpected—even unprecedented —dangers and opportunities. There is nothing in this to dismay the courageous. Problems equally intractable have been approached in the past, difficulties equally dangerous surmounted. Only when Jewry refuses to respond to the challenge of an age, and fears to grasp new opportunities and adventures as they are offered, will Jewish history come to an end. That time is not yet.

Epilogue

IN the preceding chapters no attempt has been made to survey all the problems with which the contemporary Jewish world is faced. Attention has been concentrated only on those matters which throw light on that complex highway which binds together Israel, the Jewish communities elsewhere, and the Gentile world. Israel has its own urgent problems, and the solution of some of them will strengthen or weaken the links which have been here discussed. She offers all kinds of possibilities as a country which is both eastern and western. But at the moment the most immediate implications of that fact are not such as to suggest a future creative unity ; since she tends today to become a country in which all the important posts, educational, political, and administrative, are held by the western group only. She must solve the problem of her relations with the Arab world ; but at present she is tied down by domestic difficulties even over the property of her own Arab population, much of which has been declared 'abandoned,' and turned to other uses. She must solve her relations with the Christian Churches if peace is to return to Jerusalem ; but there again she still has difficult property questions to solve, in view of her own extreme poverty. She must keep open her doors, but she is increasingly puzzled as to how to feed and set to work those who enter. So one could continue to raise difficulties out of the present position in examining the affairs of every Jewry in the diaspora ; and one great Jewry, that of the Soviet Union, has scarcely been mentioned in the previous pages at all.

There has, then, been a selection of the questions to be raised in this book ; but it is not a chance selection. For those questions lie at the heart of the matter, whether they have dealt with Jewish life a thousand years ago, or have looked towards the future For in the last thirty years the whole situation of the Jews has been radically changed. The solutions which appeared adequate after the first world war, and which were believed capable of offering 'a final solution of the Jewish question,' have proved completely superficial; and more tragedy and adventure have been packed into those thirty years than in any comparable period in the long history of this extraordinary people. The whole of her past has risen, both to judgment and to fulfilment, in the short span of a single generation. In that brief moment of time a single generation of Jews has been called on to take part in a drama which has been three thousand years in preparing.

Moreover, the elements in the challenge thus offered are peculiarly Jewish in their quality. Like the huge folios of her rabbinical commentaries, they are compounded of an infinity of little issues. There is no point at which Jewry can solve a problem by some superb gesture of generosity or of renunciation. These vast issues on which her whole future depends can be solved only step by step, ' here a little, there a little ' in the cut and thrust of political activity, or in detailed plans of social reform, or again in those scarcely perceptible tendencies of thought and conduct by which normal people in their normal lives produce what, in retrospect, has ultimately the force of a revolution.

The demands which are made on the Jewish people would be the more easily met if we were able to expect some sudden emotional revival, such as has at times stirred other nations. Jews are not like that. If millions of pounds and dollars have to be raised, they must be raised dollar by dollar and pound by pound ; if God, the ultimate source of their religious inspiration, is to become more real to them, it will be by no pulpit oratory suddenly filling the synagogue ; but by a touch here, a new note of conviction there, a door opening unexpectedly, and a fresh perspective revealing itself.

There has been an inevitable undertone, as subject after subject has been raised, of a conviction that what Israel and the Jewish people do about this matter or that is of still wider significance, that it concerns the Christian and Gentile world, that it may ultimately take its place among the factors that shape the future destiny of mankind. Yet nothing would be more unbalanced than a Jewish conviction that the world waited on their lightest word. Foolish and dangerous things have been said under the emotional banner of the ' mission of Israel.' And some of the utterances of Israeli statesmen have seemed to suggest that already they were preparing to be a light to the nations, and that the Zion of their activities was the Zion to which the world would turn. A child must walk before it can run ; the problems which Israel needs to solve she needs to solve for her own sake ; and the right solution will be that which meets her own needs, whether the outside world notices it or not.

186

It would be well for her if, for a period, she would forget the glowing prophecies of the consequences of restoration which fill the prophets. And yet not wholly forget, for the words have been spoken, and they can be a summons to courage as well as a call to humility.

> ' Thus saith the Lord of hosts : It shall yet come to pass, that there shall come people, and the inhabitants of many cities :
> ' And the inhabitants of one city shall go to another, saying, Let us go speedily to pray before the Lord, and to seek the Lord of hosts : I will go also.
> ' Yea, many people and strong nations shall come to seek the Lord of hosts in Jerusalem, and to pray before the Lord.
> ' Thus saith the Lord of hosts ; In those days it shall come to pass, that ten men shall take hold out of all languages of the nations, even shall take hold of the skirt of him that is a Jew, saying, We will go with you : for we have heard that God is with you.'
>
> ZECHARIAH viii, 20-23.

APPENDIX

A Christian Apology for Israel

a study in the thought of James Parkes

by Robert A. Everett

Perhaps on no other issue are Christians quite as perplexed by the Jewish experience as by the State of Israel and its meaning to Jews. There is simply no parallel in the Christian experience which couples land and people, religion and politics, piety and society. Throughout the Jewish tradition, the land of Zion has been an integral part of the Jewish consciousness as reflected in the unbroken covenant between God and His people Israel. The geo-political dimension of Jewish theological self-understanding has always been a stumbling block to Christianity, and the debate in Christian circles over the State of Israel reflects the continuation of Christian difficulties with a Jewish state.[1] Except for a small, but vocal group of Christians, official Christian attitudes, i.e. World Council of Churches, National Council of Churches, Vatican etc., reflect either indifference to the Jewish state or outright hostility. While Christian opponents of Israel deny that their opposition is motivated by antisemitism, their inability to deal with the success of the Jewish state reflects a long-standing tradition in Christianity which stated that Jews should always remain in a subjugated state of existence. The refusal of the Vatican to officially recognize Israel as a state can be seen as an example. The refusal of Christians to appreciate the centrality of the Land in the Jewish

[1] Uriel Tal, 'Jewish Self-Understanding and the Land and State of Israel', *Union Seminary Quarterly Review* (New York), vol. 26, XXVI. No. 4, Summer 1971, 352.

experience reveals, I think, a determination to continue to define Judaism solely in Christian categories, rather than coming to terms with Judaism itself.

Within Christian circles, James Parkes, the British clergyman, theologian and historian, has been the most articulate apologist for Israel. Parkes has written extensively on many of the issues related to Israel, and his work represents the most sustained effort yet made by a non-Jew to defend the creation of the Jewish state. He has written on the political problems associated with Israel's statehood, dealing at length with the British Mandate, Zionism and Arab reactions.[2] However, Parkes has devoted most of his attention to an examination of Jewish claims to the Land, and his work can properly be seen as an attempt to justify those claims on the basis of theological, historical and moral grounds. While sympathetic to Zionism, Parkes is often critical of Zionist historiography and propaganda. He believes that the Zionist experience is but one part of Israel's claim to statehood, and he believes that Israel's strongest case is to be made on other grounds. At the root of his work is the desire to show how Jewish claims to the land are based on a long religious and historical connection to the land, which spans nearly 2,500 years. It is here, not in twentieth century politics, that Parkes believes Israel can make its strongest claim to the land. In this paper, I shall examine the way in which he constructs his version of the case for Israel, particular attention being given to Parkes's own historical methodology.

I

There are two unique features in Parkes's work. Being both an historian and theologian, he draws on theology as well as history for material on which to build his argument. The religious dimensions of the Jewish claims are just as essential in his view as are the historical factors. This does not mean that he believes God gave the Jews the Land and no one else can have it. Parkes is not a Biblical fundamentalist. But he takes very seriously the role which the Land has played in the development of Jewish theological self-identity, and he views this role as crucial to any interpretations of the Jewish point of view He realizes that this is often where non-Jews become confused about the Jewish position, since neither Islam nor Christianity have such a

[2] There are three books by Parkes one should consult on these problems: *The Emergence of the Jewish Problem* (London 1946); *Whose Land?* (Harmondsworth. 1970); *A History of the Jewish People* (Chicago 1963)

190

relationship with a particular land. Thus, Parkes goes to some length to explain the religious dimensions of the Jewish claim.

The other unique feature is the emphasis Parkes puts on the history of Palestine itself. Unlike many histories of Israel which begin with an examination of the Zionist movement in nineteenth century Europe, he looks just to Palestine to begin understanding the Jewish claims.

Although Parkes was writing about the Zionist question in 1939, his sustained study of the question of a Jewish state began in 1946. In that year, he travelled to Palestine to see for himself what the situation was. He saw immediately how incompatible the Jewish and Arab claims were, and he perceived the inevitable failure of the British Mandate. What impressed him most was the ignorance on the part of all concerned of even the most basic historical facts concerning the Land and its people. On his return to England, he undertook the task of writing a history of Palestine and the relationship which the three different religious traditions and peoples had with the Land. He gives the following explanation for undertaking this task.

I had three assets. I was not personally involved in the issue. I was concerned equally with Jews, Christians, and Moslems, and I had no *parti pris* ... Secondly I was as much a theologian as a historian, and again was concerned with the whole theological background Jewish, Christian, and Islamic. Thirdly as a historian I was concerned with the whole of Jewish history, so that any discoveries I made about Palestinian Jewish history, found an inevitable background in my knowledge of Jewish history outside Palestine at the time with which I was concerned.[3]

The results of Parkes's efforts during this two year period was the book *Whose Land: A History of the Peoples of Palestine*. It dealt with the changing history of Palestine over a 2,000 year period, and examined the links which Christianity, Islam, and Judaism all had to it. This research led him to the conclusion that the Jewish claims to the land were unique among the three claims. As he points out, Islam appeared in Palestine around 636. As far as Muslims were concerned, the land of Palestine was not a Holy Land; rather their interest was in Jerusalem as a Holy City. It was said that from Jerusalem the prophet Muhammad had been transported up to heaven where his vocation was recognized by his prophetic predecessors. In Islamic tradition, Jerusalem is the third holy city. For Christians, Palestine was a Holy Land because it was where Jesus had lived and conducted

[3] James Parkes, *Notes on the Long Haul to Peace in the Middle East* (no publisher 1969), 2 (my copy).

his ministry. It never became a centre of the Christian religion nor did Christians believe that living on the land was a religious obligation. Christians concerned themselves mainly with the security of holy places and access for pilgrimages.

It is only when one turns to Judaism that one finds the Land itself viewed as being of ultimate value and importance. Within Judaism, the land is an integral part of the covenant between God and His people, the Jews. It is the 'Promised Land', and Parkes points out that this is very distinct from the Christian concept of Palestine as the Holy Land. He writes:

For Jews the Land is a Holy Land in the sense of being a Promised Land, and the word indicates an intensity of relationship going beyond that of either of the other two religions. As it is for Christians, the Land is unique; but the nature of its unique appeal goes further, and has throughout the centuries involved the idea of settlement and return, and an all-pervading religious centrality possessed by no other land.[4]

In Parkes's view, this is the key for understanding the basis of the Jewish claim. The Land is a unique factor in Jewish life and identity. The full implications of the Land in Jewish history are reflected in the very nature of the Jewish religion.

Throughout his work, Parkes defines Judaism as a religion which is communally oriented. 'The centre of Judaism', he writes, 'is the natural community. Its whole emphasis is on man as a social being, related to other men through righteousness and justice. It insists on human responsibility', on definable and achievable objectives.'[5] The covenant between God and Israel is one in which emphasis is placed on the way men should live their lives in a community. Compared to Christianity or Islam, Judaism is little concerned with questions of the after-life; rather, the emphasis falls on the life in the world, in the community. The covenant which called Israel forth as a people also included in it the promise of a land in which Israel could be a nation and a people. Parkes points out that from Biblical times onwards this land has always been believed by Jews to be Palestine. He writes:

The history of a community cannot be divorced from its geographical and historical setting and it is the historical fact that this setting was Palestine during the whole formative period in Judaism which gives to the soil of Palestine its unique place in

---

[4] James Parkes, *Whose Land?*, 135.

[5] James Parkes, *Prelude to Dialogue: Jewish-Christian Relationships* (New York 1969) 217. See also my article on Parkes's Theology in CHRISTIAN ATTITUDES ON JEWS AND JUDAISM, no. 52, February 1977.

Jewish thought and life, a place which remains unique even among those Jews who have followed the secularist tendencies of the age in their attitude to religious tradition and revelation ... For the Jew the intimate geographical link is, however, not concerned only with the past. The 'promises' concern the future also.[6]

Parkes's view of the interplay between history and theology is evident in this discussion of the Land and its intimate connection with the life of the people. Obviously there are historical realities which contribute to this relationship, but these realities have often been expressed religiously within the Jewish tradition. Parkes's understanding of the role the Land plays is found in the following lengthy passage.

The intimate connection of Judaism with the whole life of a people, with its domestic, commercial, social, and public relations as much as with its religion and its relations with its God, has historically involved an emphasis on roots in physical existence and geographical actuality such as is found in neither of the other two religions. The Koran is not the history of the Arab people; the New Testament contains the history of no country ... But the whole religious significance of the Jewish Bible — the 'Old Testament' — ties it to the history of a single people and the geographical actuality of a single land. The long religious development which it records, its law-givers and prophets, all emerge out of, and merge into, the day by day life of an actual people with its political fortunes and social environment. Its laws and customs are based on the land and the climate of the Land; its agricultural festivals follow its seasons; its historical festivals are linked to events in its history — the joyful rededication of the Temple at the feast of Hanukkah, the mourning for its destruction in the month of Ab, and above all the commemoration of the original divine gift of the Land in the feast of Passover. The opening words of the Passover ritual conclude with the phrase: Now we are here — but next year may we be in the land of Israel; Now we are slaves, but next year may we be free men. And the final blessing is followed by the single sentence 'Next year in Jerusalem'.[7]

In this passage, Parkes gives his account of the role the Land plays in developing both the theological and historical consciousness of Judaism. While the 'Promised Land' is rooted in the divine covenant between God and Israel, it also provides the backdrop for even the most mundane activities of the Jews. In Parkes's interpretation, removing the Land as a factor in Jewish history and identity would leave one bewildered as to the meaning of Judaism and its tradition. The concept of peoplehood, so central to Judaism, would have no meaning if not linked somehow to the land. It is out of this very intimate connection between the Land and all which is considered Jewish that Parkes discovers the roots of the Jewish claims to the Land.

[6] *Prelude to Dialogue*, 111.
[7] *Whose Land?*, 137.

Parkes has written that 'it was only in the course of this study (in 1946) that the uniqueness of the Jewish relationship and its amazing quality became clear. I did not acquire the idea ready made from any previous writer.'[8] Contrary to many Zionist historians who begin their histories of the state of Israel with an examination of the events in late nineteenth century Europe, Parkes argues that Zionism is unintelligible without a complete understanding of how the Land is intimately linked to Jewish identity and survival. As far as he is concerned, the Balfour Declaration of 1917 and the League of Nations Mandate of 1920 merely recognize the connection of the Jewish people to the Land and their right to a Homeland. He believes that if the Arab reaction to this decision — 'Palestine is an Arab country which Great Britain had no right to give to the Jews' — is countered by the Jewish reaction — 'Jews have claimed nothing which has not been legally granted to them' — the Arabs have the stronger case. In Parkes's words: 'If these two statements really represented the whole of the facts, the Arab refusal to recognize the whole transaction would be morally justified. Political legality is not in itself an unchanging moral authority, and in any case, a legal document could not make moral anything if it were fundamentally immoral'.[9] Parkes is not saying that the decision for a Jewish Homeland was wrong, but he is expressing his own concern that Zionist arguments in Israel's defence often miss the point. His own research had led him to conclude that: (1) It misses every essential quality of the country in its long recorded history to say simply that Palestine is an Arab country. (2) The Jewish case does not rest on the legality of two twentieth century documents, but on a unique and unbroken historical relationship.[10]

Parkes believes that his discovery of the unique quality of the relationship between the Land and the people would not have been such a surprise had Jewish historians been writing about it. However, its very uniqueness was the reason no one felt the need to explain it. It was such an essential part of Jewish life and identity that Jewish historians simply took it for granted. While this is understandable to Parkes,[11] he believes that the neglect of this issue became problematic when Arab nationalism began to challenge the Zionists. As he writes, 'it was only when the Jewish primary interest was challenged by Arab

[8] *Notes*, 3 (see note 3).
[9] James Parkes, *Arabs and Jews in the Middle East: a tragedy of errors* (London 1967), 6.
[10] Ibid., 6.
[11] James Parkes, 'The Palestinian Jews: did someone forget?' *The New Middle East* (London), no. 13, October 1969, 49.

nationalism and its supporters that the *quality* of the Jewish relation-ship (to the land) became a matter of supreme significance; and by that time, the argument from legality, so strong in Jewish minds because of Jewish history, had assumed unchallengeable authority in Zionist and Israeli publicity'. Parkes believes this to be a serious error, and one that had led Zionist apologists to construct their positions without access to the strongest factors in Israel's favour.

A second criticism raises questions about the whole enterprise called Jewish history. In Parkes's view, the reason the Jewish rela-tionship to the Land was ignored by most Jewish historians can be traced back to the authority of Heinrich Graetz. Parkes argues that Eastern European Jewry, Jewish mysticism, and oriental Jewry were viewed through 'nationalist' eyes and thus not given the attention they deserved. Parkes points out that 'up to the present the whole tradition of Jewish historiography has been to present the Jew of Europe and later of America, as the heir to an earlier Jew of the Middle East ... Because of the long stagnation of the area, the Jewish historian decided to forget that substantial Jewish communities went on living there, except when there was a European Jewish irruption such as the population of sixteenth century Safed'.[12] In his view, such histo-riography gives an unbalanced and incomplete picture of the Jewish experience, and it distorts Israel's strongest claims. 'A true picture of Jewish history', writes Parkes, 'must balance the essential contributions of both West and East and expound why the Western appeared of exclusive significance during the formative years of the modern age'.[13] Parkes argues that although Zionism manifested itself in the late nineteenth century as a purely European affair, usually in secularist and political forms, its roots lay deep in the qualities and hopes of Judaism itself. Without an awareness of these roots, Parkes believes, Zionism cannot be correctly understood or interpreted.

The third criticism Parkes has of Jewish historiography concerns its neglect of Palestinian Jewry. He believes that an essential clue to Jewish history is found in the Palestinian Jewish experience. Yet, conditions at the turn of the century had caused that community to suffer a serious decline, and thus it is not surprising that the early Zionists overlooked its importance. Parkes argues, however, that at very crucial times in Jewish history, it was the Palestinian community which provided the necessary energy and life-force needed to keep Judaism alive. In addition, Palestinian Jews were responsible for

[12] *Prelude to Dialogue*, 126.
[13] Ibid., 127.

keeping a physical Jewish link to the land, and the continual presence of this Jewish community marks the most important argument in favour of Jewish claims. Parkes also believes that the Jewish presence in Israel was of vital importance to the Jews living in the diaspora.

We now need to mention Parkes's interpretation of Jewish history and the role played by Israel. In his opinion, Jewish history has been based on a tension between universalism and particularlism. In religious terms, this has been expressed as the experience of Exile and Return. The Land plays an important role in providing the framework within which one important key to Jewish history and survival is to be found. Parkes argues that the exilic experience has always been understood and made bearable by reference to the land of Zion and the hoped-for restoration. Psalm 137 is the classical expression of this experience. Parkes writes: 'A diaspora community shows itself, on the one hand, conscious of its "exile" and its need to "return" to the homeland. But, on the other hand, it regards itself as autonomous, it creates its own religious forms; and it accepts influences from its non-Jewish environment'.[14] Israel, on the other hand, keeps the diaspora community aware of its Jewish identity, and prevents it from total assimilation into the non-Jewish world. He speaks of this mutual relationship as follows.

The diaspora community feeds into the heart of Jewry in Israel the experience, spiritual, cultural, social, and material which its garners in its life with the Gentile world. Israel feeds back into each diaspora community the same experience digested and transiented by the values inherent in the Jewish way of life.[15]

Parkes believes that this constant exchange between Israel and the Diaspora is the key to understanding Jewish history.

Two ideas are at work here. First, Parkes is trying to establish the centrality of the Land of Israel in the whole of Jewish history. Second, he is attacking the idea that since there is now a Jewish state all Jews should move there. 'Nothing could be falser', he writes, 'than the conception, which has found too frequent expression in recent years, that the appearance of Israel has made the survival of the diaspora unnecessary'.[16] In his view, neither assimilationists nor extreme Jewish nationalists have a proper view of Jewish history and its meaning. He argues that Jewish survival is concerned with both

[14] James Parkes, *Israel and the Diaspora* (London 1952), 12. Historical Society, 1952, 12.
[15] James Parkes. *End of an Exile* (London 1954), 171.
[16] Ibid., 178.

a moral and a geographical identity, and it would be disastrous to Jewish survival to choose one or the other.[17] Both are essential since neither alone represents the whole Jewish experience. 'In the permanent relationship between Israel and the diaspora there is a spiritual as well as a material thread. For the reinterpretation of Judaism can only be achieved by drawing on the total experience of the Jewish people, and the Israel of today represents a fraction of that experience as will indeed the Israel of the future'.[18]

In Parkes's view, Jewish history is a combination of non-cosmopolitan universalism and non-exclusive particularism. It is Israel which prevents the universalism from degenerating into cosmopolitanism; it is the diaspora which saves Israel from becoming arrogant, or parochial in her particularism.[19] Without Israel, the diaspora would collapse into an ethical monotheism or a universalist position devoid of Jewish identity. Without the diaspora, Israel would become another Levantine state which would lack spirit and energy. Parkes sees this as a condition found throughout Jewish history, and this condition remains true today. Whereas the dangers in the past had been in forgetting Israel (a reference made in his criticism of Jewish historiography), today the dangers are in letting Israel overshadow the importance of the diaspora. It was in the diaspora that Jews began to shed their separatism and develop universal ideas and intellectual activities. But it is in Israel where these pursuits were constantly filtered through the Jewish experience. In Parkes's view, 'the main reason for Jewish survival lies in those Jewish qualities which Jews recognized to be obligatory to all men, but found to be better taught and practised within the Jewish fold than outside.' In his opinion, this is only possible if there is a constant flow of ideas and activities between Israel and the diaspora.[20] This has been the important characteristic of Jewish history.

Parkes appreciates the need for a place where Jews can be Jews, and such a place is the state of Israel. The centrality of the Land and its Jewish community is, however, according to him only one half of the determinative factors in Jewish history. The other is the influence the diaspora has had on the Jewish experience, as a counter to Jewish parochialism. It cautions against extreme nationalism which Parkes

[17] *Israel and the Diaspora*, 38.
[18] *End of an Exile*, 176.
[19] Ibid., 164.
[20] *Israel and the Diaspora*, 37. See also Parkes, *Israel and the Arab World* (New York 1967), 12-15.

believes would reduce the function and importance of Israel in Jewish life.

Whether one can view Jewish history as being a struggle between universalism and particularism is a matter of debate. Jewish historians do not usually talk in these terms, and Arthur Hertzberg has pointed out that these categories could well reflect Parkes's Christian background. Christians are usually troubled by the tension in Judaism between universalism and particularism, and Hertzberg suggests that Parkes may be reflecting this concern in approaching Jewish history in this manner.[21] However, one should not dismiss Parkes on this point. I would suggest that Parkes's view of Jewish history reflects his sensitivity to both non-Jewish hostility to Israel and the situation of Jews in the diaspora. Parkes attempts to explain why all Jews needn't move to Israel, while maintaining the importance of having a Jewish state. The use of categories not usually employed by Jewish historians may reflect Parkes's recognition of his role as an apologist for Israel to non-Jews, and thus he uses categories familiar to them in making his case.

II

Parkes admits that the case for Israel is often difficult to appreciate because it is so complex. Israel's critics can simply say that the Jews took Arab land which wasn't theirs to take. Obviously, Parkes does not believe this but he does believe that Jewish claims need to be carefully presented if they are to counter the claims of Israel's critics. As he writes:

The Jewish case . . . rests on a long history little known even to many Jews and not easy to assess in terms of a politicial decision. But without some knowledge of that past association, no fair judgement can be made; and, however dimly appreciated, it was acceptance of that past connection which moved many Englishmen, Lord Balfour among them, to make a unique decision.[22]

Parkes, therefore, presents Israel's claims by stressing the unique historical relationship the Jews have had with the Land. In this way, he hopes to counter the idea that Jews took land that wasn't theirs, as well as demonstrating that this long historical connection is the core of Jewish claims. To do this, Parkes describes what he calls the 'Five Roots of Israel'.

[21] This was pointed out to me by Professor Hertzberg in a seminar on Zionism, Columbia University, Spring, 1978.
[22] *End of an Exile*, 3.

198

He sums up these five roots as follows:

The tree of Israel springs from five roots deeply embedded in the experience of the Jewish people. The first and deepest is Judaism as the religion of a community. The second is the Messianic hope, intimately connected ever since the destruction of the Jewish state with the expectations of a return to the Promised Land. The third is Jewish history, and the long experience of dispersion and insecurity. The fourth is the continuity of Jewish life in Palestine. The fifth is the unique relationship between the Jewry of Palestine and the whole Jewish people.[23]

From these five roots, Parkes constructs his position concerning Israel's right to exist as a nation among nations in the Middle East.

We have already mentioned Parkes's definition of Judaism as the religion of a community, and the consequences of such a definition regarding the Land of Zion. Parkes is aware that this is often a most difficult concept for Christians to understand. To the outsider, Judaism presents the paradox of claiming to be a universal religion, while being bound up at the same time with the Jewish nation. 'The nature of Judaism,' writes Parkes, 'is such that, in all his wanderings, each individual Jew was conscious that he was a member of a single people — he would not have understood had he been asked whether that people constituted a religious or national community — and that the fulfilment of his own destiny was inextricably bound up with the safety and restoration of his people'.[24] Parkes believes that this is such a fundamental part of Judaism that even secular Zionists must admit the influence it had on their own thinking. Despite the debate between religions and secular Zionists concerning the nature of Zionism, Parkes maintains that 'the deepest root from which the state of Israel has sprung is the Jewish religion'.[25]

Parkes argues that at Sinai Israel was chosen to be a particular people with a particular relationship to God, and out of their covenant with God came a unique relationship to the Land. Non-Jews frequently misunderstand the Jewish concept of 'chosenness' as implying special privileges. The Prophets and Rabbis, however, viewed being God's chosen People as a responsibility given to the Jewish people. It is always to the people or nation of Israel that this responsibility was given, along with God's promise to the Land. The themes of Exile and Return in Jewish tradition have been bound up in this covenant, exile being seen as punishment for Israel's refusal to keep the covenant,

[23] Ibid., 3.
[24] Ibid., 5.
[25] Ibid., 5.

199

restoration of the Land as a sign of God being faithful to His people. Even non-religious Zionists, many of whom rejected outright the religious orthodoxy of their day, often explained their mission in similar terms. Secular Zionists also spoke of Jews as being 'chosen' for a special role in history, but 'chosen' for reasons more in tune with political needs of the time. Israel would be the great Socialist state, or democratic state, etc.[26] Thus, Parkes believes that secular Zionists express a feeling inherent in Judaism, and he argues that, inspite of their rejection of religious orthodoxy, they are really the heirs of a deep-seated feeling for the whole people implanted by religious orthodoxy.[27]

There have been movements in Judaism which have tried to make Judaism into a purely ethical monotheism, which often spiritualized the concept of the people and the Land. For years, Liberal or Reform Judaism opposed the Zionist movement *per se*. Opposition also came from ultra-orthodox wings who believed that only the Messiah should restore Israel. On the whole, however, Parkes's understanding of Judaism and the religious roots of Israel's claims to the Land seems to be solidly established in Jewish tradition.

The Messianic hopes which run through Jewish tradition are the second root of Israel in Parkes's view. Messianic hope is common to both Jews and Christians, but Jewish hopes differ greatly from Christian hopes. This difference is often a source of great misunderstanding between the two religions. Unlike Christians, Jews have never understood the Messiah as simply a redeemer of souls. Rather, the hoped-for Messiah would restore Israel to all its glory. As Parkes understands it, 'the Messiah's prime function was the gathering in of the dispersion, and the restoration of the Jewish people to the land of their fathers, the land they believed theirs by divine promise'.[28] Secular Zionists would discount this, but in many ways, secular Zionism had its own messianic consciousness about itself. Many secularists spoke of the gathering-in of the dispersion and restoring the Land in a way very reminiscent of religious messianic hopes. Despite the early debate between the 'practical' and 'political' Zionists over where to establish a homeland, the messianic image which many Zionists had of themselves is closely related to traditional messianic thought. Parkes sees

[26] See Arthur Hertzberg's introduction to *The Zionist Idea* (New York 1970), 15-101, for a historical survey of Zionist positions.
[27] *End of an Exile* 8.
[28] Ibid., 11.

this as more evidence of the influence Judaism as a religion had on the Zionist enterprise.

Parkes considers the historic situation which Jews found themselves in while living in Christian and Muslim societies as being the third root of Israel — 'based on long experience of inequality and insecurity under the rule of both Christianity and Islam, and on the shattering disillusion which followed the high hopes of complete emancipation in the liberal democracies in Europe.'[29] This situation produced an urgent need for a homeland for the Jews where they would not be a subjugated racial or religious minority. Parkes believes there to be a correlation between this situation of the Jews and the fact that messianic hopes were kept alive over centuries of alien rule; the restoration to the Land was always viewed as a solution to the problems.

He also observes that the Jewish experience in the diaspora contributed to the feeling among Zionists that appeals to the legal aspect of their claims provided them with their strongest case. Jews were often at the mercy of Christian and Muslim authorities, and so they had an interest to establish their legal rights. Parkes suggests that this dependence on legal documents heavily influenced Zionists in their desire to establish Jewish claims to the Land *via* legal documents. Believing that Jewish claims are founded on stronger grounds, he argues that appeals to legality do more harm than good and he strongly urges Zionists to reconsider their position on this issue.

Looking for the *rationale* behind Zionism, he finds the late nineteenth century provided the necessary framework in which a political expression for the Zionist impulse could be manifested; but, he says, it is a serious error to view Zionism as simply a western version of Jewish nationalism. That Zionism became politically active in the nineteenth century is more an accident of timing rather than necessity. What is more essential, in Parkes's thinking, is how Zionism manifested impulses long in existence within Judaism, and how the historical situation of Jews contributed to its manifestation at a particular time.

While the first three roots in Parkes's scheme establish the place the Land has in Jewish tradition, the fourth and fifth attempt to establish the actual physical links which Jews have had with the Land. Parkes believes that the continuity of Jewish life in Israel constitutes the strongest argument on behalf of Jewish claims — the fourth root. The actual number of Jewish inhabitants is meaningless to him

[29] Ibid., 18.

because the population was often subject to radical changes due to outside pressures. As he writes, 'if the number of Jewish inhabitants has constantly varied, it has been because of circumstances outside Jewish control, and not because Jews had themselves lost interest in living in their "promised land." On the whole it may be said that it was always as large as was possible in view of conditions existing at any one time'.[30] According to Parkes, the Jewish population of Palestine was always considered to be the ambassador of the Jewish people; the physical reminders of the long-awaited return to the land of Zion.

The charges against Israel as being a creation of western imperialism or that Jews took land from Arabs are challenged by the fact that there has been a Jewish presence in the land for centuries. Parkes also points out that this root is not religious in nature and cannot be dismissed out of hand by atheists or secular critics.[31] Jews had always struggled to preserve their presence in Palestine, and had been immigrating in varying numbers for centuries. The Zionists were a new type of immigrant, but certainly not unique. 'They were the successors and reinforcement to a Jewish community which through all vicissitudes had remained a part of the land of Israel.'[32] It was not true that Jews suddenly reappeared in 1948 to take land away from Arabs, they had never left the land. That Zionist immigrants increased the Jewish population is held to be no more nefarious than the fact that the Arab population also grew *via* immigration during this time.

Parkes believes that Zionist propaganda has often been its own worst enemy by not giving enough attention to this aspect of Jewish history. He writes:

The Zionists ignored not merely their strongest argument but their real case. They were not bridging a gap of 2000 years. They were augmenting a Jewish population which had never ceased to exist in the country, and which survived largely because every successive Muslim ruler recognized that it had a right to be there. The Zionists ignored this vital relationship, probably because they were in opposition to the religious conservatism of eastern European Judaism, and simply saw the existing Jews of Palestine as exponents of a religious fanaticism they disliked. But from the point of view of Arab reaction, the real justification of the Zionist presence is that the Jewish population of Palestine has always been as large as could find the humblest means of existence in the Land of Israel.[33]

The fifth root of Israel, closely related to the fourth, also relates back at Parkes's criticism of Jewish historiography. Believing that

[30] Ibid., 19.
[31] *Whose Land?*, 138.
[32] *End of an Exile*, 23.
[33] *Arabs and Jews in the Middle East*, 21

Palestinian Jewry played a fundamental role in shaping Jewish history, he argues that at four crucial points in Jewish history it was they who provided Jewry with direction and leadership. He writes:

There would be neither Jewish people nor Judaism, without the *scholars of Jabne,* who evolved a Judaism which needed no geographical centre, no sanhedrin, no political or religious hierarchy; the Masorites of Tiberias who produced a text of the Old Testament, and recalled Jewish scholars to its significance, at a moment when the centre of Jewish life was moving from Islam to Christendom, and so provided one vital link between the two religions; the mystics of Safed who created an inner world of light and joy opened to the Jewish communities of Eastern Europe during centuries of otherwise intolerable denigration and derilections; and the *founders of Zionism* who alone offered a physical and psychological redemption to the survivors of the Holocaust.[34]

'The Rabbis of Galilee', writes Parkes elsewhere 'laid the foundation which allowed the Jewish people not only to survive, but to retain their creative power.'[35] One also finds the creation of the Talmud and the beginnings of Biblical studies rooted in this community. Christians, as well as Jews, came to benefit from this activity.

These are the five roots of Israel on which Parkes builds his case for Israel. It will probably be noted that little mention of antisemitism has been made as a contributing factor to Israel's creation. The third root of Israel dealing with the historical situation of Jews in Christian Europe of course includes this problem, but Parkes believes that European antisemitism should not be seen as an essential factor. The Arabs would be rightly indignant over being told that they had to pay the price of Europe's evil. Parkes believes that Israel's case rests soundly on events and ideas central to Judaism and the Jewish people themselves rather than on problems imposed on Jews from the outside. He attempts to demonstrate the legitimacy of Jewish claims to the land on religious, historical, and moral grounds.

The writings of James Parkes on Israel and the Middle East are a most valuable contribution to the literature devoted to this topic. Its unique quality rests on the fact that such a defence of the Jewish state comes from a Christian thinker. It is hoped that this paper has been able to present Parkes's position in such a way that its richness and depth are properly appreciated, while pointing out its most distinguishing features.

[34] James Parkes, *Israelis and other Palestinians in the Perspective of History* (Southampton 1973), 7-8.
[35] *End of an Exile,* 27.

Introduction to Articles by Reinhold Niebuhr in The Nation,
January and February, 1942

The outstanding interpreter of Zionism, as perceived by a
Christian, was Reinhold Niebuhr (1892-1971), minister of the
United Church of Christ (Congregational-Christian-Evangelical
-Reformed), professor of Applied Christianity and vice-
president of Union Theological Seminary in New York City from
1928 to 1960, essayist and author of a score of books, founder
of Americans for Democratic Action and the American Christian
Palestine Committee, and pre-eminent philosophical theologian
of the twentieth century. In the winter of 1941-42, shortly after
America's entry into World War 11, and at the time authentic
reports were coming from Hitler's "Festung Europe," of the
Nazis' sworn intention to extirpate European Jewry, Niebuhr
published in the pages of The Nation two articles entitled, "Jews
After The War." Four decades later these eloquent, carefully
reasoned pleas for the affirmation of the right of Jews to live
anywhere in the world they might choose to, and the recognition
of the need to fulfill international promises (the Balfour Declaration, the League of Nations Mandate for Palestine, etc.), on
behalf of a Jewish national home, are as powerful and cogent,
valid and significant as when Niebuhr presented them.

One of his great admirers in the British Isles was James
Parkes, with whom he had a warm and close friendship. They
were constantly in touch with each other, both by correspondence
and by personal visits abroad and in the United States. Parkes
considered Niebuhr the foremost mind in American Protestantism,
and the one person most sensitive to the Zionist aspirations of
the Jewish people and the tangled problems of Great Britain's
Realpolitik in the Middle East. Both men spoke as Christians
who had identified with the Jewish people in their sufferings and
in their hopes to achieve normalcy and dignity in the establishment of Israel as the Jewish national homeland.

In 1946, when James Parkes came to America to deliver the
Charles W. Eliot Lectures before the students, faculty, and
friends of the Jewish Institute of Religion (now the New York

School of the Hebrew Union College-Jewish Institute of Religion)
at the invitation of its president, his great and good friend,
Rabbi Stephen S. Wise, he also spoke in various institutions
all over the country, and often conferred with leaders of the
new movement which was supported by Christians to aid the
Zionists in that crucial post-war period. He was particularly
interested in the newly formed American Christian Palestine
Committee which is described in the following article, written
as a chapter in Essays in American Zionism, edited by the
distinguished historian, Dr. Melvin Urofsky, for the Herzl
Press as the 1978 Herzel Yearbook.

Parkes had for some time been active in the British counterpart, the British Association for a Jewish National Home, and
had sage words of counsel and encouragement to offer. Never
sparing in his critical comments, Parkes told his friends in the
American Christian Palestine Committee that they should not
slavishly follow the Zionists in their ideology and political tactics
without balanced reservations and viewpoints of their own. He
also wanted his American colleagues to be aware of Great
Britain's difficulties, both at home and throughout its far flung
Empire during the days of recovery from the exhausting,
traumatic years of 1939-1945. He was intent on reminding the
American cousins that they, too, had responsibilities in a world
where isolation had been a cheap luxury and where the consciences of Christians were either insensitive or all too often
unawakened. He was equally sharp in his caustic comments
about Jews in America who were blind to their obligations to
their fellow Jews; but to American Christians he spoke bluntly
and candidly. Hence, his strictures echoed through the ACPC.

Just as James Parkes had a spiritual and intellectual affinity
with Reinhold Niebuhr, so did he have a kinship of mind and heart
on the Jewish-Christian relationship with Paul Tillich, the famous
German Protestant philosopher at Marburg, and then at Frankfurt-
am-Main, until he fled Hitler's tyranny in 1933 and came to Union
Theological Seminary. Parkes had known Tillich in Europe
when the British clergyman of the Anglican persuasion had served
in the late 1920s and early 1930s as an executive of the International Student Service (now known as World University Service),
and when Tillich was so active in the group he helped to organize
and lead in Germany: the Religious Socialists. At that time

Tillich, as a socialist and as an internationalist, was in favor of assimilation for the Jewish people, and was not in favor of Zionism. Not until later years did Tillich become pro-Zionist, especially when the Holocaust drove him in that direction and he reassessed Jewry, Judaism, and Zionist thought.

When Parkes visited America in 1946-47, he met Tillich again and enjoyed their lively exchange of ideas, because their respective views now tended to coincide more and more, especially with respect to the relationship of the Jews to what was then still Palestine, and was in May of 1948 to become the new Jewish State of Israel. But another memorable reunion came in 1954 when Parkes, accompanied by his wife Dorothy, returned to the United States at the invitation of the American Christian Palestine Committee and the Union of American Hebrew Congregations. As Parkes met with rabbis at "Clergy Institutes" in various Reform synagogues throughout America, and talked with interfaith groups gathered under the auspices of the American Christian Palestine Committee, he found that Tillich had considerable influence on rabbinical thought (just as Martin Buber did on Christian thought); and here, in Parkes and Tillich, there was truly a meeting of the minds. Parkes found that Tillich had moved in new and creative directions.

Carl Hermann Voss

JEWS AFTER THE WAR

By REINHOLD NIEBUHR

THE POSITION of the Jews in Europe and the Western world is by no means the least of the many problems of post-war reconstruction which must engage our minds even while our energies are being exhausted in achieving the prerequisite of any reconstruction, that is, the defeat of the Axis. It is idle to assume that this defeat will solve the problem of the Jews ; indeed, the overthrow of Nazism will provide no more than the negative condition for the solution of any of the vexing problems of justice which disturb our consciences.

PLIGHT OF THE JEWS

Millions of Jews have been completely disinherited, and they will not be able to obtain the automatic restoration of their rights. An impoverished Europe will not find it easy to reabsorb a large number of returned Jews, and a spiritually corrupted Europe will not purge itself quickly of the virus of race bigotry with which the Nazis have infected its culture. It must also be remembered that the plight of the Jews was intolerable in those parts of Europe which represented a decadent feudalism—Poland and the Balkans—long before Hitler made their lot impossible in what was once the democratic world.

The problem of what is to become of the Jews in the post-war world ought to engage all of us, not only because a suffering people has a claim upon our compassion, but because the very quality of our civilisation is involved in the solution. It is, in fact, a scandal that the Jews have had so little effective aid from the rest of us in a situation in which they are only the chief victims. The Nazis intend to decimate the Poles and to reduce other peoples to the status of helots ; but they are bent upon the extermination of the Jews.

LIBERAL FALLACIES

One probable reason for the liberal world's failure to be more instant in its aid to the Jews is that we cannot face the full dimensions of this problem without undermining the characteristic credos of the democratic world. Even the Jews are loath to bring the problem to our attention in all its tragic depth. We will not face it because we should be overwhelmed by a sense of guilt in contemplating those aspects of the problem which Hitler did not create but only aggravated. Some Jews have refused to face it in dread of having to recognise that the solutions provided by the liberal Jewish world have failed to reach the depths of the problem.

The liberal world has sought to dissolve the prejudice between Jews and Gentiles by preaching tolerance and good will. Friends of the Jews have joined the Jews in seeking to persuade their detractors that the charges against them are lies. But this does not meet the real issue. The real question is, why should these lies be manufactured and why should they be believed ? Every cultural or racial group has its own characteristic vices and virtues. When a minority group is hated for its virtues as well as for its vices, and when its vices are hated not so much because they are vices as because they bear the stamp of uniqueness, we are obviously dealing with a collective psychology which is not easily altered by a little more enlightenment. The fact is that the relations of cultural and ethnic groups, intranational or international, have complexities unknown in the relations between individuals, in whom intelligence may dissolve group loyalties and the concomitant evil of group friction.

American theories of tolerance in regard to race are based upon a false universalism which in practice develops into a new form of nationalism. The fact that America has actually been a melting-pot in which a new amalgam of races is being achieved has given rise to the illusion that racial and ethnic distinctions can be transcended in history to an indeterminate degree. Russian nationalism has the same relation to Marxist universalism as American nationalism has to liberal universalism. There is a curious, partly unconscious, cultural imperialism in theories of tolerance which look forward to a complete destruction of all racial distinctions. The majority group expects to devour the minority group by way of assimilation This is a painless death, but it is death nevertheless.

JEWISH POSITION UNIQUE

The collective will to survive of those ethnic groups in America which have a base in another homeland is engaged and expressed in their homeland and need not express itself here, where an amalgam of races is taking place. The Finns need not seek to perpetuate themselves in America, for their collective will to live is expressed in Finland. But the Jews are in a different position. Though as an ethnic group they have maintained some degree of integrity for thousands of years, they are a nationality scattered among the nations. Does the liberal-democratic world fully understand that it is implicitly making collective extinction the price of its provisional tolerance ?

This question implies several affirmations which are challenged by both Jewish and Gentile liberals ; it is therefore important to make these affirmations explicit and to elaborate them. One is that the Jews are really a nationality and not merely a cultural group. Certainly the Jews have maintained a core of racial integrity through the ages. This fact is not disproved by the assertion that their blood is considerably mixed. There are no pure races. History develops new configurations on the bases of nature, but not in such a way as to transcend completely the natural distinctions.

208

Who would deny that the Germans have a collective will to live, or think that this simple statement can be refuted by calling attention to the admixture of Slav blood in people of German nationality ?

The integrity of the Jews as a group is of course not purely biological ; it has also a religious and cultural basis. But in this Jews are not unique, for there are no purely biological facts in history. The cultural and religious content of Jewish life transcends racial particularity, as does the culture of every people, though never so absolutely as to annihilate its own ethnic core. The one aspect of Jewish life which is unique is that the Jews are a nationality scattered among the nations. I use the word "nationality" to indicate something more than "race" and something less than "nation." It is more than race by reason of the admixture of culture and less than nation by reason of the absence of a state. The Jews certainly are a nationality by reason of the ethnic core of their culture. Those Jews who do not feel themselves engaged by a collective will to live have a perfect right to be so disengaged, just as Americans of French or Greek descent need feel no responsibility for the survival of their respective nationalities. But Jews render no service either to democracy or to their people by seeking to deny this ethnic foundation of their life, or by giving themselves to the illusion that they might dispel all prejudice if only they could prove that they are a purely cultural or religious community.

THE RIGHT TO SURVIVE

The fact that millions of Jews are quite prepared to be *spurlos versenkt*, to be annihilated, in a process of assimilation must affect the programme of the democratic world for dealing with the Jewish question. The democratic world must accord them this privilege, including of course the right to express the ethos of their history in purely cultural and religious terms, in so far as this is possible, without an ethnic base. The democratic world must resist the insinuation that the Jews are not assimilable. They are not only assimilable but they have added to the riches of a democratic world by their ethnic and cultural contributions. Civilisation must guard against the tendency of all communities to demand a too simple homogeneity, for if this is allowed complete expression it results in Nazi tribal primitivism. The preservation of tolerance and cultural pluralism is necessary not only from the standpoint of justice to the Jews but from the standpoint of the quality of a civilisation.

The assimilability of the Jews and their right to be assimilated are not in question ; this conviction must prompt one-half of the programme of the democratic world, the half which consists in maintaining and extending the standards of tolerance and cultural pluralism achieved in a liberal era. But there is another aspect of the Jewish problem which is not met by this strategy. That is the simple right of the Jews to survive as a people. There are both Jews and Gentiles who deny that the Jews have such a survival impulse as an ethnic group, but the evidence of contemporary history refutes them, as does the evidence of all history in regard to the collective impulses of survival in life generally. Modern liberalism has been blind to this

209

aspect of human existence because its individualist and universalist pre-suppositions and illusions have prevented it from seeing some rather obvious facts in man's collective life.

THE WILL TO SURVIVE

One proof of the Jews' will to survive is of course that they have survived the many vicissitudes of their history. They have survived in spite of the fact that they have been a nationality scattered among the nations, without a homeland of their own, since the dawn of Western European history. They are a people of the diaspora. Modern assimilationists on both sides sometimes suggest that the survival of the Jews through the centuries was determined on the one hand by the hostility of the feudal world and on the other by the toughness of an orthodox religious faith ; and they suggest that the liberal era has dissipated both the external and the internal basis of this survival. They assume that liberal ideals of tolerance are infinitely extensible and that the breaking of the hard shell of a traditional religious unity will destroy the internal will to live.

The violent nationalism of our period proves the error of the first assumption. While we need not believe that Nazism or even a milder form of national bigotry will set the social and political standards of the future, it is apparent that collective particularities and vitalities have a more stubborn life than liberal universalism had assumed. The error of the second has been proved by the Jews themselves. For Zionism is the expression of a national will to live which transcends the traditional orthodox religion of the Jews. It is supported by many forces in Jewish life, not the least of which is an impressive proletarian impulse. Poor Jews recognise that privileged members of their Jewish community may have achieved such a secure position in the Western world that they could hardly be expected to sacrifice it for a Zionist venture. But they also see that for the great multitude of Jews there is no escape from the hardships a nationality scattered among the nations must suffer. They could, if they would, be absorbed in the Western world. Or they could, if they desired, maintain their racial integrity among the various nations. But they know that the price which must be paid for such survival is high. They know from their own experience that collective prejudice is not as easily dissolved as some of their more favoured brothers assume.

THE IMPULSE OF ZIONISM

These poorer Jews understand, out of their experience, what is frequently withheld from the more privileged—namely, that the bigotry of majority groups toward minority groups which affront the majority by diverging from the dominant type is a perennial aspect of man's collective life. The force of it may be mitigated, but it cannot be wholly eliminated. These Jews, therefore, long for a place on the earth where they are not " tolerated," where they are neither " understood " nor misunderstood, neither appreciated nor

210

condemned, but where they can be what they are, preserving their own unique identity without asking " by your leave " of anyone else.

It is this understanding of a basic human situation on the part of the less privileged portion of the Jewish community which has given Zionism a particular impetus. There are of course individuals in the more privileged groups who make common cause with the less privileged because they have the imagination to see what their more intellectualist brothers have not seen. But on the whole Zionism represents the wisdom of common experience as against the wisdom of the mind, which tends to take premature flights into the absolute or the universal from the tragic conflicts and the stubborn particularities of human history.

The second part of any programme for the solution of the Jewish problem must rest upon the recognition that a collective survival impulse is as legitimate a " right " as an individual one. Justice, in history, is concerned with collective, as well as with individual, right. Recognition of the legitimacy of this right must lead, in my opinion, to a more generous acceptance of the Zionist programme as correct in principle, however much it may have to be qualified in application.

UNIVERSALISM NO SOLUTION

The Jewish religionists, the Jewish and Gentile secularists, and the Christian missionaries to the Jews have, despite the contradictory character of their various approaches, one thing in common. They would solve the problem of the particularity of a race by a cultural or religious universalism. This is a false answer if the universal character of their culture or religion demands the destruction of the historical—in this case racial—particularism. It is just as false as if the command " Thou shalt love thy neighbour as thyself " were interpreted to mean that I must destroy myself so that no friction may arise between my neighbour and myself.

The author, who happens to be a Christian theologian, may be permitted the assertion, as a postscriptum, that he has his own ideas about the relation of the Christian to the Jewish religion. But he regards all religious and cultural answers to the Jewish problem which do not take basic ethnic facts into consideration as the expressions of either a premature universalism or a conscious or unconscious ethnic imperialism.

*

I offer " a " solution rather than " the " solution to the problem of anti-Semitism precisely because a prerequisite for any solution of a basic social problem is the understanding that there is no perfectly satisfactory formula. A perennial problem of human relations can be dealt with on many levels of social and moral achievements, but not in such a way that new perplexities will not emerge upon each new level. The tendency of modern culture to find pat answers and panaceas for vexing problems—one aspect of its inveterate utopianism—has confused rather than clarified most issues with which it has occupied itself.

I have previously suggested that the problem of the relation of the Jews

211

to our Western democratic world calls for at least two different approaches. We must on the one hand preserve and if possible extend the democratic standards of tolerance and of cultural and racial pluralism which allow the Jews *Lebensraum* as a nation among the nations. We must on the other hand support more generously than in the past the legitimate aspiration of Jews for a " homeland " in which they will not be simply tolerated but which they will possess. The type of liberalism which fights for and with the Jews on the first battle line but leaves them to fight alone on the second is informed by an unrealistic universalism. If its presuppositions are fully analysed it will be discovered that they rest upon the hope that history is moving forward to a universal culture which will eliminate all particularities and every collective uniqueness, whether rooted in nature or in history. History has perennially refuted this hope.

A " DOUBLE STRATEGY "

The late Justice Louis D. Brandeis illustrated in his person and his ideas exactly what we mean by this double strategy. Brandeis was first a great American, whose contributions to our national life prove that justice to the Jew is also a service to democracy in that it allows democracy to profit from the peculiar gifts of the Jew—in the case of Brandeis and many another leader, the Hebraic-prophetic passion for social justice. But Brandeis was also a Zionist ; his belief in the movement was regarded by some of his friends, both Gentile and Jewish, as an aberration that one had to condone in an otherwise sane and worthy man. Brandeis's Zionism sprang from his understanding of an aspect of human existence to which most of his fellow-liberals were blind. He understood " that whole peoples have an in-dividuality no less marked than that of single persons, that the individuality of a people is irrepressible, and that the misnamed internationalism which seeks the elimination of nationalities or peoples is unattainable. The new nationalism proclaims that each race or people has a right and duty to develop, and that only through such differentiated development will high civilisation be attained."* Brandeis understood in 1916 what some of his fellow-Jews did not learn until 1933 and what many a Gentile liberal will never learn. " We Jews," he said, " are a distinct nationality, of which every Jew is necessarily a member. Let us insist that the struggle for liberty shall not cease until equal opportunity is accorded to nationalities as to individuals."

It must be emphasised that any programme which recognises the rights of Jews as a nationality and which sees in Zionism a legitimate demand for the recognition of these rights must at the same time support the struggle for the rights of Jews as citizens in the nations in which they are now established or may be established. This strategy is demanded, if for no other reason, because there is no possibility that Palestine will ever absorb all the Jews of the world. Even if it were physically able to absorb them, we know very well that migrations never develop as logically as this. I cannot judge whether Zionist estimates of the millions which a fully developed Palestine

---

* From an essay first published in 1916 and reprinted by the *Jewish Frontier* (*New York*) in its October, 1941, issue.

could absorb are correct. They seem to me to err on the side of optimism.
But in any case it would be fantastic to assume that all Jews could or would
find their way to Palestine, even in the course of many centuries.

It is more important, however, to consider what democracy owes to its
own ideals of justice and to its own quality as a civilisation than what it owes
to the Jews. Neither democracy nor any other civilisation pretending to
maturity can afford to capitulate to the tendency in collective life which
would bring about unity by establishing a simple homogeneity. We must
not underestimate this tendency as a perennial factor in man's social life.
Nor must we fail to understand the logic behind it. Otherwise we shall
become involved in the futile task of seeking to prove that minority groups
are not really as bad as their critics accuse them of being, instead of understanding that minority groups are thought " bad " only because they diverge
from the dominant type and affront that type by their divergence. But to
yield to this tendency would be to allow civilisation to be swallowed up in
primitivism, for the effort to return to the simple unity of tribal life is a
primitive urge of which Nazism is the most consistent, absurd, and dangerous
contemporary expression. In the case of the Jews, with their peculiar
relation to the modern world and the peculiar contributions which they have
made to every aspect of modern culture and civilisation, any relaxation of
democratic standards would also mean robbing our civilisation of the special
gifts which they have developed as a nation among the nations.

NECESSITY OF A HOMELAND

The necessity for a second strategy in dealing with the Jewish problem
stems from certain aspects of the collective life of men which the modern
situation has brought into tragic relief. The Jews require a homeland, if for
no other reason, because even the most generous immigration laws of the
Western democracies will not permit all the dispossessed Jews of Europe to
find a haven in which they may look forward to a tolerable future. When I
say the most " generous " immigration laws, I mean of course " generous "
only within terms of political exigencies. It must be observed that the
liberals of the Western world maintain a conspiracy of silence on this point.
They do not dare to work for immigration laws generous enough to cope
with the magnitude of the problem which the Jewish race faces. They are
afraid of political repercussions, tacitly acknowledging that their theories do
not square with the actual facts. Race prejudice, the intolerance of a
dominant group toward a minority group, is a more powerful and more
easily aroused force than they dare admit.

A much weightier justification of Zionism is that every race finally has
a right to a homeland where it will not be " different," where it will neither
be patronised by " good " people nor subjected to calumny by bad people.
Of course many Jews have achieved a position in democratic nations in which
the disabilities from which they suffer as a minority group are comparatively
insignificant in comparison with the prestige which they have won. A
democratic world would not disturb them. Their situation would actually
be eased to an even further degree if the racial survival impulse were primarily

213

engaged in Palestine. Religious and cultural divergences alone do not present a serious problem, particularly under traditions of cultural pluralism. But there are millions of Jews, not only in the democratic world but in the remnants of the feudal world, such as Poland and the Balkans, who ought to have a chance to escape from the almost intolerable handicap to which they are subjected. One reason why Jews suffer more than any other minority is that they bear the brunt of two divergences from type, religious and racial, and it is idle for Jews or Gentiles to speculate about which is the primary source of prejudice. Either would suffice, but the prejudice is compounded when both divergences are involved.

Zionist aspirations, it seems to me, deserve a more generous support than they have been accorded by liberal and democratic groups in Western countries. Non-Zionist Jews have erred in being apologetic or even hostile to these aspirations on the ground that their open expression might imperil rights' painfully won in the democratic world. Non-Jewish liberals have erred equally in regarding Zionism as nothing but the vestigial remnant of an ancient religious dream, the unfortunate aberration of a hard-pressed people.

POLITICAL ARRANGEMENTS

Whether the Jews will be allowed to develop a genuine homeland under their own sovereignty, within the framework of the British Empire, depends solely upon the amount of support which they secure in the two great democracies, for those democracies will have it in their power, if Hitler is defeated, to make the necessary political arrangements. The influence of the American government will be indirect but none the less effective—which is why American public opinion on this issue cannot be a matter of indifference. It is obviously no easy matter for British statecraft to give the proper assurances and to make basic arrangements for the future while it is forced to deal with a vast and complex Arab world still in danger of falling under the sway of the Nazis. Yet it must be observed that the Arabs achieved freedom and great possessions in the last war, and that this war, in the event of victory for the United Nations, will increase the extent and cohesion of their realm. The Anglo-Saxon hegemony that is bound to exist in the event of an Axis defeat will be in a position to see to it that Palestine is set aside for the Jews, that the present restrictions on immigration are abrogated, and that the Arabs are otherwise compensated.

Zionist leaders are unrealistic in insisting that their demands entail no " injustice " to the Arab population since Jewish immigration has brought new economic strength to Palestine. It is absurd to expect any people to regard the restriction of their sovereignty over a traditional possession as " just," no matter how many other benefits accrue from that abridgment. What is demanded in this instance is a policy which offers a just solution of an intricate problem faced by a whole civilisation. The solution must, and can, be made acceptable to the Arabs if it is incorporated into a total settlement of the issues of the Mediterranean and Near Eastern world ; and it need not be unjust to the Arabs in the long run if the same " imperial "

214

policy which establishes the Jewish homeland also consolidates and unifies the Arab world. One may hope that this will not be done by making the Jewish homeland a part of an essentially Arab federation.

STATUS QUO ANTE NOT SUFFICIENT

It must be noted in conclusion that there are both Jews and Gentiles who do not believe that Palestine is a desirable locus for a Jewish homeland though they do believe that a homeland must be created. They contend that there is as yet no evidence of Palestine's ability to maintain an independent economic existence without subsidies ; that the co-operative agricultural ventures of the Jews, impressive in quality but not in size, offer no hope of a solid agricultural basis for the national economy ; that the enmity of the Arab world would require the constant interposition of imperial arms ; that the resources of Palestine could not support the millions whom the Zionists hope to settle there ; and that the tendency to use Arab agricultural labour may once more create a Jewish urban caste. It is difficult to know to what degree such criticisms are justified. The fact that 25 per cent. of the Jewish settlers in Palestine are engaged in agriculture tends to refute the argument that the Palestinian economy has no adequate agricultural base. The criticism that Palestine cannot, under the most favourable circumstances, absorb all the Jews who must find a new home and security after the war is more serious. However, even if fully borne out, it would not affect the thesis that the Jews require a homeland. It would simply raise the question whether a different, or an additional, region should be chosen. It is barely possible that a location ought to be found in Europe.

The whole matter is so important that it should be explored by an international commission, consisting of both Jews and Gentiles, both Zionists and non-Zionists. The Jews were the first, as they have been the chief, victims of Nazi fury. Their rehabilitation, like the rehabilitation of every Nazi victim, requires something more than the restoration of the *status quo ante.* We must consider this task one of the most important among the many problems of post-war reconstruction. We cannot, in justice either to ourselves or to the Jews, dismiss it from our conscience.

The American Christian Palestine Committee

By Carl Hermann Voss

In the annals of support of Zionism by non-Jews, few chronicles are as heartwarming and reassuring as that of the American Christian Palestine Committee, whether of its antecedent groups, the American Palestine Committee originated in 1932 and the Christian Council on Palestine begun in 1942, or the merger of the two organizations into the American Christian Palestine Committee in 1946. The interfaith cooperation, interethnic amity, and interpersonal understanding on the part of the ACPC's staff and members were of a high order; and aided greatly in strengthening Jewish efforts to interpret Zionist aspirations to an American public, then singularly callous and uncaring about the rescue of Jewish refugees from annihilation by Hitler and not at all concerned with the future of a Jewish national home in Palestine.

During the fateful mid and late 1940s the American Christian Palestine Committee played a significant, often strategic role in mobilizing public opinion on behalf of opening Palestine's gates to the remnant of European Jewry spared the Nazis' gas chambers and of helping establish the foundations of the newly proclaimed Jewish state of Israel on May 14, 1948.

The American Palestine Committee,[1] publicly launched at a dinner in Washington, D.C. on January 12, 1932, and attended by members of both Houses of the U.S. Congress and many other dignitaries of the U.S. Government, including Vice-President Charles Curtis, was organized primarily by Dr. Emanuel Neumann, an American member of the World Zionist Executive. Neumann had become deeply concerned in 1931 about the retreat by the British Government from the commitments of the 1917 Balfour declaration and their League of Nations Mandate for Palestine, just as in 1930 he believed the publication of the

Labor Government's White Paper on Palestine presaged disaster for Zionist hopes.

Encouraged and guided by Zionism's "elder statesman" and *"éminence grise,"* U. S Supreme Court Justice Louis D. Brandeis, Neumann gathered for this meeting of non-Jewish sympathizers with Zionist objectives an array of outstanding government officials who, he hoped, would make American influence felt in British governmental circles and perhaps turn the unfavorable tide: Senator Robert M. LaFollette, Jr. of Wisconsin, Senator William H. King of Utah, New York's Congressman Hamilton Fish, Jr., Assistant Secretary of State James Grafton Rogers, and Idaho's doughty Senator William E. Borah (who had another engagement but agreed, at the urging of Rabbi Stephen S. Wise, to serve as honorary chairman). Neumann prevailed on the controversial Felix Frankfurther of Harvard University's Law School faculty to address the dinner, a task he performed with characteristic skill.

A more impressive moment of the evening, however, was the reading of a letter from President Herbert Hoover:

> I am interested to learn that a group of distinguished men and women is to be formed to spread knowledge and appreciation of the rehabilitation which is going forward in Palestine under Jewish auspices, and to add my expression to the sentiment among our people in favor of the realization of the age-old aspirations of the Jewish people for the restoration of their national homeland. I shall appreciate it if you will present my cordial greetings to those attending the dinner in Washington on January 17th to advance this enterprise.

Yet the American president actually said nothing new, for he was merely giving a qualified approbation whereas on several occasions Woodrow Wilson had spoken of his "personal approval of the [Balfour] Declaration" and had written in 1919: "I am . . . persuaded that the Allied Nations, with the fullest concurrence of our Government and people, are agreed that in Palestine shall be laid the foundations of a Jewish commonwealth." President Hoover only echoed what, with perhaps less reflection and comprehension, had been said to Zionist delegations and conventions by his predecessors, Warren G. Harding and Calvin Coolidge, in the 1920s.[2]

Considerable publicity emerged from this initial dinner of the American Palestine Committee; but the APC, so well started, soon lapsed into desuetude because its guiding spirit, Emanuel Neumann, left for Palestine soon afterward to assume duties there in the Zionist Executive, not to return until 1941. By that time, the British White Paper of 1939 on Palestine had been issued; and an end to Jewish immigration to Palestine was a real threat. The pressures of World War Two on British policy seemed to spell doom for any prospects of establishing a Jewish national homeland.

The APC began again, however, in 1941. Dinner meetings in Washington were held once more, primarily to remind non-Jewish leaders in governmental circles that the American government had, by presidential approval through the years and Congressional action on several occasions, given sanction to the 1917 Balfour Declaration. No less important in the eyes of the APC leaders of that time—and subsequent years as well—were the imperatives of the League of Nations Mandate given to Great Britain (and approved by the Congress, despite nonmembership of the United States in the League) that the Mandatory Power was to "put into effect the Balfour Declaration," to "facilitate Jewish immigration," to "encourage close settlement by Jews on the land," and to "be responsible for placing the country under such political, administrative and economic conditions as will secure the establishment of the Jewish National Home." These words of 1917 by Balfour and of 1920 by the League's Permanent Mandates Commission had an incalculable effect on the non-Jewish supporters of Zionist aims. They respected the sacredness of the pledged word and believed in the validity of international law, as in the assignment of responsibilities by the Mandates Commission of the League, despite America's rigid isolation and neurotic aloofness from international responsibilities.

By 1942, when the United States was at war with the Axis Powers and firmly yoked to Great Britain as an ally, the British Government sought but failed to impede holding the annual dinner of the American Palestine Committee. On that banquet evening at the Mayflower Hotel in Washington, an international broadcast from Great Britain brought the voice of the famous Lord Josiah Wedgwood across the Atlantic to startle the audience, composed of 55 outstanding Americans—governors, editors, college presidents, and congressmen—as he said, "There is no longer any hope from the British administration. . . . Seek to get your America to act—to press for arms and justice—to accept the Mandate—to build another free land with open doors and open hearts. . . . I have tried to save for my own countrymen the glory of rebuilding Jerusalem—of doing justice and creating freedom. . . . It's no use. They won't do it! I can't help. You must turn to America and take on the job yourselves."

As Emanuel Neumann tells the story in his memoirs, Wedgwood spoke directly at (or to) Senator Robert Wagner of New York, partly as a member of the Congress and partly, it appeared, as chairman, along with Senator Charles McNary of Oregon as co-chairman, of the American Palestine Committee; he seemed to cry out across the 3,000 miles of space: "You are as proud of America as I am of England's past. Will you see where lies America's duty? Can you take on the job from our enfeebled hands? . . . The mantle of Elijah has fallen upon Elisha—not only in Palestine. It is your rendezvous with destiny."[3]

Whatever may have been the impact of Wedgwood's extraordinary appeal on the continued reluctance of Britain to fulfill the Mandate in Palestine and on the traditional hesitancy of the United States to assume responsibility, one thing was certain: the issue was now to the fore. American Christians were being urged to demand that their government bethink itself of what it might say and do on the matter.

The American Christian Palestine Committee was still only the American Palestine Committee; not for another four years would it combine its program with that of the soon-to-be-born Christian Council on Palestine. The APC, however, had broadened its constituency; no longer did it number only congressmen and senators, but now it included hundreds of additional public figures: Paul Kellogg, editor of the *Survey* magazine; Johns Hopkins University's William Foxwell Albright; soil expert Walter Clay Lowdermilk; radio commentator Raymond Gram Swing; columnist Edgar Ansel Mowrer of the *Chicago Daily News;* critic and essayist Lewis Mumford; and other molders of public opinion, including many clergymen and teachers of religion.

But there was need for a specific group of ministers, of Christians whose vocations labeled them as such. From that awareness there grew the Christian Council on Palestine in 1942-43. The urgency of the times, when the first reports of Hitler's destruction of European Jewry began to trickle through from Nazi-occupied lands, impelled men like Stephen S. Wise, a leading Zionist and foremost rabbi, to join with his younger colleagues, Rabbis Milton Steinberg and Philip S. Bernstein, to offer aid from the Emergency Committee for Zionist Affairs and enlist the support of such outstanding Protestant leaders as Henry A. Atkinson, secretary-general of the Church Peace Union and the World

219

Alliance for International Friendship Through the Churches, Daniel A. Poling, editor of the *Christian Herald*, and Reinhold Niebuhr and Paul Tillich of Union Theological Seminary.[4]

As chairman *pro tem* and later the elected chairman of the Christian Council on Palestine, Henry Atkinson convened a meeting at the Hotel Pennsylvania in New York City and made clear the motivating conviction: "The destiny of the Jews is a matter of immediate concern to the Christian conscience, the amelioration of their lot a duty that rests upon all who profess Christian principles."

A large, genuinely concerned group attended and heard addresses by Professor S. Ralph Harlow, formerly a missionary in the Middle East and a convinced pro-Zionist, at this time a well-known faculty member at Smith College; the widely hailed social liberal, Methodist Bishop Francis J. McConnell; the world renowned archaelogist, William Foxwell Albright (who was prevented from attending because of illness in his family but who sent a message of support); Mrs. Inez Lowdermilk, wife of Walter Clay Lowdermilk, the world's authority on Palestine's "absorptive capacity"; the great Stephen S. Wise; and, outstanding among them all, Reinhold Niebuhr, the preeminent theologian in Protestantism. On that occasion, as in many earlier instances and throughout the remaining 29 years of his life, Niebuhr's word on Zionism, Jewry, and Judaism was forthright and sane.

The previous winter Niebuhr had published two scintillating articles in the *Nation* on "Jews After the War,"[5] in which with logic and emotional power he had argued for a two-fold emphasis: first, Jews should be guaranteed the right to migrate to any land upon the face of the earth, especially since they had been deprived of rights in so many lands and suffered persecution and expulsion through the centuries; and secondly, they should be granted a national homeland, preferably Palestine because of their historic tie to the land and the internationally assumed obligations in recent decades on behalf of Zionist pleas, made all the more urgent by the persecution of Jews under the Nazis and the threat then being carried out to "solve the Jewish problem" by wiping them from the human race, "a final solution."

With these thoughts, widely publicized by both the *Nation*, then a magazine of considerable prestige, and a reprint of the articles in the tens of thousands under the imprint of the American Palestine Committee, Niebuhr built another structure, namely, that of "The Jewish State and the Arab World." He faced the realistic threat of Arab hostility by asserting: "It is quite apparent that the formation of a Jewish state in Palestine cannot be achieved by the simple consent of the Arab world," because "no solution acceptable to the Arabs will give such a state any realy integrity." In response to those who accepted the Ichud/Judah Magnes/Martin Buber formula of a bi-national state, he contended that "an Arab-Jewish federation in Palestine would certainly not solve the problem, for it would merely perpetuate animosities into the indefinite future."[6]

He had no illusions about the ease with which the solution was to be achieved:

> Those who believe in the justice of the Jewish claims to Palestine are persuaded primarily by the desperate necessity of the Jews for a homeland and the comparative justice of their claim to Palestine in terms of ancient and historic considerations. With these claims the actual present possession of the disputed territory by the Arabs is in conflict. It is not pretended that there can be a simply "just" solution of such a conflict, when competing claims move on such various levels.

Niebuhr was, however, more practical and, yet at the same time, more prescient than the other speakers, for on that December 14, 1942, he was able to discern the future and foresee what had to be accomplished:

> It is, however, possible in such a circumstance to satisfy the Jewish claims essentially under the compulsion of their great need; and to seek compensation for the Arabs by a total settlement of Near Eastern claims. The Arabs will not have made any substantial contribution to the defeat of the Axis if and when it occurs. It would, however, be a wise statesmanship to allow the Arab world to be federated and to give it this higher unity in compensation for its loss of rights in Palestine.

Anticipating what might ensue in the 1950s, 1960s, and 1970s, Niebuhr went on to say:

> Such a *quid pro quo* would have to involve a genuine disavowal of sovereignty over a sufficient part of Palestine to permit a Jewish state to be established which would have territorial integrity, political independence within the framework of a commonwealth of nations,

221

and the means of economic survival. It would also demand a genuine improvement of the Arab situation in terms of a greater unity and independence of that world.

He warned, however, that "the settlement would require some rigorous self-abnegation on the part of the Great Powers" and admonished: "They will have to cease the policy of establishing particular zones of influence in this or that Arab state and develop a larger policy of mutual security."

Fully aware of the fact that British power in that region was "embarrassed with the problem of the relation of the Arab to the whole Moslem world, . . . [an] embarrassment for Britain [which] has undoubtedly made the solution of the Palestinian problem more difficult than some of Britain's critics have been willing to admit . . ." and that "French imperial claims [in the area], which have no reality in power or in justice . . . [must undergo an] abridgement of imperial rights wherever they come in conflict with the necessity of an overall settlement of the vexing Jewish-Arab problem and the Jewish-world problem," Niebuhr had a word of advice for his own government:

> There is no reason, however, why America should mold its policy according to such embarrassments or according to French imperial claims. . . . American arms [due to the invasion of North Africa by United Nations forces, primarily American, the previous month] have brought us into a dominant position in that very portion of the world where this issue must be solved. It would be ridiculous ot use our power merely to underwrite the past when we have a chance to underwrite the future and to help in granting justice to a people who have been the first, and most cruelly used, of Hitler's victims.

Although Niebuhr was to be chosen treasurer of the Christian Council on Palestine that very day and began to assume a major role in formulating decisions among Christians of Zionist sympathies, this kind of *Realpolitik* did not become an integral part of the approach the organization was to take in the following years. On the contrary, more simplistic, elementary approaches were characteristic of the CCP and ultimately of the American Christian Palestine Committee, when the APC and CCP united forces, partially in 1944 and fully in 1946. This less complex outlook was reflected in three of the leading Christians committed to Zionist goals but who steered clear of such tortuous, yet rigorously honest and realistic thinking—Henry Atkinson, Walter Clay Lowdermilk, and Eduard Lindeman.

222

Atkinson, originally a Methodist but ordained a Congregationalist, was a product of the Social Gospel in American Protestantism. He pioneered in the founding in 1910 of the Department of Church and Labor, later to become the Social Service Commission, and the Department of Social Relations of the Congregational churches, and then the Council for Social Action, a model for many other denominations. In 1919, he became secretary-general of the Church Peace Union, a Carnegie-funded interfaith organization bent on world organization and international peace. Atkinson spent much of the year in Geneva, Switzerland, working with the League of Nations Secretariat and the International Labor Office, cooperating with Protestant leaders in the early days of the ecumenical movement, and traveling to many parts of the world. On close terms of friendship with such international leaders as Raymond Fosdick, Sir Eric Drummond, Field Marshal Jan Christiaan Smuts, and Lord Robert Cecil, he firmly believed in the League's intentions with reference to the Balfour Declaration and its assignment of the Palestine Mandate to Great Britain.

Foremost in his makeup was a strong religious belief in the cause of Zionism, so basic that he always said, "I had imbibed my Zionism with my mother's milk, and she fortified it with teachings from the Bible." Thus when Wise, Bernstein, and Steinberg asked him to organize the Christian Council on Palestine, he greeted them as fellow-clergymen and fellow-Zionists, energetically getting the Council under way but naively believing a letter-head organization would swiftly achieve the objective.

When he brought me from my pastorate in Pittsburgh, Pennsylvania in the winter of 1942-3 to serve as executive secretary on a half-time basis, spending the other half of the time at the post of extension secretary of the Church Peace Union and the World Alliance for International Friendship Through the Churches, he advised me, "You'll soon be devoting all your time to the CPU and the World Alliance, for this Palestine stint will be a short term job. As soon as the British see that list of men on our stationery—Niebuhr, Tillich, McConnell, Albright, Sockman, and Poling—they'll open the gates of Palestine and let those Jewish refugees come pouring in. Then we'll disband the committee. It's as simple as that." Shortly before his death in 1960, I reminded him of that prediction; and he ruefully confessed, "How wrong I was, how very wrong."

There was about Atkinson on openness of mind, a heartiness of manner, a down-to-earth quality, all redolent of the open spaces of the

West whence he had come; he was always something of the pioneer, not only in social action and the ecumenical movement, but also in the struggle against fascism, especially, however, in the battle against American isolationism, from the days when Woodrow Wilson went down to defeat at the hands of "a little group of willful men" until the attack on Pearl Harbor, and in the fight against anti-Semitism and in his life-long espousal of a Zionist solution.

The indomitable, crusading spirit emerged dramatically one day in February 1944, when he appeared in Washington before the Committee on Foreign Affairs of the House of Representatives on behalf of a House Resolution supporting a Jewish national home in Palestine. He defined the Christian Council on Palestine, which he represented, as having been founded "for the purpose of bringing to the American people through Christian leadership and membership of churches the conviction that in the post-war settlement Palestine should be made accessible to Jewish refugees from lands of persecution and that the ultimate destiny of the Jews depends upon the reaffirmation and fulfillment of the Balfour Declaration."

He summed up the basic religious conviction of the CCP by asserting:

> We have had our consciences hurt by the recognition that it is only in so-called Christian lands where things like that which happened in Germany could start. Outside of places where there are Christians, the less Christian they are, the more liberty there is for the Jewish people apparently; and we feel the time has come when we ought to face up to the responsibility and recognize that there's hardly a Jewish problem in the world, but there is a very serious Christian problem that we have to face.
>
> We believe that this problem is basically a Christian problem, and thus we appeal on behalf of our members and the people in their churches. We are convinced that the open door of a strongly established and recognized Jewish homeland in Palestine offers the only real hope for most of these suffering men, women, and children, who today linger in misery and ignominy under the heel of Hitler.

In words which visibly moved the members of the House Committee and did not leave untouched anyone present that morning in Washington, he concluded with this plea:

> I firmly believe . . . that Palestine is not only a means of salvation for the Jewish people, but in a larger sense is also a means of safeguarding

our democracy. . . . The attack on the Jews was the entering wedge by which the liberties of all the free people in all the nations were attacked, and the Jew was attacked because he was the most vulnerable in Germany at the time.

Therefore, Mr. Chairman, ladies and gentlemen of the Committee, in the name of humanity and in the name of justice, I strongly urge the passage of these resolutions [Nos. 418, 419—Wright-Compton] in order that we may begin the establishment of a just and durable peace by affirming rather than denouncing and nullifying the Balfour Declaration, the best and most constructive single document that emerged from World War I.[7]

More soft-spoken, yet equally rugged in physique and strong of character, was Walter Clay Lowdermilk, who suddenly sprang into fame in March of 1944 with the publication of a new book, *Palestine: Land of Promise*. A nationwide gathering of the American Palestine Committee and the Christian Council on Palestine, in cooperation with the Free World Association, the Union for Democratic action [later known as Americans for Democratic Action], the American Federation of Labor, the Congress of Industrial Organizations, and several other organizations, met in Washington to unify Christian and other non-Jewish sentiment on behalf of the rescue of Jews from Hitler's Europe and the rebuilding of Palestine as a Jewish national home. On that day a copy of Lowdermilk's *Palestine: Land of Promise* (1944) was given to each of the thousand delegates. The book, a lucid, scientific treatment of Palestine's potential to settle several million people on its once rich but now parched earth, had been long in the making; but now the copious prose had been edited to readable proportions. It presented a message of hope for Jewish pioneers and gave the lie to those who said the "tiny notch of land" (Lord Balfour's words) was "not big enough to swing a cat around in" (Lord Passfield's phrase).

Lowdermilk, a conservation specialist with the Department of Agriculture, had visited Palestine for the first time in 1939 on his return to the United States from China. Fired by what he saw, he declared in speeches and articles that "the Jews of Palestine have done the finest reclamation of old land I have seen on four continents. Theirs is the most successful rehabilitation of land and people in modern times."[8]

When he wanted to tell the story in a longer exposition and perhaps publish it, the British Mandatory officials tried to dissuade him and brought pressure to bear on their American friends to discourage

Lowdermilk from the idea of a book on the subject; the American State Department heeded their British colleagues' entreaties and tried, though unsuccessfully, to head Lowdermilk in other directions. Justice Louis Brandeis, still alive when Lowdermilk began putting his prolix sentences on paper, urged him on; and when, several years after Brandeis's death, the book was published, Lowdermilk traced the basic inspiration to the great jurist. Ultimately it went into fourteen printings and was reissued in paperback editions with translations into six languages.

One of the concepts in *Palestine: Land of Promise* was the National Water Carrier Project of Israel which was later begun by Lowdermilk in 1951. It was carried to completion within five years with such success that the Haifa Technion founded in his honor the Lowdermilk School of Agricultural Engineering, a thriving institution of which he was the first director.

An unfinished project of Lowdermilk's is the Jordan Valley Authority by which he hoped—and his disciples still hope, not without reason—to harness hydroelectric power by the 2400 foot drop between the Mediterranean Sea and the Dead Sea.

When Lowdermilk, aided by his indefatigable wife, Inez, spoke in forums and conferences of the American Palestine Committee and the Christian Council on Palestine, as well as to innumerable Zionist groups, audiences were impressed by their mystic love of the Land of the People and the Land of the Book. Everyone, Jew and non-Jew alike, could not help being stirred by Lowdermilk's oft-repeated statement: "If Moses had foreseen the destruction mankind would bring upon the world, he would have added an Eleventh Commandment dealing with man's responsibility to the Holy Earth." That Eleventh Commandment, engraved on a tablet which graces a wall in the Haifa Technion, reflects Lowdermilk's Christian concern for Israel:

Thou shalt inherit the Holy Earth as a faithful steward, conserving its productivity and resources from generation to generation. Thou shalt safeguard they fields from soil erosion, thy living waters from drying up, thy forests from desolation, and protect the hills from over-grazing by thy herds, that thy descendants may have abundance forever. If any shall fail in this good stewardship of the earth, thy fruitful fields shall become sterile, stony ground or wasting gullies, and thy descendants shall decrease and live in poverty, or perish from off the face of the earth.[9]

226

Quite different from Atkinson and Lowdermilk was the celebrated authority on mass psychology and both urban and rural sociology, the widely hailed "father of adult education in America," Eduard Lindeman of the New York School of Social Work. As deeply religious as they, though a humanist/naturalist/non-theist, Lindeman was an immigrant who had endured hardship in his youth and attained his education only in later years. His sympathy with the Jews and the problems of homelessness sprang from his own origins, his fight for identity and survival in earlier decades of a distinguished career. When he spoke at an APC/CCP conference in Philadelphia in the autumn of 1944, he gave as his topic, "Palestine: Test of Democracy," and noted that he was "a fairly recent convert to the idea of a Jewish state, having resisted the appeal of this movement for a great many years."

Lindeman had not "forsaken the idea that democratic strength comes from diversity, not from uniformity," but had "finally come to see that democracy cannot fully succeed unless there is a Jewish state." Then he proceeded in this address, delivered all over America, to list his reasons "why non-Jews should be heartily and thoroughly in favor of building up a strong Jewish state:"

> *In the first place:* there is a moral issue involved — a multi-faceted promise to be kept, . . . an historic promise in the spirit, the hearts, and the minds of Jews, and it will not die; a promise internationally, . . . the Balfour Declaration,. . . . and . . . Mr. Woodrow Wilson assented . . . and a resolution in Congress in 1922, . . . stating we were committed. . . .
>
> *Second:* . . . I want to bring dignity to all Jews everywhere. I believe that Jews all over the world will walk straighter and that all the furtiveness imposed upon them by their dispersion will disappear once there is a place which will ultimately be not merely an autonomous state but a sovereign state, with all the rights and privileges of sovereignty, brought into existence, managed, and supported by the genius and the labor of Jews . . . They must cease to be the only homeless people on earth.
>
> *Third:* . . . I believe that the Jewish homeland should be established now, before the War is over, . . . in order to provide a solution for the very large group of Jews among the so-called uprooted people of Europe.
>
> *Fourth:* A Jewish homeland . . . will help solve the entire problem of minorities. If the Jewish minority can solve its difficulties, then all the other minorities will take hope and learn the methods, devices and

techniques which have helped solve the Jewish question. If the Jewish question remains unsolved, then the status of all minority groups will continue to worsen. . . .

Fifth: The minority question is no longer purely European as it was after the last war. It is now an American disease, too, and we must help the rest of the world to solve this problem if we wish to avoid in this country the same kind of trouble which has bedeviled Europe for the last eighty to ninety years. . . . I feel we can no longer assume that there cannot be a strong, anti-Jewish movement in this country. It could be ignited very easily among . . . fifteen million so-called "Christians." It is therefore for our own sakes as Americans that we must help to solve the Jewish problem.

Sixth: A Jewish National Homeland will not only bring dignity to Jews, but remove from non-Jews the stigma of anti-Semitism. Unless we are rid of that stigma, it seems to me we can become neither Christian nor democratic.

Seventh: I am in favor of a Jewish Palestine because I believe that only with its aid can the Near East be developed and enabled to support a huge population. . . . The energy, skill, and devotion which young Jews have brought to the building of Palestine demonstrate how the whole Middle East can be expanded.

Eighth: Palestine is already a going concern. Why should we turn our backs on something which has been so successful that within the years of turmoil, when great capitalistic societies like England and the United States were almost having their death trial and suffering an unprecedented depression, Jews were building a new economic society upon new cooperative principles? Palestine is a pragmatic success, with an investment of a half billion dollars, a growing population, increased health, increased welfare, even for the Arabs, rising standards of education, culture, art. I do not think it is too much to say that there is no other example in modern history of a state building itself, lifting itself by its own bootstraps and building itself out of its human energy. There is no epic in modern history so magnificent as this Palestine experiment. . . .

Finally: The Palestine question is the acid test of democracy. . . . the acid test of the peace. A peace which leaves the Jewish question unresolved, will leave us who believe in democracy vulnerable to all the future Hitlers, all the malcontents, who will use this historic scapegoat to build up their nefarious movements. If we should enter into such a peace as leaves no room for the solution of the problem of which Palestine is the symbol, then there will be no peace.[10]

228

The Niebuhr emphases were not without meaning for the Christian Council on Palestine and its sister organization, the American Palestine Committee; but these organizations' basic *leitmotif* was that of the Atkinson/Lowdermilk/Lindeman view, namely, the Christian conscience which had been touched and was now aroused, the love of the Land and its sacred, responsive soil, and an awareness of what tiny Palestine meant to the democratic world and its democratic ethos, especially in terms of the future of the Jewish people and the awakening of the entire Middle East.

The year 1944 meant a broadening of the program of the APC and the CCP, brought about by the advent of Howard Marion LeSourd who combined the efforts of both groups; he, on a fulltime basis, and I, on a part-time arrangement with the Church Peace Union and the World Alliance, served as co-directors. Seminars and conferences in cities throughout the country were planned. A speakers' bureau, Club Program Service, was organized, thus making it possible for service clubs, church groups, community forums, and university convocations to secure knowledgeable, able speakers such as Helen Gehagan Douglas, Eleanor Roosevelt, Welthy Honsinger Fisher (widow of Gandhi's friend, Bishop Fred Fisher), Lucille LeSourd, George Fielding Eliot, Wendell Phillips, Frank Gervasi, Carl J. Friedrich, Edgar Ansel Mowrer, and Charles Turck.

Literature, especially the publication, *Palestine* (issued by the American Zionist Emergency Council, through which the APC and the CCP were financially supported), and such books as Lowdermilk's *Palestine: Land of Promise,* Frank Gervasi's *To Whom Palestine?,* Ellen Thorbecke's picture-and-text book on *Palestine: Land of Miracles,* Carl Friedrich's *American Foreign Policy and Palestine,* and my own *Answers on the Palestine Question* (issued in continually updated versions) were all widely distributed, especially to the now several thousand members of both organizations and to libraries throughout the land.[11]

LeSourd, a well-known clergyman and educator, was available for the director's post because war-time mobilization had shrunk the graduate student body at Boston University where he had been dean of the Graduate School. He brought both imagination and experience to the position and launched many new projects, not the least of which was an attempt to form a World Committee on Palestine.

Quotations from two letters, one in May 1945, and the other in mid-summer of that year, give some indication of the breadth and depth of the ACPC's program at the time. Immediately after the Allied forces' victory had been achieved in Europe, we joined with Helen Gehagan Douglas, congresswoman from California and national secretary of the ACPC, in sending a letter to every member of the United States Senate and House of Representatives:

The American Christian Palestine Committee, expressing widespread Christian conviction, believes that every effort must be made now to fulfill the international promises made to the Jews concerning their national homeland in Palestine.

The Nazi regime in the course of its monstrous campaign of systematic murder and torture has almost annihilated the Jewish communities of Europe; and for millions of Jews, the end of the war in Europe comes too late. Horrible disclosures concerning the Buchenwald, Maidenek, Oswiecim, and other prison and concentration camps have shocked the civilized world. Hitler waged his war against the helpless Jews of Europe with a barbarity and determination which we in this country have only now begun to realize. At this moment we must do all we can to insure justice to the remnant of European Jewry and make impossible a repetition of this tragedy. Therefore we are asking you and the other members of the Senate to sign the enclosed letter addressed to President Truman as a current reiteration of our traditional national policy. The party platforms of both Republicans and Democrats affirm their support of the opening of Palestine to unrestricted Jewish immigration and colonization so that in accordance with the full intent and purpose of the Balfour Declaration, Palestine may be constituted as a free and democratic Jewish Commonwealth.

The results were gratifying, and there emerged a wave of support which was as overwhelming as it was surprising. There is no question about the influence this had on the White House and President Truman's slowly growing interest in and sympathy for the restoration of a Jewish national home.

The other letter, dated July 30, 1945, reflected something of the hope and relief of V-E Day and foreshadowed the dramatic events of the following three years in which the activities, limned in these paragraphs, came to fulfillment; for Howard LeSourd and I had high hopes, many of which eventually achieved reality:

By the time this letter reaches you, we will have traveled to England by plane. Our trip is at the invitation of Sir Wyndham Deedes, chairman of the British Association for a Jewish National Homeland, and Mr. David Ben-Gurion, chairman of the Jewish Agency for Palestine. We have been asked to attend, as observers, the World Zionist Conference in London at the end of July.

Then we outlined our plans for regional conferences in the coming months; told of the Memorial Sunday in May 1945, we had chosen to commemorate the loss of six million Jews at the hands of the Nazis and the hope we expressed that each year there would be some kind of remembrance; described the National Seminar held in early July at the Princeton Inn, with countrywide representation and a roster of resource persons including Carl J. Friedrich, Reinhold Niebuhr, Eduard C. Lindeman, Edgar Ansel Mowrer, and David Ben-Gurion; noted the nationwide radio program we sponsored with the aid of Morton Wishengrad as writer and Paul Muni as star actor; mentioned our sending to President Truman a petition with the signatures of 39 governors gathered at a Mackinac Island conference which asked for "the opening of Palestine to unrestricted Jewish immigration and the land's transformation into a Jewish commonwealth," the resolutions of 33 state legislatures seeking the same objectives, and a letter Senator Robert Wagner brought to President Truman with the signatures of 54 Senators and 256 Representatives (which had indeed been "as overwhelming as it was surprising"); told of a significant meeting held with "leading religious editors [all Protestants but no Roman Catholics], where plans were discussed by which the weekly and monthly magazines reaching the constituency of our Christian churches could be covered more effectively, . . . particularly through a news service with material on Palestine and the present need of the Jewish people"; spoke of the ever growing work of the speakers' bureau, Club Program Service; and then mentioned the most important project of the ACPC:

The prime purpose of our visit to Great Britain is to discuss with Sir Wyndham Deedes the possibility of holding an International Christian Conference in Washington, D.C. next November. There are more than a score of pro-Palestine committees throughout the world—a dozen in the Western Hemisphere, several on the European Continent, and a half dozen in Great Britain and the Dominions, all of which are in basic accord with the principles of the

American Christian Palestine Committee and seek, as do we, to mobilize Christian opinion on behalf of Jewish aims and hopes in Palestine. We shall be able to discuss this project more intelligently and specifically . . . after our return from the British Isles.[12]

From that time on for the next thirty-three and one-half months, until mid-May of 1948 when Israel was proclaimed an independent Jewish commonwealth, the activities followed that pattern, all at a whirlwind pace. The seminars, meetings, petitions, and conferences, especially the World Conference, held in Washington that November of 1945 as planned, brought a mounting pressure to bear on Washington and London and on the United Nations at Lake Success.[13]

The 1946 testimony of Reinhold Niebuhr before the Anglo-American Committee of Inquiry on Palestine served, according to Richard H. S. Crossman, a British member of the Committee,[14] to clarify the group's mind and set the members thinking along pro-Zionist directions. Likewise, the documents presented by the ACPC to the United Nations Special Committee on Palestine in early 1947 were not without influence, especially because now there was a flood-tide of protest against Jewish national homelessness and on behalf of the partition of Palestine as proposed by UNSCOP's findings and as voted by the General Assembly on November 29, 1947.

Before and after the partition vote by the United Nations, the American Christian Palestine Committee found itself linked with dozens of organizations, Jewish and non-Jewish, pressing for the adoption of the UNSCOP plan, and then for its swift, effective implementation. No longer did the ACPC feel itself to be something of a voice crying in the wilderness. On the contrary, there was now a host of groups, among which was the influential World Christian Committee for Palestine, speaking out on behalf of what was to become a strong and vibrant new country, the State of Israel.

The American Christian Palestine Committee continued for another thirteen years of strong and meaningful programs, interpreting the new Jewish state to the Christian community, and then dissolving its status, firm in the knowledge it had known an heroic, unique hour in the history of the world.

There were, however, grave limitations in the program of the American Christian Palestine Committee, not the least of which were the *ad hoc* nature of the Committee from its very start and the lack of an informed, concerned constituency on which to draw. Only the grievous crisis of World War Two and the increasingly credible reports of Hitler's annihilation of European Jewry finally galvanized some—all too few—Christians into action. Even when the political stakes became increasingly visible and it was clear that a strong, knowledgeable Christian voice was the necessary ingredient for any kind of solution, a man as courageous and forthright as Henry A. Atkinson insisted on caution, a muted protest, the blunted criticism. During 1946 and 1947, Reinhold Niebuhr frequently expressed anxiety about too harsh an indictment of Great Britain for her failure to administer the Mandate in such a way that Jews might be rescued and the foundations for a Jewish state laid forthwith.

It was difficult to structure a definite, consistent program, except to stir public opinion and carry on as broad and specific an educational project as possible, especially through pamphlets and booklets, radio debates and public forums. We had to rely on letters-to-the-editor and petitions to Congress, protests to the State Department and pressure on the American delegation to the United Nations, especially in the final months from the August 1947 report of the Special Committee on Palestine through the adoption of partition by the General Assembly in late November 1947, on to the incredible reconstitution of the Third Jewish Commonwealth on May 14, 1948. Christians did play a part but not as significantly or as definitively as they should have. They had been conditioned against such action by centuries of deeply ingrained anti-Semitism, conditioning which could not be undone in a few short months or even years.

The American Christian Palestine Committee had all the assets of "a good cause," namely, an urgency and a righteous objective, an elemental justice to secure and a concrete objective to attain, a Christian ethic to hold as its standard and a sensitized conscience to be its guide. But it also had liabilities: a lack of ample funds (although the American Zionist Emergency Council, representing the major Zionist groups among Jews on the American scene, rendered support as generously as possible),[15] a lack of sufficient time in such a crisis to work out a long-term, carefully defined strategy over many years, and an insufficiently "briefed" constituency, for while many Christians "cared," there were not enough of them. Even these few knew precious little of the historical background and even less of the complex circumstances in the Middle East and its power struggles, especially in the latter days of two expiring empires, the British and the French, and the rise to heady

233

power by two imperial giants, the Soviet Union and the United States.

Sudden decisions were often inadequately considered, then ineptly executed. Pronouncements, solemnly, often ardently made in the heat of controversy, appeared later to have been hyper-emotional and ill-conceived. Enthusiastic adherent to the cause turned out in many instances to be fainthearted and, at times, cowardly. Officers of the Committee, working on a voluntary, unpaid, genuinely committed but nevertheless distracted basis, were not always available for consultation and decisions. The organization inevitably suffered from the lag between an urgent need for a statement or an action, on the one hand, and the difficulties, on the other, of formulating carefully reasoned announcements and attaining chosen objectives. This was essentially a propaganda war from beginning to end, a tragic beginning with Hitler's sworn intention to wipe out all the Jews in the world, and a triumphant end, Israel's establishment and the rescue of the remnant of European Jewry.

The greatest problem among Christians lay in their unwillingness, perhaps their inability, to commit themselves to this cause amid so many confused and confusing issues. Indecision and inaction seemed the easiest way out of a dilemma. Most disturbing was the average Christian's willingness to listen to the anti-Zionist diatribes of denominational officials, especially missionaries, who looked askance at Zionism and listened uncritically to Arabists in the U.S. State Department.

Despite the uncertainty and timidity of many Christians, however, there was indeed a Christian voice; and it was expressed, though imperfectly and often ineffectually, by the American Christian Palestine Committee. The founders and the leaders were prophetic—that is, in the ancient meaning of that word, they "spoke for God"—but one is compelled to echo Moses: "Would to God that all His people were prophets"!

FOOTNOTES

1. *Encyclopedia of Zionism and Israel*, 1:34-36; 1155; files on "American Palestine Committee," "Christian Council on Palestine," and "American Christian Palestine Committee" are to be found in the Zionist Archives and Library, New York; also Emanuel Neumann *In the Arena: An Autobiographical Memoir* by (New York, 1976), *passim*.
2. Carl Hermann Voss, *The Palestine Problem Today: Israel and Its Neighbors* (Boston, 1953), p. 11.
3. Neumann, *In the Arena*, pp. 172-73. A full page advertisement in the *New York Times*, Friday, December 31, 1943, lists not only Robert Wagner as chairman and Charles McNary as co-chairman, but also includes an executive committee, consisting of Claude Pepper, U.S. senator from Florida, Eric A. Johnston, president of the U.S. Chamber of Commerce, Arthur H. Vandenberg, U.S. senator from Michigan, Philip Murray, president of the CIO (Congress of Industrial Organizations), William Green, president of the AFL (American Federation of Labor), William H. King, U.S. senator from Utah, Msgr. John Ryan, executive vice-president of the National Catholic Welfare Conference, and Elbert Thomas, U.S. senator from Utah. See also Hertzel Fishman, *American Protestantism and a Jewish State*, (Detroit, 1973), *passim*.
4. Archives of Christian Council on Palestine, Zionist Archives and Library.
5. *Nation* 154 (February 21 and 28, 1942): 214-16, 253-55.
6. Reinhold Niebuhr, "The Jewish State and the Arab World," a paper read on December 14, 1942 at conference of Christian clergy at which the Christian Council on Palestine was founded; available in *précis* in files of American Emergency Committee for Zionist Affairs, Zionist Archives and Library, also in Abba Hillel Silver Archives, Temple Tifereth Israel, Cleveland, Ohio.
7. Atkinson concluded his remarks by saying: "We are horrified by the indescribable brutality of Hitler and his oppressors, and conscious of the tragic plight of millions of Jews in Europe today. We urge that the United States Government help provide appropriate measures to the end that the doors of Palestine be opened for further entry of homeless, stateless Jews of war-torn Europe. We urge that there be full opportunity for colonization in Palestine so that the Jewish people may reconstitute that country as a free and democratic Jewish commonwealth." *Hearings Before the Committee on Foreign Affairs, House of Representatives, Seventy-Eighth Congress, Second Session on H. Res. 418 and H. Res. 419, Resolutions Relative to the Jewish National Home in Palestine, February 8, 9, 15, and 16, 1944, etc.*
8. Quoted in Emma Kimor, "Walter Clay Lowdermilk—Pioneer Environmentalist: A Man Who Cared For the Earth," in *Jerusalem Post*, March 24, 1976.
9. *Ibid.*; also quoted in Inez Lowdermilk, *Modern Israel: Fulfillment of Prophecy—A Christian Speaks Out*, published by the California Christian Committee for Israel [1975 or 1976]. The obstacles Lowdermilk encountered and then overcame in publishing *Palestine: Land of Promise* are described in an 800-page unpublished autobiographical manuscript which is available in the National and Israeli Library of the Hebrew University, Jerusalem, Israel, and the Library of the Haifa Technion in Haifa, Israel.
10. Dr. Eduard C. Lindeman, "Palestine: Test of Democracy," was published by Christian Council on Palestine and American Christian Palestine Committee, 1945.
11. The later (1950-59) publication of the American Christian Palestine Committee, *Land Reborn*, edited by Karl Baehr (from 1947 the extension secretary of the ACPC) and myself, had not yet begun publication. The pamphlet/booklet, *Answers on the Palestine Question*, was thoroughly revised and rewritten in 1953 and published by the Beacon Press of Boston as *The Palestine Problem Today: Israel and Its Neighbors*. Other publications included "Addresses and Messages Delivered at the Second Annual Dinner of the American Palestine Committee" (1942), "Common Purpose of Civilized Mankind: Declaration by 68 Members of the Senate and 194 Members of the House . . . on the Occasion of the 25th Anniversary of the Balfour Declaration" (1942), "Congressional Leaders Petition Pres. Roosevelt For a Jewish Homeland in Palestine" (1943), "Memorandum On Rescue of Jews Submitted to the State Department by Christian Spokesmen" (1944), "United Nations and the Jewish National Home in Palestine" (1942), "Voice of Christian America: Proceedings of the National Conference on Palestine, Washington, D.C., March 9, 1944," "The Jewish Case: The Place of Palestine in the Solution of the Jewish Question" (1945), "Questions and Answers on Palestine" (1945), "To the American People" (1945), "A

Christian Point of View" (Presented to the Anglo-American Committee of Inquiry), 1946, "Benjamin Franklin on Palestine" (1946), "The Truth About Palestine" (1946), "The Arab War Effort" (1947), and "People Speak on Palestine" (1948).

12. Files of American Christian Palestine Committee, Zionist Archives and Library.

13. In his book, *Zionism at the UN: A Diary of the First Days*, (Philadelphia, 1976), Eliahu Elath, director of the Middle East division of the Jewish Agency's Political Department from 1934 to 1945, writes in his entry for June 1, 1945:

> I spent a large part of the evening with Dr. Henry Atkinson, who has returned to San Francisco [from his office at the Church Peace Union in New York City] as an adviser to the American delegation. He gave me a detailed picture of the American Christian Palestine Committee he heads. It was founded at the end of 1942, and is made up of Christians of all denominations. It has a membership of more than two thousand. One of the Committee's first moves was to declare its support for the Biltmore Program [ed. note: in so many words, no; but moving slowly toward this goal]. Atkinson expressed his satisfaction at the fact that among the founders of his committee are some of the most eminent Christian theologians: Reinhold Niebuhr, John Haynes Holmes, Paul Tillich, and Ralph Sockman. Most members are Protestant, but there are also Catholics, some of whom are well known, such as Msgr. John A. Ryan. Dr. Daniel Poling, editor of the *Christian Herald*, one of the most important and widely circulated Protestant periodicals, is an active member of the Committee (p. 234).

14. Richard H. S. Crossman, *Palestine Mission* (New York, 1947).

15. In an otherwise scholarly, readable book, Howard Sachar inexplicably and erroneously writes (*A History of Israel: From the Rise of Zionism to Our Time* [New York, 1976], p. 289) that the American Christian Palestine Committee was "a front group" through which the American Zionist Emergency Council "activated labor leaders, the press, and clergymen, etc., etc." It must be stated categorically the ACPC was anything but a "front." It was a cooperating organization, founded and fostered by leaders within the AZEC, but characterized by independent status and an independent mind which expressed itself in many unique ways. The story is much more complex, interesting, and full of creativity than Sachar allows himself to infer from the ACPC's history or to imply in his handful of words about its programs.

236

James Parkes: Christianity without Anti-Semitism

Rose G. Lewis

In 1946, after some 17 years of research into Judaism and
Jewish history, the Rev. Dr. James Parkes went to Palestine
for the first time. During a three-month visit, the Anglican minister asked a great many historical questions to which, he found,
he could get no satisfactory answers. Upon his return to England,
therefore, he looked into the records for himself. His resulting
history of the peoples of Palestine is still being widely read in a
popular Penguin paperback titled Whose Land. The book remains
unique as a brief, comprehensive account of the country and stands
virtually alone, in English, at any rate, in its attention to the years
between the subjugation of ancient Judea and the rise of modern
Israel.

Among other things, Parkes had been surprised to find that the
Jews in Palestine had not "returned after 2000 years," as he had
long heard Zionists proclaiming. He discovered, on the contrary,
that the Jewish presence in the country had been continuous throughout those forgotten centuries. He remained sympathetic to the problems of the Arabs, and was naturally concerned with the status of
the Christians, but he concluded nonetheless that the history of the
Middle East supported the right to self-determination of the Palestinian Jews. He had been persuaded of Israel's title deeds by its
Mideast rather than its European connections: by the endurance
and accomplishments of Palestinian Jewry under Arab domination,
by the historic oppression of the Jews under Islam, by the claims
of the Mideast Jewish refugees who are a majority of Jewish
Israelis.

Parkes closed his history, however, with sharp criticism of
all the parties to the Israeli-Arab dispute, including the Zionists.
Each of them, he charged, had in crucial ways been short-sighted
and self-defeating.

Parkes's broad perspectives and cool judgments did not make
him a hero to factions on any side: the Arabs tried to bribe him
into silence; English Arabists, in and out of the Foreign Office,
were actively hostile; and Zionists for the most part ignored him,

giving little publicity to the numerous books and pamphlets in which he continued steadily to defend as well as to criticize Israel.

Israel's political legitimacy was not the first Jewish issue with which James Parkes had chosen to confront the world in his double vocation of clergyman and historian. As a young man, in the 1920s, he had taken on Christian "antisemitism"* itself. At that time also he had stumbled upon a historical vacuum. He had been unable, when he needed them, to find any unprejudiced books which would explain anti-Semitism to Christian students. He promptly embarked upon his own research and authored several classics in the modern study of Jewish-Christian relations.

On the question of anti-Semitism, too, Parkes did not flinch from his preacher's task of expounding the relevant texts and reading the moral lessons. In the end, he called upon the Church for an admission of theological error and asked for Christian recognition of Judaism as a sister religion, independent and valid in its own right.

Parkes's reputation as a historian rests upon his rigorous scholarship and his pioneering inquiries into primary sources. But he did hold a point of view, and it was quite frankly that of a deeply believing Christian and a political interventionist. He studied the past, he said, in order to intervene in the present. "I was always conscious," he wrote, "that historical research was justified because it was necessary for the understanding of a contemporary evil and its eradication, and it was here that my main task lay. Much as I loved history, it was never an end in itself."

Parkes considered it to be the responsibility of the Church to cooperate with a benevolent God in the cause of human progress and social justice. This was, of course, not so fashionable an idea in his youth as it is today. Yet very early in his career he had begun to search for a Christian doctrine of politics. He

*Parkes urged the spelling: "antisemitism." He felt that "anti-Semitism" gives a false substantive look and invites Arabs to argue that they, too, are Semites and therefore cannot be anti-Semitic, etc. Since the word means anti-Jewish and nothing else, he thought this spelling would avoid irrelevant semantic quibbling.

wanted to find "a real theological interpretation of the divine
relation to our social and political life." When he became involved in the battle against anti-Semitism, this turned out to be
for him both an end in itself and also the means toward his
wider goal.

Parkes's combination of purposes, added to an uncompromising
independence of mind, led him down a rather lonely road. He
had little encouragement from his own Anglican Church. Christian conservatives found his deviationism unacceptable, particularly since he was outspoken in demanding such things as re-
visions of New Testament interpretations and the abandonment
of Christian missions to the Jews. At the same time, he is
relatively little known among Jews, who have on the whole not
given his far-reaching ideas a very ample hearing.

London's Jewish Chronicle once wrote of Parkes that
he falls between two stools: many Christians regard
him as having been Judaized, and many Jews look
upon him with suspicion as a Christian who knows
all the Jewish answers. . . . But when allowance
has been made for mistrust born of ignorance of
his real views, is it not a measure of our community's inability to make the best use of the
material which is available that it has failed to
recognize the role which he is playing in pro-
jecting a positive picture of Judaism to the non-
Jewish world?

James Parkes at the age of 20 was a British soldier in World War 1,
and he studied for the ministry at Oxford in the years directly after.
His was, he said, "a generation which had seen too much of the
reality of war, and which saw too clearly the immense gaps in the
Christian tradition insofar as human community was concerned."
Parkes took an active interest in student political activities, and
founded the university's chapter of the League of Nations Union.
After his ordination he worked with the Student Christian Movement in London, then went to Switzerland to begin there an experiment in European cultural cooperation for a new organization
called the International Student Service.

Parkes's job with the ISS was to arrange inter-university study
conferences "to deal with sore spots in the body academic, conflicts

of nationality, of race, and of political party." Often, in effect, he had to introduce the very idea of open discussion to students on the continent to whom "English debating was still an inexplicable mystery." His task was to bring about the face to face confrontation of antagonists "in an atmosphere where duels were out, and walking out of the room was discouraged."

Examining the many political and ethnic quarrels within European universities at the time, Parkes found that "the worst of them was antisemitism. Universities were closed because of antisemitic riots. Jewish students were actually killed in the universities, and so," he wrote in his autobiography, "I thought I'd better get down to the problem of antisemitism as one of the keys to the situation." In 1929, therefore, Parkes planned a first meeting between nationalist and Jewish student organizations. He arranged it for a cold damp week in January in an isolated 17th-century French chateau with only one properly heated meeting room, because if there had been two warm rooms "I knew that in between the formal meetings all the Jews would go into one room, all the antisemites into the other."

For Europe, it was already too late. But for Parkes, it was the beginning of a lifetime's devotion to the study of Jewish-Christian relations. He had discovered, to his considerable astonishment, that there existed no adequate Christian scholarship on the subject. Only the Jews had been able to bring to his seminars any competent lectures. "We had combed Europe unsuccessfully for a Christian scholar who could talk objectively either about Jewish history or about the contemporary Jewish situation," he recalled.

And so he became such a Christian scholar. To satisfy the immediate need, he prepared a first short study, and after that there was no turning back. He returned to Oxford, since it seemed evident that "if I were going to get anywhere in so controversial and difficult an issue, I had to become Herr Doktor. It was not that any doctor was automatically a learned man, but that, if a man was not even a doctor, he could not be a learned man." His doctoral thesis became The Conflict of the Church and the Synagogue, still considered the most authoritative survey of the origins and nature of Christian anti-Semitism.

Reflecting upon his early years in Geneva, Parkes said that
> it would have surprised me greatly at that time to
> have been told that my studies of a contemporary

social evil would lead me through history into theology, and into the reappraisal of theological statements which I had previously seen no reason to question. But I soon found that contemporary antisemitism was incomprehensible without a knowledge of Jewish history, and that there was no clue to Jewish history without an understanding of Judaism. As I began to understand historic Judaism, I began also to realise that it impinged far more deeply and disturbingly on my Christian preconceptions of its nature than I had ever suspected.

Clearly, James Parkes could not be satisfied merely with preaching tolerance and ecumenical goodwill. The historian in him was aroused, to begin with. There was a unique and irrational misanthropy in Christian anti-Semitism: Why? How had it started? He was already aware from early readings of Greek and Latin authors that Jewish minorities in cities of the ancient world had often been viewed as exclusive and intolerant, and that Gentile hostility had been aroused further by the special privileges and exemptions which Jews were granted in the Roman Empire. But this hostility seemed to him unexceptional, a normal example of xenophobia or of discordant group relations, and quite obviously based upon perceptions of reality.

Similarly, it was not difficult to understand the friction between Jews and early Christians. The dissension began within the Synagogue, where growing differences of belief and practice led inevitably to bitter dispute. Here Parkes places considerable emphasis upon the proselytizing activities of both Jews and Christians, which aggravated their rivalries in relation to the pagan world as well as to each other. Nonetheless, evidence indicated to him that for many years the battle had largely been one of words. The theologians had been busy hurling abusive scriptural texts at each other, but the people continued to pursue their common interests with no unusual economic or social divisiveness. Both sides were intolerant, to be sure, and inclined to "the occasional violence of exasperation." But even this seemed an insufficient explanation for what came after.

Parkes now shifted his inquiry from history to theology, and "was completely unprepared for the discovery that it was the Christian Church and the Christian Church alone, which turned

241

a normal xenophobia and normal good and bad relations between
two human societies into the unique evil of antisemitism." Sifting
carefully through records and writings of the first four centuries,
he came to see that what the Church had done was to create a
Jewish enemy from theological exegesis and not at all in response
to contemporary reality. The early Christian polemic of vilifica-
tion proved to be altogether unrelated to actual persons or ob-
servable fact or even historical memory. Instead, a fictional
Jewish people had been deliberately extracted from the words of
the Old Testament. Its malevolent image had been fabricated
simply by cutting into two separate parts the actual Jewish people
of the Bible and of history.

"The Old Testament is very frank about Jewish sins," Parkes
writes. "But it also dwells on the love between God and Israel
. . . . So long as both elements in the story are accepted as being
about a single people, a lofty balance is retained. But Christian
theologians divided it into the story of two peoples--the virtuous
Hebrews, who were the pre-incarnation Christians, had all the
praise and promise; and the wicked Jews had all the crimes and
denunciations."

For the Jew his Bible was naturally a unity, "with its combination of denunciation and encouragement, of threat and promise.
But the moment these were separated and all the promises applied to one group, and all the curses to an entirely separate
one, an appalling falsification took place." By the 4th century,
the Church historian, Eusebius, had gone so far as to make the
biblical Jews into two biologically distinct races.

Parkes found, here, the big lie at the very core of Christian
anti-Semitism. The Jews whom the Church taught herself to
hate, it turned out, were Jews from the Old Testament rather
than from the New. The Jewish reader is likely to be struck at
the outset by the lesser importance which Parkes gives to the
story of the Crucifixion. The basic motive for anti-Semitism, it
seemed, was not the Jewish rejection of Christianity, but rather
the Christian denial of Judaism, the deep need of the Church to
remove from her own view all trace of the continuing Synagogue,
authentic Jews, and actual Jewish history. This was done so effectively that Parkes was able to remark upon the modern Christian "rediscovery that Jews are a living people and Judaism a
living religion."

What was it, then, that impelled the Church? What was the inner necessity which so distorted her vision? The reason, it would appear, lies less with Calvary than with Sinai. It is impossible to read Parkes, or indeed other Christian theologians of similar concerns, without noticing the centrality to them of the Covenant at Sinai. Put simply, what the Christian needs, and has needed from the beginning, is assurance of his participation in the ancient Covenant of God with Israel, and his own full and recognized share in its blessings and promises. Christianity does not begin with Jesus, who was in any case a faithful Jew. It is rooted in Judaism, and the Covenant at Sinai is the deepest root of all and the primary source of comfort and legitimacy.

The early Church, furthermore, required the strength of Jewish authority and continuity in order to establish her position and defend her claims, even to protect her concept of God, without whom Jesus in Gentile hands was in danger of being turned into a pagan deity. As long, therefore, as the Synagogue might appear to be still in possession of Covenant and Bible, the Church could not feel secure. Even in this century, as though to illustrate the historic point, an Austrian theologian is able to write:

> We Christians. . .need God. We begrudge Him those
> to whom He previously revealed Himself, to whom
> belong the Fathers, the Covenant and the Promise.
> Despite two thousand years of Christian history, we
> still retain the uncertainties peculiar to upstarts. . . .
> It annoys us less that they / the Jews / do not acknow-
> ledge Christ as that along with this--with a few excep-
> tions such as Rosenzweig, Buber, and Schoeps--they
> deny our own tie with God. *

And the Methodist clergyman, Roy Eckardt, points to "the nature of the Christian problem" by asking yet again: "If it is so that the Lord has pledged His faithfulness to Israel, the question is: how may His abiding Covenant be extended to us who are poor pagans?"**

The Church found a way, during those first quarrelsome centuries. With neither rabbis nor priests in fact disposed to attempt a sharing of the tradition, the Church began a process of appropriating it all

*G. Molin, "Warum kann ein Christ kein Antisemit sein?" Judaica, XIX, 2, June 1963, p.108.
**A. Roy Eckardt, Your People, My People. New York, 1974. p. 223.

to herself and dispossessing the Synagogue altogether. The covenant at Calvary was proclaimed to have absorbed and superceded the Covenant at Sinai. Arbitrarily cutting the biblical Jews into two peoples made it possible for Christians to select for themselves their own Jewish heritage from the prophets and sages and all the "good" Jews, while at the same time abusing their Jewish neighbors as heirs only of the "bad" Jews.

To explain the stubborn loyalty of the Jews to their own religion, Christian theologians further read into the Old Testament a satanic and deicidal Jewish role which is based upon a theory that among them only a remnant ultimately remained faithful and righteous. These few then carried into the Church all that was valid in Judaism, while the rest of the nation, who had abandoned God, were in turn abandoned by Him. About this central Christian doctrine, Parkes said bluntly, "The spiritually-minded remnant, withdrawn from the main stream of national life, is a figment of Christian imagination." The belief rests, he pointed out, upon a falsification of history which paints the period from Ezra to Jesus as years of decline and decay for Judaism, when it was demonstrably a period of abounding vitality, innovation, and spiritual growth.

If Parkes had found an answer, he also had raised many questions. He called this the "theological whodunit" of his life: the search for a unifying vision of the works and the purposes of an intelligent, responsible, and benevolent God. Good theology, he insisted throughout, cannot be based upon bad history. He could no longer accept those Christian teachings concerning Judaism which he now knew to be historically false. But what then? Was Christainity's self-definition dependent upon a slandered and negated Judaism? Could the Church stand tall only if she felt her feet planted upon the body of a battered prostrate Synagogue? Was it possible to have a Christian religion without anti-Semitism?

Parkes read more and more deeply in the Talmud, in rabbinic writings, in Jewish history and literature. He collected a rich library of books and pamphlets on Christian-Jewish relations. He wrote further on medieval Jewry as well as on contemporary Jewish problems. There were those who chided him as "ganz verjudet." Others noted that "it has never happened before that a Christian had been so deeply soaked in Judaism without becoming a Jew."

244

Nonetheless, Parkes remained a Christian, and he went on steadily preaching to Christians. Early experiences had involved him in the tangled doctrinal and emotional problem of Christian missions to the Jews. With typical quiet humor, he chose to formulate his position on the issue when he was invited to Oxford to preach the McBride Sermon, which had been endowed "with an especial view to confute the aruguments of Jewish commentators and to promote the conversion to Christianity of the ancient people of God." Parkes had started down new paths. He told his startled audience:

> The Gentile Church to which we belong does not possess the whole truth. The Synagogue of rabbinic Judaism does not wholly lack it. Gentile Christianity and rabbinic Judaism are two parts of one whole: the separation of the Church from the Synagogue was the first and most tragic of all the schisms in our history and, like all schisms, it left truth divided. . . .We have failed to convert the Jews, and we shall always fail, because it is not the will of God that they shall become Gentile Christians; antisemitism has failed to destroy the Jews, because it is not the will of God that essential parts of His Revelation should perish. Our immediate duty to the Jew is to do all in our power to make the world safe for him to be a Jew.

Gradually, there had evolved for Parkes a doctrine which became the answer to his own questions and which has continued to challenge other theologians. God revealed Himself at Sinai and at Calvary, Parkes believes, with Covenants of equal validity and equal permanence. Between the two Covenants, God in His omnipotence had neither corrected nor contradicted Himself. The two Covenants are separate and distinct, each emphasizing a different channel of God's activity, each speaking to a different aspect of man's needs.

God's Covenant with the Jews, Parkes writes, is a Covenant with a whole nation, an inclusive natural community of people as they are, good and bad, here and now. At Sinai God presented a doctrine of social order, a way of life to guide men in society. The revelation of Torah therefore emphasizes justice and righteousness and law, both within and among the nations. It is concerned with mutual obligation, with attainable goals, with the general welfare. The Promises are of a Messianic Age in which God's justice and righteousness and peace shall be achieved in this world for all mankind.

God's Covenant at Calvary, Parkes continues, is a communication to individuals, a call to the few and the elect from among the nations to choose the narrow way. It emphasizes man as person and encourages singular aspiration to the highest, even if unattainable, ideals. The revelation of Calvary speaks to man in himself of personal salvation. The stress is upon faith, and the Promises are of spiritual rewards in a heavenly world and of a Messiah whose return will usher in a heavenly kingdom.

Thus, says Parkes, "an intelligible doctrine emerges which claims for Judaism the flow of the divine purpose into the life of the community, for Christianity the flow of the same purpose into the life of man as person." Parkes has no doubt that the relationship of tension between the two Covenants is intended to be both continuing and creative. He argues, therefore, that Judaism and Christianity "are neither identical nor interchangeable, so that neither can be said to be superfluous." Both, in his view, are part of a single divine plan.

Parkes was finally brought full circle, back to his first uncomfortable youthful realization that "there was nothing central in the Christian tradition which could be called a doctrine of the natural community. . . . but that there was a strong and uninhibited Christian tradition which denied the relevance of the Christian insight to the political field, and even relegated ethics themselves to a completely secondary place of importance." It was Judaism, he decided, which held the inspiration and the understanding of divine imperative in community or, as he had once put the question to himself, a coherent and creative theology of politics. When, therefore, the Church had rejected Judaism and had instead chosen accommodation with Rome and Empire, she had also in practice rejected the discipline of Sinai and abandoned its mission.

Parkes believes that the Christian's claim to the Sinaitic Covenant through Jesus the Jew is not to be denied. He holds, however, that Calvary has demonstrably not superceded Sinai, and that Christianity continues to lack precisely that which Sinai offers. "Not only has Christianity not absorbed Judaism, historically speaking," he writes, "but, theologically speaking, it would not have absorbed it if all Jews individually accepted baptism in the different existing Christian churches. They would have gained Jews, but they would have lost Sinai."

In thus urging the validity and permanence of both religions, Parkes explained: "I may be innovating, but I am completely orthodox in refusing to recognize inequality within the Godhead. Judaism and Christianity are to me equal partners in the task of bringing mankind to the Messianic age, and neither can replace the other."

James Parkes' ideas did not, of course, find their way into the Sunday sermons of very many parish churches. He himself pointed unhappily to the gap between Church practices and modern scholarship.

> For me as an Anglican, the situation is become spiritually intolerable. In theological colleges and universities, in books and scientific periodicals, an entirely new conception of the nature of the writings of the Old and New Testaments has become a universally accepted basis for further research. But there is no trace of this conception in the doctrines of the Anglican Church or in the use of the Scriptures in worship, and there is very little in religious education.

Parkes has, however, had a considerable impact upon a growing number of Christian theologians who have come to share his concern with the problem of anti-Semitism. To this problem "James Parkes has given /us / a more radical and more valid answer," wrote Rev. John T. Pawlikowski of the Catholic Theological Union in Chicago. "His model and vision need expansion and refinement. But in his writings we have witnessed a terribly important breakthrough. . . .Once again he has set us in the right direction, just as when in the 30's and 40's he reestablished the validity of Judaism as an independent religion."*

Rev. Robert Everett, pastor of Emanuel United Church of Christ in Irvington, New Jersey finds that Parkes "has provided Christian theology with many of the historical and theological correctives needed for the quest for a theology without antisemitism

---

* John T. Pawlikowski, "The Church and Judaism: The Thought of James Parkes," Journal of Ecumenical Studies, Fall, 1969. p. 573.

to succeed. . . .What Parkes proposes is a new Christian theology which is theocentric in nature, but which does not destroy Christian self-identity nor exclude Judaism as a valid source of divine revelation."**

Noting that in James Parkes "we are blessed by an Anglican of the Anglicans," Roy Eckardt points out that Parkes welcomed "the trend away from the calculated blurring of differences that was prevalent during an earlier day. To be sure, a Judaism that was prepared to reduce the events of Sinai to an interesting piece of folklore and a Christianity that was prepared to relegate Jesus's claim to divinity to a Hellenistic mystery relic could easily join hands. But the price had to be a denial of the essential truths embodied in each religion. . . ."***

Inevitably, many rabbis have been ambivalent about Parkes's work. Certainly, they are grateful for his concern and they have a high regard for his scholarship. They respect the unflinching integrity of the historian, the honesty and courage and simple decency of the man. But it is the Anglican priest with whom they are, finally, uncomfortable. Parkes wrote, to be sure, in a spirit of Christian self-examination. Yet he deals with matters which, for Jews, have radiations of meaning--where does he lead? Thus far, discussions of the sorts of questions he raises have been largely confined to the more scholarly religious journals, and there has been relatively little Jewish participation. And among Jews, as among Christians, recent enlargements of biblical and historical perceptions have not noticeably filtered into the awareness of religious congregations and popular forums.

Parkes from the outset had his difficulties with the Orthodox Jewish establishment in England, which regarded him with some suspicion. "They must understand," he said patiently, "that I cannot at the same time be a liberal in regard to the New Testament and a conservative in regard to the Old. If I am to say that the Gospels exaggerated and even falsified the evidence and that Paul was wrong, then I cannot accept literally every word of the Old Testament either."

For its part, Orthodox Jewry in the United States has determined

---

**Robert Everett, "James Parkes and the Quest for a Christian Theology Without Antisemitism," Christian Attitudes on Jews and Judaism, February, 1977.
***A. Roy Eckardt, Elder and Younger Brothers, New York, 1967, pp. 82-89.

to shun altogether any Jewish-Christian dialogue touching upon questions of religious dogma or interpretation. An operative guideline by Rabbi Joseph Soloveitchik, Professor of Talmud at Yeshiva University, asserts that "the whole idea of a tradition of faiths and the continuum of revealed doctrines which are by their very nature incommensurate and related to different frames of reference is utterly absurd, unless one is ready to acquiesce in the Christian theological claim that Christianity has superceded Judaism." Soloveitchik denies that Jews are related to any other faith community as "brethren" even though "separated" and he insists that Jews must refrain from suggesting to the Christian community any "changes in ritual or emendations of its texts. . . . It is not within our purview to advise or solicit . . . . Non-interference with and non-involvement in something which is totally alien to us is a conditio sine qua non for the furtherance of good-will and mutual respect." At the same time, Soloveitchik speaks firmly of God's "private covenant" with the Jews and of their "exclusive covenantal confrontation."

Parkes received a wider hearing from Reform rabbis, and over many years had warm personal and working relationships with, for example, Stephen Wise and Maurice Eisendrath. More recently, however, he was included in a bitter attack upon some of the most prominent Christian clergymen within the ecumenical movement, which was published in the magazine Religion in Life (Summer, 1972) by Rabbi Levi A. Olan, former president of the Central Conference of American Rabbis. Parkes's doctrine of equality for the two Covenants is not really as equal as it may appear, Olan contends. Calvary follows Sinai, chronologically as well as schematically, and thus Christianity is free to absorb Judaism's inspiration and teaching concerning community. But Judaism alone, Parkes seems to suggest, remains deficient in answering man's personal needs. Olan denies that this is so, and finds Parkes's perception of such a deficiency in Judaism to be an insuperable bar to further free discussion. "Parkes does not understand," Oland writes, "that to a Jew, Judaism is the total answer."

Leaving aside the matter of whether, in fact, Parkes did not understand this--which is questionable, to say the least--one may wonder whether Olan is not quarreling here with Parkes's Christian faith itself. If Parkes had not believed that Christianity is an enlargement, he would presumably long ago have converted to Judaism. Certainly, the Christian sees Judaism as inadequate. Similarly, the Jew sees Christianity as unnecessary. These are the very hallmarks of our identity.

Even more, however, Olan denies the reality of history. Although he himself recognizes the "inherent" and "abiding need of Christianity to dialogue with Jews," he nevertheless repeats that "Christianity is for Judaism a wholly new and different religion, totally unrelated to the Covenant. Its Jewish origin is an accident of history. If Christians can accept themselves in this role, then dialogue can be fruitful between Christians and Jews. . . ."

But, of course, the point is that Christians do not accept themselves in this role. Nor have they ever. That is what James Parkes's histories are all about. Today's Christian response to the Jewish rejection is more courteous than it used to be, but it is just as unequivocal. Recalling a second-century heresy which tried to cut the Church free from Judaism, the magazine's editor firmly answered Olan: "We Christians are not Marcionites, we are Jews. . . . Now that the range upon range of insight, judgment and relation behind Jesus in Judaistic memory is in better view we can comprehend better. . . under it all there is a faith Jesus was and is and it's Jewish. . . ."

But very well, the editorial went on. If it must, then let the conversation continue on this basis or on any basis. Rosemary Radford Ruether, however, is less compromising. Ruether has, with Parkes, been in the vanguard of those Christians struggling to rid Christianity of its anti-Semitism. In her oft-quoted book, Faith and Fratricide, she writes: "The question of a new covenantal theology cannot be solved or even adequately discussed from one side alone. It would be the area where Christians and Jews would have to enter into discussion of their contrary traditions about the nature of covenantal peoplehood. Each of the traditional propositions proves inadequate before the facticity of the other people. . . ."

To be sure, the rabbis are right that Judaism can stand alone, self-sufficient. And it is also true that Christianity cannot. One way or another, the Jewish faith and the Jewish people must continue to occupy a central place in Christian theology. If Jews will continue to live among Christian majorities, then, can it be altogether a matter of Jewish indifference that there does exist today a serious search among some Christians for a Christian theology without anti-Semitism?

True to his early resolve, James Parkes never withdrew into his study, nor did he avoid any fight in a good cause. While writing in Geneva, he helped to rescue Jews from Germany, to resettle uprooted students, to expose anti-Semitic forgeries, and to so enrage the Nazis that he only narrowly escaped assassination at their hands. Back in England for the war years, he found himself drawn into political discussions about Palestine, and here faced a painful dilemma. Certainly he sympathized with the plight of European Jews—but Palestine was surely in another and guiltless world?

Once again, Parkes was to come upon an unexpected history when he visited Israel in 1946: the story of the loyalty and persistence of the Jewish people in maintaining a corporate existence and unbroken claim to their homeland throughout its long Arab occupation. It was Mideast history which put a new complexion on the matter for him, and during the rest of his life he worked to bring this overlooked dimension of the issue to public attention. Just as he had been tireless in preaching to the Christians, so now he was resolute in exhorting the Jews.

The Palestinian Jews--Did Someone Forget?was the title of one of his pamphlets. He wrote of Israeli and Other Palestinians. One of his most interesting and persuasive historical treatments is called The Five Roots of Israel.

"The disaster was," he said, "that the Jewish appeal was to the legality of the Balfour Declaration and the Mandate, and not to the / Mideast / history and tradition which alone made the Declaration and the Mandate not only reasonable but right."

Parkes wrote in Whose Land:

> It was perhaps inevitable that Zionists should look back to the heroic period of the Maccabees and Bar-Kochba, but their title deeds were written by the less dramatic but equally heroic endurance of those who had maintained a Jewish presence in The Land all through the centuries, and in spite of every discouragement. This page of Jewish history found no place in the constant flood of Zionist propaganda, much of it as violent as it was one-sided. The omission allowed the anti-Zionist, whether Jewish, Arab or European, to paint an entirely

251

false picture of the wickedness of Jewry trying to
re-establish a two-thousand-year-old claim to the
country, indifferent to everything that had happened
in the intervening period. It allowed a picture of
The Land as a territory which had once been 'Jewish'
but which for many centuries had been 'Arab.' In
point of fact any picture of a total change of population is false. . . .

Parkes pointed to Arab responsibilities rather than innocence.
He saw Israel as a country emerging "from the long stagnation of
foreign rule." He tried to keep in sight the fact that it is "numer-
ically a typical middle-eastern country. An enormous section of
the population has never known any environment except that of the
Middle East, though this fact is rarely, if ever, used by Israeli
speakers before the United Nations, or published in their
propaganda.

Commenting upon the historic continuity of Jewish life in the
Middle East, Parkes said often that "it is one of my great regrets
that the Israeli government will never make us--not of 'this
argument' but of this basic fact--in its presentation of the case
for Israel on every possible international occasion, and especially
in the United Nations."

Parkes's writings strongly support Israel's rights and legitimacy,
but, for the most part, they remain unpublicized.

"The Zionist organizations don't like me," he commented
recently.

"Why not?" I asked.

"Because I insist on treating the whole subject," he answered.
"They don't like my insistence on a total historical approach.
Then the secularists don't like me because I'm religious. And the
religious. . . ." he sighed. "They just can't believe I don't want
to convert them."

This past summer, a few months shy of what would have been
his 85th birthday, James Parkes died, after a long illness, in
Southampton, England.

Many years ago he said that he regarded his life's work as
that of "reversing a stream that has flowed in the wrong direction
for 1900 years." When he was asked how long he thought the job
would take, he guessed "about three hundred years."

252

For those who come after him, James Parkes has left a rich legacy of pioneering research and provocative thought. In addition, his extensive personal collections of books, historical records, and ephemera have gone to the University of Southampton to be The Parkes Library, a continuing center for the study of relations between the Jewish and the non-Jewish worlds.

The Parkes Library

5

BY JAMES PARKES, *England*

IN 1956, just at the moment when I was suffering from the popular complaint of a coronary thrombosis, there came into existence an educational charity — technically 'a Company limited by guarantee' and registered with the British Board of Trade — called *The Parkes Library* to which I handed over with thankfulness the collection of books on many different aspects of 'the Jewish Question' which I had accumulated during my thirty years of concern with the problem.

I felt a natural diffidence about labelling the collection with my own name, but there was really no alternative unless I brought the detestable phrase 'non-Jew' into the title, and this I was absolutely determined not to do. Quite early on in my career I had asked a distinguished professor of the Sorbonne to lecture at a conference which I was organising, and he had said that it would be better to ask a Jewish scholar to deal with a Jewish subject. I rashly replied that, as I wanted to convince antisemites who would believe nothing a Jewish professor told them, I was looking for 'un non-juif.' I just got out of the room with my life, but I retained a very clear impression that other people had positive allegiances and loyalties as well as Jews, and that they expected to be identified by them, and not by the fact that they happened not to be Jews! As 'Christian' was too narrow and 'Gentile' too obscure, 'non-Jew' had to go into the sub-title in an impersonal form — 'a Centre for the study of relations between the Jewish and the non-Jewish worlds' — and the institution itself had to be called the Parkes Library.

I was delighted that this turning of the library into a charity would preserve the collection which I had built up. I hope it will go on as a Centre with an active staff; but, should that cease to be possible, then the statutes compel the governors to find some suitable body to receive the books. They would not be sold and dispersed. Naturally, since I have never been a collector with a private income, the library does not contain the treasures of a bibliophile. It has no manuscripts and only two incunabula. On the other hand, it has a very adequate collection of books on the subjects with which I have been successively concerned, and which were acquired primarily for the practical purpose of aiding the study of those subjects. They are, not unnaturally, mainly written in languages which I can understand, and it is only by accident that I have passed outside the range of English, French, German, Latin and Greek. Many will be surprised that I have not included Hebrew; but I had very early in my career to decide whether I would know Hebrew or know Jews, and the latter seemed to me more important. To explain this more fully, it will be easiest to say something of how the library came into existence.

In 1928 I was asked to go out to Geneva to help *International Student Service* to develop a cultural programme. It had hitherto been trusted universally in the European universities under its first name of European Student Relief because it had confined itself to practical relief and reconstruction, and had kept out of politics. Hence it came only slowly to the decision to start a cultural department, whose business would be to rush in where angels feared to tread across all the lines of division and hatred which separated country, class, and nationality within the European universities. But in 1928 it decided to take the risk, and called me from my job with the Student Christian Movement in London to be the first director.

I very soon discovered that no problem was more widespread or more bitter than antisemitism; and I actually got together a group of Jewish and antisemitic student leaders to discuss whether I.S.S. could help them in any way to ease relations. The conference itself, which took place in France at the Chateau de Bierville near Étampes, was a remarkable experience. It led to the conviction of both sides that there was work which we could do. But when we looked for the scholars who would help us to do it, we could find only Jews who could give us an objective and scholarly presentation of the subject; on the other side, alas, we could muster only ignorance or prejudice. So I was asked by the executive assembly of I.S.S. to give as much time as I could to a study of the subject. And that is the beginning of the Parkes Library thirty years ago in 1929.

My immediate field was the European university world; my environment was the growing antisemitism of the '30's. That is why I decided to know Jews rather than to know Hebrew. With my continual travelling in central and eastern Europe, I had unusual opportunities for meeting Jewish scholars and leaders of all sorts, and for seeing something of Jewish life.

However, part of 'knowing Jews' had to be acquired from books, and my spare time in Geneva was occupied with voluminous reading. My first acquisition was an English edition of Graetz in five volumes. I read them from cover to cover, and made pages and pages of notes, analyses and lists of dates.

The next stage was to build up two groups of people whom I could call upon for help. The first group consisted of Jews of various kinds who would allow me to come and ask them innumerable questions. Though in listing them I am bound to leave out people who should have been included, I would like to mention some. Journeying to central or eastern Europe, I always tried to stop off at Vienna on the outward or return journey in order to discuss things with Dr. Alexander Teich, one of our executive members and head of the Jewish student organisation for social welfare in that university. His knowledge of personalities all through eastern Europe was enormous and invaluable. When in England, I tried to spend some time with Dr. Israel Mattuck in London and with Mr. Herbert Loewe in Cambridge — I thus acquired liberal and orthodox interpretations of Judaism from two wonderfully fair exponents of their subject. Later I got to know Dr. Claude G. Montefiore. Rabbi Dr. Maurice Eisendrath was my first contact across the Atlantic, when he was still in Toronto. When I got to New York I met Dr. Louis Ginzberg, and time with him became a 'must' on every visit to that city. Then there was Dr. Nathan Feinberg in Geneva itself, who is now in Jerusalem. And there were Messrs. Victor Jacobson and Leo Motzkin to lecture me interminably on the Comité des Délegations Juives and its woes, and to make sure that I was not deceived by the advocates of Assimilation. To balance them I generally went to see Mr. Lucien Wolf when I could find him at Geneva, and tried to shake his conviction that people like me were increasing antisemitism by talking about it! All these people advised me about books in which to find further answers to my questions; and, as far as my very limited resources would allow, many of them were added to my library.

I also had two booksellers to whom my debt was enormous, and who were far more to me than just purveyors of books. They were invaluable counsellors from their vast experience, and would sometimes tell me that the book I asked them for was not the one I wanted, because something else of which I had not heard was much better. One of these was Louis Lamm in Berlin and the other was Nathanson — I do not remember his first name — in the Rue Gay-Lussac, Paris. I saw Louis Lamm last in Amsterdam, and he died during the war: I have not been able to find any trace of my good friend in Paris. Many were the hours which I spent in their shops, sitting generally on the top of a ladder looking at books and asking questions. Both were men whom I could trust implicitly. Louis Lamm issued admirable specialised catalogues before the war; and sometimes, instead of ordering precise books on a subject on which he knew far more than me, I would write and tell him that I could spend so much at the moment and would he give me the best selection he could for that modest sum. Now that I know much more about books, I realise how honest and generous he was with me in those early days. As for Nathanson, his prices always went down when I came into his shop. Their memory is indeed 'for a blessing.'

So the library was built up, gradually and systematically, according to the subject which at that precise moment I was trying to understand. From the time when I came back to England in 1935 there was a little more money for buying books, and I had Mr. Herbert Ashbrook as research secretary until 1939. He was already an experienced bibliographer and is now in business in the antiquarian book trade. There were also purchases from second-hand catalogues, and occasional prizes when *bouquinant sur les quais de Paris* or some other city. All except one of the books here illustrated were obtained in this last way, and in every case I was ignorant at the time that I had obtained a treasure. I only slowly realised that most people thought that the first edition of Basnage (Fig. 1) was in five volumes, not in the six I had; and I really believed in Rabbi Moses Levi (Fig. 2) and his history of the religion of the Jews and their establishment in Spain, and so entered it in my catalogue, thinking that I had got a prize in a seventeenth century description of Judaism, written in French. For I had already become aware that one of the historical problems was the mystery of a religion whose books were unreadable by the ordinary

Christian, so that I was concerned with the beginnings of explanations in a European language. Later, for example, I got Ricci's list of the 613 Commandments in Latin (1515), Abendana on the synagogue liturgy in English (1706), and had several editions of the *Sepher Toldoth Jeshu* in European languages. I found the curious book of devotions (Fig. 3) at Dijon where it was published. It is a reminder of the problem of *no-break-at-the-Reformation* in Roman Catholic countries, and does something to explain how the windows of St. Gudule, Brussels, could actually have been inserted in the early 19th century with their graphic and detestable pictures of another imagined 'Hostienschändung'. The binding illustrated (Fig. 4) came from Nathanson, who had acquired a number of books from Drumont's library, and was dividing them among favoured customers.

Thus, from the beginning, I was building up the collection 'in depth', getting the picture of past centuries from their actual works. For a small collection, built up with constant economies, I have a good range of early printed books. In Jewish-Christian relations I would include Reuchlin, Margarita, and Van Eck among others; among Christian Hebraists, Lightfoot, Spencer, Selden, Buxtorf, Surenhuis; in that new department created by a leisured class wishing to be interested in what was *merkwürdig* and *curieuse*, Schudt, Bodenschatz, Addison, Bünting; in emancipation history, Grégoire, Mirabeau, Dohm, Mendelssohn (in the collected edition of 1843), Riesser (in that of 1867-8), and a good many English pamphlets dealing with the issue from a hostile as well as a friendly standpoint; in travels to the Holy Land, Sandys, Dapper, Roger, Surius and Doubdan (whose experiences are a particularly interesting illustration of the hostile attitude of local Muslims to Christian pilgrims in the seventeenth century). As for modern antisemitica, I have Toussenel and the curiously rare Gougenot des Mousseaux, Gobineau, and the famous pamphlet of Wilhelm Marr, *Der Sieg des Judenthums über das Germanenthum, vom nicht-confessionellen Standpunkt aus betrachtet*. My copy of the *Dialogue aux Enfers entre Machiavel et Montesquieu* was one of the books which the Nazis had intended to steal when they tried to murder me in Geneva in 1935. In 1934 there was a 'protocol trial' at Berne, and from time to time 'students' came to my appartment, asking me what it was all about. Naturally I explained, and showed them what I had in the way of documents. Moreover at my appartment they were likely to meet refugees from Nazi Germany, either students or more important persons. Only afterwards did I discover that most of these 'students' were spies, either from Germany or from the Swiss Nazi organisation, the Iron Front. They were acting for the *Antisemitische Weltdienst* of Erfurt, and apparently reported that I appeared to be a king-pin in the Anti-Nazi plottings at Geneva. The *Weltdienst* decreed my elimination and the collection of all available material from my appartment — facts which emerged in the subsequent trial of leaders of the Iron Front. Luckily the attempt miscarried, but as the *Weltdienst* was particularly interested in my copy of Joly's *Dialogue*, it lives on my shelves under a false title. Judging that, if they repeated the attempt, they would be least interested in the Bible, I gave it the title of

'The Pentateuch: Revised Version.' Another of my rarities is the 1865 edition of the German translation of the book, entitled *Gespräche aus der Unterwelt*.

But my first main objective was to build up the historical side, for in early years I was concerned with history more than with either the Middle East or the relations of the two religions. With the help of my two book sellers I learned what were the important books in each country and period, books such as Reinach's *Textes des Auteurs Grecs et Latins*, Aronius' *Regesten*, Stobbe, Schürer, Caro, *Gallia Judaica*, *Germania Judaica*, Prynne, Tovey, Fritz Baer, Amador de los Rios, Mendes dos Remedios (both parts) and many local, provincial, and similar studies of which the *Urkundliche Beiträge zur Geschichte der Juden in . . . . .* were the most numerous. Gradually I was able to accumulate most of them, and at prices which today seem fantastically small. If I want to refer to a fact of Jewish history I have rarely to go outside my own work room.

The library now consists of six main sections: Judaism, Jewish History, Biography, Sociology, External Contacts and Relations, and the Middle East. I have both subject and author catalogues on cards and I try to catalogue as many serious articles as I can from periodicals as well as from books. Copies of these catalogues are available at the Wiener Library, 4, Devonshire Street, London, W.1., and at the Library of the Jewish Historical Society in University College, Gower Street, London, W.C.1. A good subject catalogue is, I believe, of inestimable value in a field as wide as mine. I use four printed bibliographies, *Magna Bibliotheca Anglo-Judaica* of Cecil Roth, *Katalog der Judaica und Hebraica, Erster Band, Judaica* of the Stadtbibliothek of Frankfurt, Tobler's *Bibliographia Geographica Palestinae*, and the *Bibliography of Jewish Bibliographies* by Shlomo Shunami. I have, but rarely use, Moise Schwab's *Répertoire des Articles relatifs à la Littérature juives dans les Périodiques de 1665 à 1900*. It is generally a subject with which I am concerned, and not an author, and the *Répertoire* has no subject index. Speaking of indices, I discovered while *bouquinant sur les quais de Paris*, whence come nearly all my Dreyfusiana and Drumontiana, that if a French book had an index it was almost certainly antisemitic. I always wondered why!

I have always been interested to accumulate pamphlets, for they are the very essence of that ephemerality which gives the day to day savour of an actual period which a historian seeks to catch. An excellent example can be found in the sudden passion of the Jewish pamphlets of the emancipation period to prove that the ethical standards for the individual were as high in Judaism as in Christianity. It had become a real issue when the prospect of individual citizenship opened, but it is a subject which finds little place in the older polemic and apologetic. I use the *Classeurs Relieurs Colma* for my pamphlet cases. Each case will hold from fifteen to twenty five pamphlets on stout wires, which allow new pamphlets to be inserted in the logical place and any single pamphlet to be taken out for consultation. I have some seventy pretty full cases, and they deal with every section of the library.

Finally come the periodicals. I am lucky enough to possess complete sets of the *Jewish*

Quarterly Review, English and American, the *Revue des Études Juives*, and the *Monats-schrift für Geschichte und Wissenschaft des Judentums*. The first and last of these series were gifts from benevolent friends; the French set I acquired through the invaluable Nathanson for less than $500 which, with many economies, I managed to scrape together. But while I am mentioning benefactors, I should add that for many years now I have had the inestimable privilege of getting books from the United States through the generosity of an American friend who settles my book bills. Without him I should be immensely impoverished. Not only are the publications of the Jewish Historical Society of America becoming every year more essential in many fields of scholarship outside purely American interests, but in two fields especially the lack of American books would be quite fatal to any attempt to keep in touch with contemporary developments. One is Judaism itself, where there is a steady stream of books of increasingly serious scholarly value, and the other is the Middle East.

To come back to periodicals, I have a good many other sets, though not all complete. I have some interesting early missionary stuff; I have the annual *Bulletins* of the Alliance Israélite Universelle from 1880 to 1913 which contain an enormous amount of information about affairs in the formative decades of modern antisemitism. I have an almost complete set of the *Verein z. Abwehr des Antisemitismus* which is also important for those seminal years.

Finally, how is all this housed? We live in a typical ancient English country house, begun round about 1500 and with floors and walls sloping in all directions; and the library spreads all over it. We need a 'pious benefactor' to build us a separate and fire-proof room where the books, pamphlets, and periodicals can live. We have spare rooms and can house scholars, as indeed we have done for more than twenty years. Books, Christian and Jewish, have in that time appeared which have owed much to the fact that this is an unusual collection, both in range and in language. I quote only one example. A research student now holding an important professorship, wrote to me to say that he understood from his tutor that two books had been written on the subject he had chosen for his thesis, but his tutor had added that someone called Parkes had apparently specialised in Jewish-Christian relations, and might be able to say whether anything else had been written. The student would be glad if I could tell him if there were such books, and could send him a précis of their contents. I replied that under that particular heading I had forty two entries in my own catalogue, and that he had better come and make his own précis! We are still open for others to come and explore our shelves.

Journal of Ecumenical Studies, 19:1, Winter 1982

IN MEMORIAM JAMES PARKES

1896-1981

6

Two prevailing memories I have of James Parkes involve spirits, though in rather different forms. I still see him, as of the third weekend in August, 1963, captivating our children Paula and Steve with tales of a mischievous "impersonating Elemental" that dwelt in his boyhood homestead on Guernsey, still among the more Norman of the Channel Islands. (Read for yourself Parkes's account of "The Bungalow Ghost" in his autobiography, *Voyage of Discoveries*.[1]) Heir to a venerable if whimsical line of persuasion, Parkes adhered to strictly empirical data—compounded, one is tempted to interject, by the marvelous fogs of Britain —to become an *orateur*, though always a chary one, for that elusive *coterie* known as ghosts. My other memory is of the expression that would light up James's handsome face when he poured the wine at dinner. His beaming in so artless a way was made possible by a standing order he had worked out with a London merchant, who agreed to keep his *clientèle* supplied with very good French wines at no higher than "seven and six" per bottle. (In those years that cost was anything but the *boutade* it would be today.)

Parkes's mother died while he was still a boy, following a long illness which left his father very poor. His brother and sister were both killed in the First Great War. He was himself gassed severely while serving as an infantry officer on the Ypres Salient. Physicians who afterwards attended him doubted that he would live out his twenties. He was eventually reduced, due to a "Dupuytren's Contracture," to typing entire manuscripts with a pencil end held in a hand he could not unclench. Yet Parkes was well on his way to eighty-five when he died on August 6, 1981, in Bournemouth. I once dared remark to him that I had recently been laid low by a coronary. He sniffed, and responded, "Oh, I've had a number of *those*!"

An individual of genius and of far-ranging interests, Parkes painted with marked creativity, and he knew the history of architecture and how to fabricate tapestries as well as he knew religious history and theology. It was as a boy of twelve or thirteen that he began to develop a tremendous interest in theology, politics, and history, all in their interrelatedness. His sense of humor was "something else." Back in 1933, he produced a handbook titled *International Conferences*, which contained the decree, "For the purposes of a conference, all museums are the same museum, all Gothic churches are the same Gothic church, all castles are the same castle, all palaces are the same palaces."

---

[1](Victor Gollanez, 1969).

For his Columbia University-Union Theological Seminary doctorate Robert A. Everett is preparing a dissertation on Parkes's life and thought. (It promises to be a beauty; I have read the initial sections.) When the student's mentors-to-be wondered aloud whether Parkes had actually "written enough" to qualify as a thesis subject, the young Everett could call attention, with more than a little scorn, to the master's list of publications totaling 329 entries by the year 1977.[2]

II

A great man has left us. Contra the chronic ignorance, near and far, of his legacy, James Parkes remains the preeminent historian-prophet of the Christian-and-Jewish worlds. (The hyphens are of the essence, in both places.) Roland de Corneille, the Canadian churchleader and politician, claims Parkes as one "who has done the most in this or any other century to destroy evil myths and legends."

Beginning in the year 1925, through his professional work in several student organizations, Parkes was appalled by the regnant Antisemitism of Christian students and others throughout Europe. The consequence was his determination to give himself to study and resolution of what was then known (with built-in shamefulness) as the Jewish problem. His first book, *The Jew and His Neighbour*, appeared in 1930 (SCM Press). Lest his developing and controversial reputation within that area needlessly compromise his endeavors beyond it, he fashioned the *nom de plume* John Hadham, under whose identity he wrote many volumes of a different genre, popular works in Christianity. (The surname was inspired by love for the Hadham villages of Hertfordshire. Even had the villages been ugly, who would not be beguiled by such an appellation as Much Hadham?) The first of the Hadham books was *Good God* (1940), the universalist and perfectionist soteriology of which so antagonized the Student Christian Movement Press that they rejected the manuscript, but the work went on to sell over 100,000 copies under the Penguin imprint. The one man was to become two best-selling authors! (His fiancée demanded, and received, two engagement rings, one from James, the other from John!)

Parkes read in five languages; his books have been translated into seven. The other major works in his primary subject include *The Conflict of the Church and the Synagogue: A Study in the Origins of Antisemitism* (Meridian Books-Jewish Publication Society, 1961 [1934]; *End of An Exile: Israel, the Jews and the Gentile World* (Vallentine, Mitchell, 1954); *The Foundations of Judaism and Christianity* (Quadrangle, 1960); *A History of the Jewish People* (Quadrangle, 1963); *Antisemitism* (Quadrangle, 1964); and *Whose Land? A History of the*

---

[2]David A. Pennie, ed., *A Bibliography of the Printed Works of James Parkes* (University of Southampton, 1977).

261

Peoples of Palestine (Taplinger, 1971). Much of his writing involved him in the case for, and the meaning of, a Jewish state. He became deeply involved in the question of Zionism and the Zionist cause.

The contribution of James Parkes to your life and mine has come out of his pioneering, singular, and unrelenting warfare against the Antisemitisms of the Christian (and, subsequently, non-Christian) world and in behalf of the God-given, abiding integrity of Judaism and the Jewish people. Parkes saw well that Antisemitism has little, if anything, to do with Jews; it is a Gentile problem from beginning to end. (Appropriately, he was honored with an assassination attempt by the official Nazi *Antisemitische Weltdienst* when he resided in Geneva.) A whole generation ahead of almost everybody else on these vital issues, Parkes was no reductionist or cushy latitudinarian when it came to church doctrine. An Anglican priest (as well as an Oxford Ph.D.), he always thought of himself as an orthodox Christian, but he kept nourishing and redeeming his orthodoxy through the resources of biblical-prophetic judgment and praxis. (Here is one explanation among several of why he always found Karl Barth's views so perverse and "abominably heretical.") During the Nazi horror, Parkes, at his rambling home/library in Barley, Royston, Herts., gave shelter to so many Jewish and other refugees, including numbers of children, that at one point there was scarcely room for him to sleep. In later years he was to resolve that a right Christian witness dictated his absence from church during Holy Week—upon the eminently moral/logical ground that that is the time when, *à outrance*, unholy things (viz., untruths) are uttered and acted out respecting the Jewish people and Judaism.

Parkes's watchword from the start to the finish of his career was: You cannot build good theology upon bad (i.e., false) history. For centuries Christian scholarship and church teaching had been disseminating a massively false but world-determining "history," born from the twin allegations that "the Jews" were guilty of deicide and that the Judaism of Jesus' time was already *spät Judentum*, a dying, even malignant thing, corrupted by inhuman legalism and rife with hopelessness. James Parkes stood in the vanguard of those who identified this entire ideology for the terrible calumny it was—and is.

On Parkes's selfsame watchword, good Christian teaching has to be relentlessly truthful concerning the actual history/life of the churches. In an address to the London Society of Jews and Christians, Parkes observed that the hatred and denigration of Jews and Judaism

> have a quite clear and precise historical origin. They arise from Christian preaching and teaching from the time of the bitter controversies of the first century in which the two religions separated from each other. From that time up to today there has been an unbroken line which culminates in the massacre . . . of six million Jews. The fact that the action of Hitler and his henchmen was not really motivated by Christian sentiments, the fact that mingled with the ashes of murdered Jews are the ashes of German soldiers who refused to obey

262

orders when they found what those orders were, the fact that churches protested and that Christians risked their lives to save Jews —all these facts come into the picture, but unhappily they do not invalidate the basic statement that antisemitism from the first century to the twentieth is a Christian creation and a Christian responsibility, whatever secondary causes may come into the picture.

How many future Christian clergy and teachers of my generation ever heard a word about any of this from their own ministers and teachers? I never did, through all the years of "liberal" divinity school and "liberal" graduate school courses—until at last Reinhold Niebuhr rescued me and enabled me to uncover the facts for myself. Of course, Parkes has not been the only scholar (Christian or Jewish) or decent/devout churchleader to point to the sin-ridden realities of church history. But the historic and all-decisive truth remains that he was among the very first to do so and, uniquely, upon the sure foundation of his own original, all-revealing researches into the ancient-to-recent Christian past. Indeed, well before the Nazis gained power in Germany he was already exposing the dread tale of Christian denigration and persecution of Jews and Judaism. Parkes acted to create a whole new anti-ideological historiography, subsequently to be elaborated and applied by such Christian scholars as Alan Davies, Edward Flannery, Franklin Littell, John Pawlikowski, Rosemary Ruether, Peter Schneider, and W. W. Simpson.

III

Parkes's views of Judaism and Christianity were distinctive and, perforce, disputatious. In total opposition to preachments declaring that the Christian church has superseded Israel in the divine economy, he bore scholarly and personal testimony to the living, dynamic, and incomparable quality of Judaism. He was especially struck by the great creativity and joy that suffused the period from Ezra to the completion of the Talmud—a period extending to a time much after "the new Israel" initiated the pretense that it has replaced "the old Israel." For Parkes, in Judaism and Christianity we are met with two quite different kinds of religion. He emphasized that at the center of Judaism is the "natural community." Although it would be absurd to assert that Judaism has no concern for the individual person, that faith's concerted stress falls upon humankind as social being, related to other human beings "through righteousness and justice." And while Christianity is not unaware of the social aspect of humanity, it has consistently subordinated that dimension "to the personal aspect of life."[3] Thus it may be adjudged that Judaism concentrates upon "the elect nation," while Christianity directs itself to "the elect from every nation." The reasoning here

---

[3] *The Bible, the World, and the Trinity*, Parkes Library Pamphlet, reprinted in *Prelude to Dialogue* (Vallentine, Mitchell, 1969).

points as well to the legitimacy of a Jewish state. Such a state finds its religious and thence political basis within the natural community. (In the specific instance of the State of Israel, the justifications of historical continuity, legality, and moral necessity are to be added to the above foundation.)

Judaism is a way of life, the religion of the attainable. Its task and contribution focus upon the norms and patterns of daily living. Christianity is a way to personal salvation and is in a certain sense, therefore, the religion of the unattainable. In an earlier article, Parkes wrote:

"God speaking to men in community through Sinai speaks with a different voice from God speaking to the hearts of men as separate persons from Calvary; and just as the church found a satisfactory doctrine of God only in the frank acceptance of the paradox of the Trinity in Unity, so we shall only find a satisfactory doctrine of man when we found it squarely on the paradox of man's dual existence as person in himself, and as member of the community in which alone his personality can exist."[4]

This one of four essays appeared under the significant general title, "The Permanence of Sinai as God's Revelation of Man in Society." The point is that Parkes was proposing an anthropological rationale and formulation for the shared legitimacy of Judaism and Christianity. In completion of the picture, humankind is in addition "a seeker called to explore and use all the riches this world provides."[5]

Correspondingly, to the understanding of God as the source and sustainer of societal Israel, and as personal redeemer, must be added a third channel (*not* persona): the action of the spirit of God in political, secular, and scientific life, or, put differently, humankind's calling and power to understand and have responsible dominion over the world. In sum, Judaism, Christianity, and scientific Humanism are to be co-related with the threefold action of God and the threefold understanding of humanity.

It should be apparent that in Parkes's trinitarian authentication of Judaism, Christianity, and Humanism he has not abandoned a Christian frame of reference. Since, as he himself taught, the two faiths of Judaism and Christianity differ essentially, it follows that the Jew will speak in a quite alternative way. I am not Jewish and I cannot represent Judaism, but I believe I am correct that the spokesperson for Judaism will testify that all three of the roles or channels Parkes depicts are underwritten within Judaism proper, without any need to introduce or call upon Christianity or Humanism. Jews will agree that, yes, their faith is fundamentally communal. But that faith also provides a fully personal dimension (cf., for example, the sublime Psalms of David). And, thirdly, Judaism has itself opened the way for humanity as seeker and ruler of the world, through its original teaching that God grants humankind dominion over the creation.

---

[4]"The Problem for the Churches Today," *St. Martin's Review*, November, 1949.
[5]"Three Channels for God's Giving," *The Times* (London), June 27, 1970.

It is not at all to the end of faulting Parkes's advocacy that I allude to a possible Jewish rejoinder to his position. That would be inappropriate in a tribute to him, but it is, in any case, not the point. I make the reference as a means, first, of underscoring Parkes's own insistence that the Jewish and the Christian outlooks are fundamentally different; and, second, of illustrating the kind of dialogue between Jews and Christians which meant so much to him and to which he devoted a large part of his life.

It remains evident, I trust, why Parkes was utterly repelled by any attempt to "convert" Jews to Christianity. The Jewish and Christian faiths are not only profoundly different; they are also of permanently equal validity.

IV

James was distressed when I saw fit to introduce "the devil" into the question of Antisemitism and the struggle against it (ghosts, *sí*; the devil, *no*). As I was more and more going the route of realpolitik vis-à-vis an Antisemitism metastasized far beyond the churches and religion, Parkes remained the Christian educationist, the rectifier of churchly sin. Contending as late as 1979 (and correctly so, as far as it goes) that "the basic root of modern antisemitism lies squarely in the Gospels and the rest of the New Testament," he drew from this the restricted and sanguine conclusion that with the aid of a radical reform of the church's liturgy and its biblical hermeneutic, Jews can be shown as "a normal, contemporary people with a normal, contemporary religion."[6] A few years earlier James had written to me that, "if for two thousand years you read the New Testament in church as the 'Word of God,' I think this is enough explanation of that subconscious and instinctive hostility which is the 'abnormal' part of antisemitism." On the other hand, Parkes did not seem to object to my usage of the concept "demonic."[7] However we may feel on the wisdom of directing energies to the reform of Christian liturgy, Parkes was surely right that the life of local Christian congregations can be a powerful force for either evil or good.

We have to keep in mind that Parkes was a wondrously reasonable man, and it was natural for him to expect everyone to be reasonable. He looked to the rationality of theological endeavor as judge of and guide to practical decision-making. Yet he forever insisted that religious understanding and claims must be assessed and chastened, not only by historical truth, but also by moral demands and ethical criteria. His threefold, dialectical devotion to reason, faith, and ethics prompted me once to denominate him an Anglican of the Anglicans. He rather enjoyed the characterization.

Parkes would often protest that while Christians have comprehended the

---

[6]Preface to Alan T. Davies, ed., *Antisemitism and the Foundations of Christianity* (Paulist, 1979).

[7]Letter to author, May 26, 1976.

person of Jesus, they have grievously denied the significance of the *religion* of Jesus, the religion of Judaism. Here erupts, in fact, the nightmarish, betraying irony of the whole history of Christianity. (One may venture to wonder, in the name of the very truthfulness that Parkes pursued so unflinchingly and at such great personal hardship, what the "person" of Jesus can ever mean in abstraction from the religious faith that possessed him and for which he gave his life.)

V

I have told of a few incidents in the life of James Parkes. I must make place for some lines from his *Autobiography*, which may better than anything else take the full measure of the man (also perhaps of the woman he married):

> Among our post-war visitors was one unusual guest, known to us as The Old Man of the Road. Some tragedy early in life had turned him into a "tramp," and he had been on the road ever since the First Great War. He took much pride in keeping himself clean; he knew that he could have a bed in our garden house when he wanted, that he could come to us when he felt ill, and that there would always be a meal for him. Once or twice we sent him to hospital, where he never stayed long. He loved the country, would tell us of its beauty and bring [my wife] Dorothy some offering of flowers or fruit culled on his way. His visits continued till we knew he was too old for the road, and we then found a place for him where he died peacefully and well loved in an old people's home.

In 1949 Parkes was elected president of the Jewish Historical Society of England, only the second Gentile to be so chosen by that date. He received fitting academic honors from, among other institutions, the Hebrew Union College-Jewish Institute of Religion, the Hebrew University of Jerusalem, and University College, London. In the mid-1960's he bequeathed his unique library of some 10,000 books, periodicals, pamphlets, and papers to the University of Southampton. He is survived by Dorothy, a redoubtable colleague in her own right. James has gone off now, *kiveyakhol*, to look up good Pope John XXIII, Reinhold Niebuhr, Cornelius Rijk, Kurt Gerstein, Heinz David Leuner, and the other departed saints of Christian redress and Christian-Jewish reconciliation. Parkes contended that either no human being survives physical death, or everyone does. If all do, "then it is into a world of growth and further understanding, not into a static world of heaven or hell."[8]

He had few peers within the category historian-cum-theologian. Nor do I know a more superb teller of tales. It may not be all that long until, over a good transfigured sherry, James Parkes will be regaling the others with his stories—

---

[8]"Parkes on Pawlikowski on Parkes," *J.E.S.* 7 (Fall, 1970): 791.

perhaps pausing to find Barth and remind him (but only the one quick time, I think) of his opinion of him. From Parkes's early years to his death (and beyond?), he has been living out the motto of his family crest, *Vous pouvez me rompre mais je ne plie pas* ("you may break me, but I do not bend"). His prodigious intellect was matched by his valor, his prophetic indignation, his steadfastness, his hopefulness. But greatest of all was his empathy. He was not a Jew, yet he was a Jew.

A. Roy Eckardt
Lehigh University
Bethlehem, PA

Index

A

Abdul-Malik, 69
Academy of Gaon Jacob, 28
Alexandria, 25, 94, 96, 132, 134
Alliance Israélite Universelle, 23, 103, 110
American Council for Judaism, 119
American Jewish Congress, 166
American Joint Distribution Committee, 7, 110, 111
Anglo-Catholicism, 160 f.
Anglo-Jewish Association, 103, 110
Anti-Defamation League, 123, 169
Antisemitism, modern, 7, 108
Aquinas, Thomas, 134
Arabs, Future, 60 f. Nationalism, 36, 37, 38 f. Refugees, 52 ff., 58 (see compensation and chap. vii *passim*). Scholarship, 97
Aristotle, 134, 135
Assimilation, 5, 7, 14, 103, 112, 165, 168
Assi, Rabbi, 118 f.
Augustine, St., 6

B

Babylonian Exile, 92 f.
Baeck, Leo, 155
Balfour Declaration, 6, 166
Bar Cochba, 19
Barley, estate in, 170
Begin, M., 150
Beirut Conference, 57
Berdayeff, N., 152
Bernadotte, Count Folke, 56
Beth Din, 169
Bodin, Jean, 160
British Union of Fascists, 166
Buber, Martin, 150, 152
Bund, 108, 110

C

Canaanites, 179
Caro, Joseph, 30, 142
Casimir the Great, 99
Chassidism, 30, 146
Christianity, attitude to Jews, 14, 28, 135 f., 138 f. ch. xiii *passim.* Hierarchy, 134. Origins, 95.
Christians, Jewish, 156
Clermont Tonnerre, 169
Cohanim, 133.
Comité des Délégations Juives, 114 f., 166
Communism, 60
Compensation to Arab refugees, 56, 58
Coon, Carleton S., 180
Court Jews, 100 f., 102
Crémieux, Adolfe, 110
Crusades, 21, 67

D

David, House of, 132
Deir Yassin, 55
Diaspora, Influence on environment, 103, 105, 106, 109 ff. Nature, 92. Relation to Israel, 93, 115 f., 171, 183. Religious core, 121, 151, 167. Part III *passim.*
Disputations, 139
Dual loyalty, 168, 172

E

Eclecticism, classical, 93
Elephantine, 92
Emancipation, 78, 102, 165
Epstein, Rabbi I., 154
Exodus, The, 11, 179

Theology, Christian, 133. Jewish,
132, 153 f., 161
Tiberias, 19, 22
Tolland, J., 160
Torah, 26
Trachtenberg, Dr., 140

U

Umar, 69
United Nations, 56

V

Vulgate, 138

W

Weizmann, Agreement with Faysal,
39 f.
White Paper, The 1939, 172
Wise, Stephen, 169
World Jewish Congress, 111, 114,
150, 165

Z

Zaddikim, 146 f.
Zangwill, I., 13
Zborowski, Mark, 147
Zionism, origins, 31, 178
Zionist Organisation, 111, 114, 150,
171